"James B. De Young does the church a great service by refuting the appeal of Universal Reconciliation in this thorough and scholarly work. In doing so, he clearly shows that if there is no everlasting hell, there is no need of the 'good news', and that this last day's apostasy must be revealed for what it is, a betrayal of the gospel of Jesus Christ."

—Dwight Douville
Senior Pastor Calvary Chapel, Appleton, Wisconsin

"I am delighted to endorse James B. De Young's new book addressing Universal Reconciliation. Jim is a gifted thinker and communicator and perhaps the single most knowledgeable source of information in the church today on this topic. I praise the Lord for his clarity and adherence to scriptural truth during our radio and television interviews and most of all, for his heart to warn those lost in aberrant ideas."

—Eric Barger
Take A Stand! Ministries

"Dr. James De Young has written another book to expose the far-reaching effects that universal reconciliation/salvation is having on Christian belief, especially as propagated in *The Shack*. Many have not thought through the consequences of embracing a view of the love of God that distorts the meaning of God's holiness and justice and that admits all humanity into heaven even apart from faith. Such a view violates the total teaching of Scripture and ends up slandering the love of God as revealed in the death of Jesus Christ on the cross. De Young here presents the fruit of his study that began eight years ago and is probably unmatched by anything else in print. If you are searching for the truth on this issue, read this book."

—Janet Mefferd
Nationally syndicated Christian radio host

"Universal Reconciliation, the teaching that all will eventually be reconciled to God and saved eternally regardless of life lived or faith professed during this lifetime, caters to the sentimentalities of people who are troubled by the idea of eternal torment in hell. I get it. There is nothing pleasant or happy about the destruction of the wicked. But there is nothing pleasant or happy about sin and rebellion either. And that is precisely what makes the gospel of Jesus Christ so wonderful. As James De Young makes clear, Universal Reconciliation is biblically groundless and is untethered from the historic teaching of the church. Further, it offers false hope to the lost and, in turn, undercuts the church's commitment to missions. With characteristic thoroughness and scholarly precision, De Young offers a devastating critique of the poisonous teaching of Universal Reconciliation. *Exposing Universalism* is an excellent one-volume guide and faithful response to Universalism's most prominent false prophets."

—TODD L. MILES
Professor of Theology, Western Seminary

Exposing Universalism

Exposing Universalism

A Comprehensive Guide to the Faulty Appeals Made
by Universalists Paul Young, Brian McLaren,
Rob Bell, and Others Past and Present to
Promote a New Kind of Christianity

James B. De Young

RESOURCE *Publications* • Eugene, Oregon

EXPOSING UNIVERSALISM
A Comprehensive Guide to the Faulty Appeals Made by Universalists Paul Young, Brian McLaren, Rob Bell, and Others Past and Present to Promote a New Kind of Christianity

Copyright © 2018 James B. De Young. All rights reserved. Except for brief quotations in critical publications or reviews, no part of this book may be reproduced in any manner without prior written permission from the publisher. Write: Permissions, Wipf and Stock Publishers, 199 W. 8th Ave., Suite 3, Eugene, OR 97401.

Resource Publications
An Imprint of Wipf and Stock Publishers
199 W. 8th Ave., Suite 3
Eugene, OR 97401

www.wipfandstock.com

PAPERBACK ISBN: 978-1-5326-4287-6
HARDCOVER ISBN: 978-1-5326-4288-3
EBOOK ISBN: 978-1-5326-4289-0

Manufactured in the U.S.A.

Contents

Preface | vii

Introduction: The Growing Popularity of Universal Reconciliation/Salvation | 1
  Impact, Definitions, Importance, Procedure of This Book | 1

Section 1: Refuting the Appeals of Universal Reconciliation | 21
  Introduction: The Four Appeals of Universal Reconciliation | 21
  Part 1: The Appeal to the Language of the Bible | 23
    Chapter 1: The Meaning of the Word "Age" | 25
    Chapter 2: The Meaning of Hell | 49
    Chapter 3: The Reality of the Belief in the Afterlife | 62

  Part 2: The Appeal to Reason and Emotion | 71
    Chapter 4: Reason Makes Hell and Judgment Unacceptable: "God is a bully." | 73
    Chapter 5: "A Loving God Cannot Punish Anyone." | 81
    Excursus: Even Reason Demands That Hell Must Be Everlasting | 99

  Part 3: The Appeal to Church History: Overview | 105
    Chapter 6: Universalism's Distortion of the Witness of the Early Church | 107
    Chapter 7: Universalism's Subversion of the Church Since the Reformation | 123
    Chapter 8: The Creeds of Universalism | 142
    Excursus: Isaac Backus: An Early American Refutes Universalism | 155

Part 4: The Appeal to Texts of Scripture | 163
    Chapter 9: The Appeal to Texts with "All" and "Whole" | 165
    Chapter 10: The Appeal to Texts Dealing with Choice and Freedom | 171
    Chapter 11: The Appeal to Other Texts That Supposedly Support Universalism | 178

Section 2: Correctly Interpreting the Bible: The Case for Everlasting Hell and Evangelical Belief | 191
    Chapter 12: The Parables of Jesus and His Additional Teaching about Hell | 193
    Chapter 13: The Apostles on Judgment and Hell: Paul, Peter, Hebrews, John in The Revelation | 208
    Chapter 14: Sixteen Questions That Expose Universalism's False Beliefs about Hell | 236
    Chapter 15: Eight Fatal Consequences Belonging to Universal Reconciliation and Summary of Nine Errors | 243
    Chapter 16: Universalism's Subversion of the Institutions of Society | 251
    Conclusion: Responding to Universalism in Fiction, Nonfiction, and Film | 258
    Excursus: An Older Persuasive Voice Defending Everlasting Punishment | 266
    Epilogue | 280

Bibliography | 285

Preface

IN THIS PREFACE I take up two matters. First, here is an outline, a summary, of what's in this book.

Twenty-One Points That Expose the Failure of Universal Reconciliation (UR) to Find Support in the Bible, in Reason, and in Church History

The following points summarize the main points of this book and form a formidable obstacle to the legitimacy, the credibility, of universal reconciliation, past and present. The following points can serve as an index and reading guide for those who have specific questions about universalism or who do not have the time to read through the entire book. I also call special attention to the Introduction—why writing this book was necessary to respond to three popular universalists and how it is arranged—and to the three excurses in the book that provide strong reinforcement for the failure of UR.

The following points are arranged in order from the more general to the more specific.

1. Overview: UR fails in every attempt to find support in the Bible (chaps. 1, 2, 3, 9, 10, 11), in reason or logic (chaps. 4–5), and in church history (chaps. 6–8).

2. Upon close examination every Bible verse that UR cites for support fails to give such support (chaps. 9–11; pp. 165–90).

3. In all of the Bible Jesus Christ makes the most statements and the strongest statements about the reality of an everlasting hell (pp. 51–7; chap. 12, pp. 193–207).

4. The Apostles of Jesus follow him in affirming the reality of a permanent hell, with the Apostle Paul leading the way (chap. 13; pp. 208–35).

5. UR is not able to find support in the book of Romans (pp. 227–31) or the rest of Paul's Epistles (pp. 231–2), in Hebrews (pp. 233–4), or in The Revelation (234–5).

6. All six major claims that UR makes about the Bible fail (203–35).

7. Every appeal that UR makes to reason and emotion fails (chaps. 4–5, pp. 73–98).

8. UR fails to find support in particular features of early church history. It is patently false to claim:
    a. that the first 500 years of church history embraced UR (chap. 6);
    b. that early major church centers supported UR (chap. 6);
    c. that Origen of the third century was doubtless an early supporter of UR (chap. 6).

9. Contrary to UR, the Bible both exhorts the need of faith in order to go to heaven—to be saved—and warns about losing one's faith and suffering judgment for unbelief (pp. 214–7).

10. UR is unable to deal with apostasy (pp. 216–9).

11. Not one Bible verse even hints that there is a second chance to believe in Jesus Christ after death, to be saved after death, to become a Christian after death (pp. 56–61, 241, 246).
    Indeed, the last state of unbelievers in hell cannot be reversed (pp. 56–61, 84, 220–2, 225–30, 233–5, 237–42).

12. UR opposes the institutions of the church, the government, and even marriage, all of which leads to anarchy (chap. 16, pp. 251–7).

13. UR falsely accuses evangelicals for teaching that there will be billions in hell and only a few in heaven (pp. 80, 240, 273, 278).

14. Since it is necessary that there be a preacher of the gospel for anyone to be saved (as Romans 10:14–5 affirms), who will be the first preacher/witness in hell (since no believers go there) (pp. 229–30)?

15. UR's insistence that the devil and his angels will repent in hell and get into heaven makes heaven forever unsafe and insecure. Such a belief is also a contradiction to logic, and entirely impossible (53, 71-98, 204, 241, 247). UR plays the devil's hand (De Young's wager: p. 248).

16. UR's insistence that the suffering in hell is corrective, to lead people to repent, is contradicted by the Bible's expressed purpose for suffering (pp. 51–6, 219, 237–8).

17. By insisting that all those in hell must repent, UR is more deterministic and coercive than Calvinism is (pp. 66, 217–9, 238–9).

18. There are many questions and aspects about hell that UR cannot answer (pp. 203–4), especially sixteen questions (chap. 14, pp. 236–42).

19. Those who fail to confess Jesus in this life will submit to him as Lord and Judge of all in the next life (pp. 220–1); they do not repent and believe. The "last state" is worse than the first (p. 221).

20. UR fails to deal adequately with the dual biblical truths of God's sovereignty and human responsibility (pp. 219–20, 228–34). There is a sense in which God's will can be thwarted (p. 217).

21. UR will come under the judgment of God at the Second Coming of Jesus Christ (pp. 226–31).

Cryptic Comments

1. According to UR, all escape hell for some reason at some time somehow (p. 182).

2. UR throws Jesus Christ under the bus driven by its own idea of God (p. 183).

3. UR is a terrible charade. There is a better chance for my dog to go to heaven than for a person to repent in hell and go to heaven (p. 190).

4. UR is theological rape of the gospel (p. 190).

5. The devil is the mouthpiece of UR. UR plays the devil's hand (pp. 246, 248).

6. Jesus became the God-man to save humans; he did not become the God-angel to save angels (p. 247).

7. UR believes that penal substitution is "one of the most diabolical doctrines ever" (p. 98).

The Heart of This Book: How Do the Love and Holiness of God Relate?

The second matter concerns what is at the heart of the legitimacy of universal reconciliation (UR). Everything written in this book ultimately leads to the issue of how the love and holiness of God relate. Those who espouse UR assert that God's supreme attribute is love and all the rest of his attributes are subjected to it. This is the major distortion—deception—of UR which I expose in this book.

Over a hundred years ago Oswald Chambers, the beloved author of *My Utmost for His Highest*, articulated this issue. In the following quotes he goes to the same heart of the matter and exposes the distortions of UR.

> Beware of the pleasant view of the Fatherhood of God—God is so kind and loving that of course He will forgive us. That sentiment has no place whatever in the New Testament. The only ground on which God can forgive us is the tremendous tragedy of the Cross of Christ; to put forgiveness on any other ground is *unconscious blasphemy* (italics mine).[1]
>
> Anything that belittles or obliterates the holiness of God by a false view of the love of God, is untrue to the revelation of God given by Jesus Christ. Never allow the thought that Jesus Christ stands with us against God out of pity and compassion; that He became a curse for us out of sympathy with us. Jesus Christ became a curse for us by the Divine decree.[2]

I return to Chambers in the Conclusion.

---

1. Chambers, *My Utmost*, 325.
2. Ibid., 326.

Introduction

The Growing Popularity of Universal Reconciliation/Salvation

Impact, Definitions, Importance, Procedure of This Book

THE SHACK IS A recent fiction by Wm. Paul Young that has captured in both a novel (2007) and in film (2017) the imagination of millions of people in recent years. The novel has risen to the top of the charts for sales of millions of copies. It has been translated into many languages. Most give it positive reviews as a bold attempt to show how a person can find forgiveness and a deeper relationship with God. But not all reviews are positive. Increasingly, people are concerned about doctrinal matters in the novel that seem to undercut the Bible's view of God and hell.

In truth, this and other fiction represent what the Christian church has struggled with through the ages—the error of universal reconciliation/salvation. This is the distortion that claims that there is no permanent hell for people or for angels (including the devil), that God is an unloving bully if he forever sends people to hell, that Jesus' death saves every single person from judgment, that God never punishes sin but "cures" it with corrective suffering before death or in hell, that the church is an institution that becomes an obstacle to God rather than a doorway, that Jesus was never separated from God as he died for the whole world.

All of these ideas are in *The Shack*. Young has written two other fictions, *Crossroads* (2012) and *Eve* (2015). The underlying doctrine permeating these is again universal reconciliation (see review of these on my web site).[1]

---

1. My website is burningdowntheshackbook.com.

Another fiction widely read in the emergent church carries the same general perspective. In *The Last Word and the Word After That* Brian McLaren asserts that the evangelical understanding of hell must be "deconstructed" in favor of a better view.

In addition, several nonfiction works, such as that of Rob Bell (*Love Wins*), have recently espoused the same ideas. It is a book making a large appeal to the general Christian audience.[2] But it offers little that is new or different from the books by McLaren, Young, or others past and present.[3]

Paul Young has also produced nonfiction as his most recent work, *Lies We Believe about God* (2017). It is the most aggressive attack on Christian beliefs.

How does one account for the popularity of these works of fiction and nonfiction in spite of their embedded errors? Why have recent years seen a general resurgence of interest in universalism as a theological option to Christian doctrine? Perhaps the answer includes the pluralism of our day, the rise of postmodernism with its debunking of objective truth, the speed of communication via the internet, the challenges of living Christianly in an increasingly polarized world (the "cultural wars"), the ease of self-publishing, and the growing biblical illiteracy in the Western world. No doubt both the cultural drift toward less and less personal accountability and the concern for politically correct speech have contributed to the new appeal of universalism. It seems also to be a viable alternative for many in the emergent church and for the younger generation of Christians seeking to do church in a new way. In many circles the questioning of the polity of the church has led to the questioning of the doctrine of the church.[4]

Many other nonfiction books espousing universalism have been published. Books by Talbot (1999), Cassara (1971), Robinson (1985), Von Balthasar (1986), and others have appeared, and writings of the universalist George MacDonald have been reissued. Other books, such as that by Parry and Partridge (2003), have sought to debate the issue. Evangelical books by Fernando (1983), Morey (1984), and Keller (2008), and collections of authors edited by Crockett and Sigountos (1991) and Morgan and Peterson (2004), have sought to defend the evangelical view. The emergent church has its own books, such as that edited by Pagitt and Jones (2007). I will interact

---

2. Rob Bell, *Love Wins: A Book About Heaven, Hell, and the Fate of Every Person* (2011). Bell has written many other books incorporating his universalism including: *Love Wins: For Teens* (2008); *Sex God: Exploring the Endless Questions Between Spirituality and Sexuality* (2012); *What We Talk About When We Talk About God* (2014).

3. See my extensive review of *Love Wins* on line: burningdowntheshackbook.com.

4. Recent (2008) polls show that almost 50% of professing evangelicals do not subscribe to the view that Jesus Christ is the only way to heaven.

with all of these texts and several more. But my chief interaction is with Young, McLaren, and Bell for reasons given in the following paragraphs.

The Impact of Universalist Fiction

The rise of literature espousing universalism within the greater evangelical scene poses a fresh challenge to evangelical faith. It is a special attempt to reach evangelical Christians. The fiction carries inherently a subtlety that may go unrecognized by the undiscerning reader of fiction. Reviews of *The Shack* make this deception all too obvious. It is because of this new challenge to evangelical faith that I have written on this topic. I will interact with the whole spectrum of universalist teaching to make this a comprehensive response.

The catalyst for my writing on universalism was the conversion of a friend, Paul Young, to universal reconciliation sometime before 2004. His conversion was without reservation. He wrote a 103-page paper (titled *Universal Reconciliation*) to defend it in a Christian forum in 2004. When he later wrote his novel, *The Shack*, I found his universalism embedded there.[5] To the unsuspecting it makes a good read, as mystery, tragedy, and theology are intertwined. It is a creative and bold attempt to introduce the reader to God, the Trinity, life after death, the way to handle tragedy, and, yes, to the basics of universalism. Yet readers suspect that all is not as it should be when compared to the teaching of the Bible.

The universalism distorts the Bible's teaching regarding divine love and justice, the nature of the death of Christ, the destiny of unbelievers and fallen angels, and why Jesus Christ died on the cross. My lengthy review of his novel is available at *burningdowntheshackbook.com*.

When other books, less informed of the background of the author, Paul Young, gave a distorted or incomplete understanding of *The Shack*, I determined to write my own book critiquing *The Shack*. In my book, *Burning Down the Shack: How a "Christian" Best Seller Is Deceiving Millions*, I both expose the distorted doctrines expressed in the novel and give a catechism of sorts of what Christians actually believe on core doctrines.

Similarly, the earlier fiction by Brian D. McLaren pursues a new view of hell.[6] While he terms his fiction a "creative nonfiction," the author also

---

5. Young, *Shack*. William Paul Young goes by his middle name.

6. Brian D. McLaren, *The Last Word and the Word After That: A Tale of Faith, Doubt, and a New Kind of Christianity*. This is the last of a trilogy of fiction. The first is *A New Kind of Christian*, and the second is *The Story We Find Ourselves In*. My interaction is with his last book since it is in this one that the author makes clear that the issue is the

calls it a "fictional theological-philosophical dialogue."[7] It is a fictional account of a pastor's search for a better understanding of hell while fully conscious of the fact that universalism is heresy. The new understanding of hell is neither exclusivist (unbelievers are excluded from heaven) nor inclusivist (all people are admitted to heaven even if they do not know about Christ's work). The author claims that it is a new way to relate justice and mercy (xiv), since God is always both. Yet he clearly faults the evangelical view of hell. McLaren would construct a "new kind of Christianity" (chap. 25) and a "new kind of Christian."

While the two fictions by Young and McLaren are quite different in format they are surprisingly alike in content, as the pages below will reveal. They are at the forefront of advocating the deconstruction of the traditional understanding of hell.

Their writing forms a special kind of fiction. They are "theological fictions"—a new (but actually old) kind of literary form that uses fiction to propagate a very deliberately formed theology. The discourse is not simply theologically informed. The fiction serves the theology; the theology does not merely serve the fiction. The focus is the theology, not the fiction. Making the theology the focus means that the authors have committed themselves to the theology and believe what they write in their fictions. They are seeking to proselytize their readers. They are apologists for a new view of hell that is really quite old.

These fictional novels are just the latest extension of the reach of universalist thinking seeking to overturn evangelical teaching. This fiction is the latest front in the conflict between evangelical thought and universalism that goes back, all the way back, to the third century AD. With the release of the film, "The Shack" (March, 2017), the propagating of universal reconciliation has reached a new level of impact and persuasion. By subliminal and overt messages the selling of universalism has become much more powerful and difficult to oppose.

Rob Bell's book is not fiction, not a novel. But it espouses the same questions about evangelical beliefs about hell, heaven, the way to God, the nature of God himself, the meaning of the gospel, and other teachings that the fictional works espouse. Indeed, the tenor of Bell's book is to question everything. Like the fictional writers, Bell interprets Jesus' claim to be the only way to God as both exclusive and inclusive (terms I'll later define)—and he ends up being inclusive (154–5). In the end he cannot accept the

---

reality of hell and he interacts with the claims of universalism which he recognizes as heresy.

7. Ibid., xvi.

teaching that the way to heaven is narrow (as Jesus said; Matt 7:13, 14, 21) because of a basic conviction that he has, and repeats at least four times: How can a God of love exert judgment on any one forever for committing a sin over a brief lifetime (2, 102, 110, 175)? He writes that we should all long for universal reconciliation (115). These views are standard fare for universalism. I answer this basic argument in the chapters that follow.

Above, I introduced Paul Young's book, *Lies We Believe about God*, as the latest in nonfiction propagation of universal reconciliation. In his twenty-eight chapters Young takes on core evangelical points of doctrine and considers them all to be lies. Examples of chapter titles ("lies") are: "God loves us but doesn't like us" (chap. 1), "God is good, I am not" (chap. 2), "God is in control" (chap. 3), "God does not submit" (chap. 4), "God is more he than she" (chap. 7), "God is a prude" (chap. 10), "You need to get saved" (chap. 13), "Hell is separation from God" (chap. 15), "God is not good" (chap. 16), "The Cross was God's idea" (chap. 17), "God requires child sacrifice" (chap. 19), "Death is more powerful than God" (chap. 21), "God is not involved in my suffering" (chap. 22), "Not everyone is a child of God" (chap. 24), "Sin separates us from God" (chap. 27), "God is One alone" (chap. 28). From this list one can see just how far reaching the beliefs of Paul Young are—and how far they depart from standard Christian beliefs.

Not surprisingly all these challenges to Christian beliefs are not peculiar to modern people. They have been discussed by Christians for hundreds of years, and satisfactorily explained and answered.[8] Indeed they arose as early as the third century. Christians then critically dealt with the challenges and found them lacking (as I will show in the following pages). "There is nothing new under the sun" (Eccl 1:9).

What Is Universalism? Definitions Are Essential

Universal reconciliation is the usual Christian form of universalism which maintains restoration after future "correction" in hell. Another form of universalism asserts that restoration takes place immediately after death. In its various forms universalism goes back a long time. In America it has a checkered history.

In 1878, at Winchester, N.H., the idea of restoration only after punishment was declared by the universalist movement in America to be the "orthodox" view. "Penitence, forgiveness, and regeneration" are all involved.[9] Earlier, due to the influence of the universalist Hosea Ballou, most

---

8. See Shedd, *Endless Punishment*.
9. Gerstner, "Universalism," 539. See the similar entry in the *Evangelical Dictionary*

universalists were persuaded through much of the 19th century that there was no hell for anyone after death but bliss alone. More recently, in 2007, the Christian Universalism Association was formed to separate universal reconciliation from Unitarian universalism. There is also a pagan form of universalism that teaches that all will ultimately be happy since all are, by nature, the creatures and children of God.[10] This view asserts that Jesus is just one of many ways to God; or that all go to heaven because Christ's death covers all people's sins whether or not they have ever heard of Jesus Christ. In this book I am specifically focusing on universal/Christian reconciliation, but much of what I write pertains to all forms of universalism.[11]

The Beliefs of Universalism

What is universalism, and in particular, what is universal reconciliation? The beliefs of universal reconciliation may be identified from the writings of its adherents, past and present. In strategic ways universalism differs from evangelical faith. Here are the salient points by which one recognizes the language of universal reconciliation. The following is the teaching of universalism.

1. God wills all his creatures, people and angels, to be saved and to acknowledge Jesus as Lord; and (this is important) God's will cannot be thwarted (Col 1:19–20; 1 Tim 2:4).

2. God's attribute of love limits his attribute of justice. It is unjust for a loving God to send people who have lived a short life to an eternal (everlasting) hell.

---

of Theology, ed. Walter A. Elwell.

10. Ibid. See also Erickson, *Christian Theology*, 1026–8, who cites other forms of universalism (universal conversion by evangelism, universal atonement, universal opportunity to respond) that are not examples of true universalism. In contrast to the classic form expressed by Origen, true universalism may take the forms of universal explicit opportunity (before or after death all place faith in Christ after explicitly hearing the gospel), universal reconciliation (reconciliation is already an accomplished fact for all), and universal pardon (in the end God will change his mind about condemning many and impute not only righteousness but also faith to all, and will forgive all). See also Erickson's "Opportunity" and his discussion of universalism in Crockett and Sigountos, eds., *Through No Fault*, 23–33. Paul Young's universalism seems to combine universal opportunity and universal reconciliation. McLaren seems to use the categories indifferently and is unconcerned that his universalism may be labeled heresy.

11. When I use the words "universalism" and "universalist" I have "universal reconciliation" primarily in mind. This wording is not meant to be lacking in precision, for I note that McLaren, Bell, Young, and others repeatedly use the broader term in their works.

3. God has already reconciled all creatures—all humanity and all angels—to himself by the atonement of Jesus Christ at the cross.

4. This reconciliation will be applied to all people either before death or after death, and to all the fallen angels, including the devil.

5. For those who do not accept salvation by *faith* in this life God will provide salvation by *sight* after they have died.

6. Faith is necessary to appropriate reconciliation in this life; God's love delivers unbelievers (and fallen angels and the devil) from hell in the next life. But, frankly, faith is often given scant attention in the writings of universalists. Young (*Lies*, 118) denies that faith is necessary for one to be a child of God.

7. The sufferings of hell and the lake of fire are not punitive, penal, or eternal, but corrective, restorative, purifying, cleansing, and limited in duration. Young (*Lies*, chap. 15) denies that hell separates anyone from God.

8. Hell and the lake of fire are not forever, but will cease to exist after all people and the fallen angels, including the devil, have been delivered from them and enter heaven.

9. God has acted as the Judge of all at the cross; there is not a future judgment for anyone. But some, such as Young, deny that any judgment took place at the cross.

10. The work of the Holy Spirit is given little, if any, attention.

11. The work of Satan, also known as the devil, is given little, if any, attention.

12. Universalism is the teaching of the Bible. It is the teaching of Jesus (universalists claim).

13. Universalism claims that it was the majority belief of the Christian church for the first five centuries.

14. The evangelical church is an obstacle to universalism. All institutions including the church, marriage, and the government are systems of hierarchy that use power to control people. Young (*The Shack* (122–4, 179) has Jesus say that they are diabolical and that he, Jesus, never created any of them.

Not all advocates of universal reconciliation would embrace all of these statements, nor the exact wording that I have used. But most do.

It is noteworthy that Young has his own peculiar UR beliefs (as noted above). In addition to those pointed out, he also asserts the following extreme (even slanderous is an appropriate word) ideas in his recent *Lies* book. (1) All people are "fundamentally good," not depraved (chap. 1); (2) God is not in control of everything; as an artist he often has to submit to humans and change his plan (chaps. 3, 4); (3) God is a sexual being, equally male and female, with whom people have a relationship (chaps. 7, 10); (4) no one needs to get saved because everyone is already saved; faith is unnecessary (chap. 13, p. 118); (5) the cross was man's idea, not God's (chap. 17); (6) all people and all creation were "created in God" and have God's nature; all are children of God; and all were included in the birth, death, and resurrection of Christ (chap. 24); (7) sin is redefined as failing to understand the nature of people rather than falling short of the absolute holiness of God (chap. 27); and (8) the Trinity as he knew it in his roots in "evangelical Christian fundamentalism" left him with a God who was distant, and the author and perpetrator of evil who tortured his child (chap. 28).

The extreme nature of Young's statements almost takes one's breath away! And the foregoing do not exhaust all that he writes, as I show in my book replying to his.[12]

The chief argument of universalism (as the reading of Young and Bell clearly shows) is the emotive appeal to God's mercy and love so that he could not bring eternal suffering to any of his creatures. The argument is: How can a loving God torment untold billions of people forever in hell, the lake of fire, for failing to believe during a lifetime of a relatively few number of years? God's justice is completely in the service of his love.[13] Universalists also appeal to Scripture, and to history, but in the end these take second place to the appeal to a sense of fairness and justice qualified by God's love in his dealing with people. God's love is his supreme attribute. Love and justice are mutually exclusive.

Yet, the matter of how God's love relates to his justice cannot be a question occurring only to moderns. It is reflected throughout the pages of Scripture. Obviously, Jesus himself, Paul the Apostle, and others through the ages have certainly thought about these matters, the nature of God and the reality of hell. Yet they teach that God is both love and just (righteous), that

---

12. De Young, *Lies Paul Young Believes about God*. I respond to each of Young's twenty-eight chapters, first summarizing his words, and then giving the "biblical response." I rearrange his chapters under four broad areas of doctrine.

13. Erickson, *Theology*, 1028, citing the universalist Ferre, *Christian Understanding*, 228. Ferre asserts that love and justice or punishment, heaven and hell, are mutually exclusive (237). McLaren, Young, and Bell are simply the most contemporary exponents of this argument, and they repeatedly make it (Bell at least four times).

all have a certain degree of knowledge of the true God as witnessed by the creation, that all have a conscience to discern right from wrong. And they assert that people are culpable and responsible for rejecting this knowledge (Romans chaps. 1-3; 10:4-18). And so the debate is engaged between those who accept these biblical statements as authoritative and those who do not.

Indeed, I will show in the following pages that God has revealed himself as, among other attributes, both love and holy. Since wrath is an expression flowing from his holiness and love, we cannot truly know God without embracing all his attributes. Those who champion relationship with a God of love but who also reject his wrath as an expression of his holiness do not know God. They cannot have a true relationship with him if they reject a significant aspect of his being or nature. *In a sense*, the Fall of Adam and Eve into sin had to occur so that they could come to know God fully including his wrath against their sin.

As an illustration, I cannot know my wife, nor she me, if either of us denies certain difficult aspects of our character and behavior and only wish to acknowledge the better traits of our character. For my wife to know me and have a full relationship with me, she must be aware of my total person including my defects and failures.

As mentioned above, universal reconciliation goes back a long time. Followers of universalism can be traced at least to the third century when Clement of Alexandria (died about 215) and Origen (died 254), the leading biblical scholar of that century, espoused such a belief. Their appeal to Scriptural arguments rests on three points: (1) the purpose of God to "restore" all things to their original excellence (Acts 3:21); Origen called this *apokatastasis*;[14] (2) the means of restoration through Christ (Rom 5:18; Heb 2:9); and (3) the nature of restoration as the union of every person with God (1 Cor 15:24-28). Yet in a future chapter I will show that what Origen believed on this matter is unclear. The great champion that universalists claim as one of their own may indeed have not been!

In response to these points the Christian church answers that the texts which speak about "all" refer not to all but to everyone who is in Christ; and that this interpretation is the only one compatible with the Bible's teaching

---

14. The word comes from Acts 3:19-21. It probably refers to the restoration of all the conditions in which people live because of sin, not the restoration of every person to fellowship with God. See Jewett, "Eschatology," 2:354-5. Also Jesus uses the term *palingenesia* ("regeneration"; Matt 19:28) to describe his coming kingdom and links it to judgment (v. 28) and "eternal life" (v. 29). And Jesus distinguishes between those who are his followers and those who are not.

on the "diverse destinies of the righteous and the wicked" (Matt 25:46; Luke 16; John 3:16; 5:29; Rom 2:8–10; 9:22–23).[15]

Another view of the future of humanity is that of annihilationism or conditionalism—that unbelievers who go to hell will suffer various degrees of punishment appropriate to their evil works prior to death, and then they are destroyed and cease to exit. In this way there is eventually no one who occupies hell or the lake of fire. All universalists reject this alternative.

Universalists Deflect Criticism

It is interesting that there is a common reluctance among adherents to universalism to confess their universalism. It is a common practice of universalists to refuse to commit themselves.[16] This agrees with the fact that it is an important element of the creed of universalism that no creed shall be imposed as a creedal test, that no adherent shall be required to "subscribe to any . . . particular religious belief or creed."[17] This allows universalists to say that they both believe and do not believe certain things. Yet over time universalists have published statements of what they believe. By comparing contemporary writers to these "creedal" statements one can uncover what they believe.

Another semantic ploy of universalism is to speak in pious tones "that I certainly hope that all those in hell will get out." Such a "hope" is found in almost all universalist literature, contemporary and past. Indeed, Origen himself used such expressions, as I will show in the section on church history. It is standard discourse found in virtually every universalist that he "hopes" that the wicked will escape from hell. But how and why should we ever have a hope for something that God clearly rejects? There is a legitimate hope which Christians have—the full realization of their salvation (see Rom 5:2–5; 8:24–25). But to hope for something to be true when it violates the clear teaching of Scripture is to view oneself as a greater authority than God himself. Hoping for universal salvation amounts to wishing for another way to God and salvation when Jesus Christ and the disciples have declared that Jesus is the only way to God (John 14:6; Acts 4:12). It is equal to the claim that there are many gods when the Bible, both Old and New Testaments, declares that there is only one true God (Isa 43:10–13; 44:6–8; 45:5–6, 14, 18, 21, 22; 46:9; Rom 3:30; 1 Tim 2:5) as proven by his total knowledge of all

---

15. Gerstner, "Universalism," 539–40.

16. This is a point made also by Orr, "Punishment, Everlasting," 2503.

17. See Mead, *Handbook*, 213. Yet isn't this denial of a creed part of their creed which they believe?

events past, present, and future (Isa 41:4, 21–29; 42:9; 43:9; 44:7; 46:10), his sovereignty over all the nations (Isa 40:10–24; 42:23–25; 45:1–3, 13, 22–24; 46:11–13; Acts 17:26), and his having created all that there is (Isa 40:25–31; 44:24; 45:7–12; Acts 17:24).

Interestingly, the contemporary authors seem to want to avoid being labeled as universalists. McLaren makes this point in the introduction and at the conclusion. He seeks to create a new "kind of Christian" who is neither inclusivist, exclusivist, conditionalist, or universalist.[18] He is purposefully non-committal, but affirms that he has "undermined conventional understanding of hell."

Why does McLaren not want to identify clearly his position? He distinctly does not want to answer the question of what position he holds because he prefers intrigue over clarity, and he wants to promote conversation instead of argument (xv). Still he seeks to deconstruct conventional concepts of hell (xvii) in hope of finding a better paradigm.

Yet McLaren writes that everyone should be at "the very least a universalist sympathizer," since God apparently is one, on the basis of 1 Timothy 2:4 (God "is not willing that any should perish").[19] If God is not willing that any should perish "neither should we," McLaren writes. This is a terribly contrived interpretation of this text, as I will show.

Similarly, Young has the Holy Spirit say that "she" has a great "fondness for uncertainty" (*The Shack*, 203). Also he asserts in print on several web sites that he "hopes" the wicked can have a second chance to get out of hell. But until the publication of *Lies*, Young has been reluctant to be identified with universalism.[20] He and his two editors have tried to deflect this and other criticisms of his novel.[21] They openly admit that they spent more than a year removing the universalism that Paul personally holds and originally had in the novel. They deny that there is universalism remaining in the novel.[22] In 2007 Young claimed that he doesn't want to be pinned down, that what one finds in reading his novel is up to the reader. This is an attempt to

---

18. McLaren, *Last Word*, xvff.; 182–3, 186–9.

19. Ibid., 183.

20. Yet in 2004 he extensively defended universal reconciliation to me and others at a Christian "think tank" or forum in his 103-page paper, titled "Universal Reconciliation." I responded and critiqued this paper at the next meeting. Paul did not hear my paper since he had ceased attending the group.

21. See the web site for *The Shack* and also www.windblownmedia.com/shackresponse.html. Jacobsen's article is titled, "Is *The Shack* Heresy?"

22. One wonders what Jacobsen and Cummings think now. Back in 2006–2007 they felt that they had influenced Young somewhat away from universalism (see Jacobsen, "Heresy," 3). Now with the publication of *Lies We Believe about God*, in which Young boldly declares that he is a universalist, it is obvious that they did not do so.

escape accountability. A careful reading of his novel and universalist literature shows that universalism is quite pervasive, that it is the foundation for *The Shack*. Others agree.[23]

I have known Paul Young for a couple of decades. As late as 2007, after his novel was completed, he affirmed to me and my wife that while he did not follow general universalism he did follow universal reconciliation (UR). But then in my home before many witnesses he asserted that he no longer believed in UR. He protested that he was not then what he was just a year before, that he was a person in process. Yet there is other evidence. Young lists at the back of his novel (in his "acknowledgements") several sources and people that have influenced him. Among these are several people (at least three) who are universalists (for example, Jacques Ellul). Also, he begins chapter 14 with a quotation from a universalist, Buckminster Fuller. Finally, many reviewers of the novel suspect the presence of universalism in the book (see the internet) without knowing Young personally. At the time this evidence seemed confusing. I document all of my history with Paul Young in my book.[24]

Now with the publication of his *Lies We Believe about God*, the "cat is out of the bag." Young confesses his open and strong adherence to universalism in a dialogue with himself. He writes (118): "Are you suggesting that everyone is saved? That you believe in universal salvation? That is exactly

---

23. See additional reviews besides mine at *burningdowntheshackbook.com*; or the reviews at amazon.com. When someone, including Young, boasts of his new belief in universalism, and berates evangelicals for their view of hell, and then after writing a popular novel for evangelical consumption seeks to disavow what he has earlier communicated, he should be held to close scrutiny to determine what he actually believes. This study is one such scrutiny that finds universalism. And his new book, *Lies*, makes this clear to all. Others (Tim Challies on his blog site; Jeffrey, "I Am Not Who You Think," 33–34; Beal, "Theology," B16–17) have discovered his universalism without knowing Young and his claims. Young seeks to deflect criticism in another way. In several interviews he has affirmed that how a person responds to his novel reveals more about the reviewer than about the book. In essence this has the effect of saying that unfavorable reviews misunderstand the book and are judgmental. Yet this seems to violate what Young asserts in the novel that judging others destroys relationships. Young would allow himself to judge others but disallow this to a negative reviewer.

24. See the Introduction to *Burning Down the Shack*. In this present book I refer to Paul's paper, "Universal Reconciliation," written in 2004 by using "UR" followed by page numbers in parenthesis. My written response to his paper, also done in 2004, is titled, "Universalism: A Response" and is identified by "Response." While I agreed to Paul's request in 2007 to stop circulating his paper (because he said it did not represent his beliefs any more) I did not agree to stop citing it, especially those portions cited in my paper as my response to his paper. But now with the publication of *Lies We Believe about God* in 2017, in which he boldly confesses universal reconciliation (118), it is clear that he has apparently believed it for at least fourteen or more years.

what I am saying! This is real good news!" Apparently Young has believed this since at least 2004, and his qualifications of 2007 were disingenuous.[25]

This bold disclosure by Young led me to write a response to his twenty-eight chapters of *Lies*. In my book, *Lies Paul Young Believes about God*, I take up all twenty-eight "lies" that Young proposes and find them to be strawman-arguments, half-truths, or fully true and not "lies."

As with the others, Rob Bell similarly writes that we should "long for" universal reconciliation (111). He too wishes to avoid the label of "universalist" but spends several pages defending the view that universalism lies within what he calls the broad stream of Christianity (107–10).

In the end it matters little what these universalists may personally affirm or deny. The question is whether there is universalism in their books. It is only the substance of their writing that we have objectively before us. And now we have Young's open confession of UR in his book, *Lies*.

Something else needs to be addressed. Universalists often accuse evangelicals of "demonizing" them, of calling them harsh or cruel names ("heretic") so that conversation becomes strident and unloving. Emotion replaces fact-finding. They warn that "fearmongering by people in power reveals the unacknowledged fragility of their own position; it can only be maintained by social threat."[26] They fault their critics as seeking personal promotion and publicity.

Yet it appears that universalists use such accusations to shield them from careful, critical scrutiny. Also, they themselves use "demonizing" language of their critics, as the quotations in this introduction reveal. In addition, McLaren himself is not reluctant to use the word "heresy" to label universalism, which is the very matter he is promoting in his novel.

I have interacted with the novel by Brian McLaren because of his significant influence in the emergent church movement. There is no doubt about his rejection of the evangelical view of hell; he clearly proclaims it. While he refuses to embrace explicitly the teaching of universalism, he speaks of his new view in such a way that leaves no doubt that the closest thing to it is universalism. There are clear parallels that McLaren has with Paul Young and with other identified universalists, past and present, including Rob Bell.

---

25. This confession occurs in chapter 13 of *Lies* titled, "You need to get saved." No one needs to "get saved" because everyone is already saved, Young asserts.

26. McLaren, *Last Word*, 183.

Universalists Dispense with the Institutional Church

It may come as a surprise to many readers that one of the tenets (if this term is appropriate) of universalism is its opposition to the institutional evangelical church. Both of the writers of fiction, Young and McLaren, are subversive to the existing form of the institutional church, and argue for a new ecclesiology. Young has Sarayu (representing the Holy Spirit) assert that the institutional church is one of many demonic systems that hinder relationship with God.[27] McLaren argues the case for the emergent church which "turns from doctrines to practices," from what one professes to believe to "how one pursues truth and puts beliefs into action through practices."[28] In his history of universalism Robinson asserts that Unitarians and universalists were brought together because of their rejection of evangelical Protestantism.[29] Similarly Rob Bell spends much time berating the traditional preaching of the gospel as infecting the institutional church with a violent view of the nature of God (because it proclaims that God will judge and punish sin) which in turn shapes us so that we act violently.[30] Young similarly berates evangelical preaching.[31]

Yet one must ask these writers: What about believing the gospel? Doesn't this new direction downplay doctrine and lead to inclusivism, so that any group can claim to be Christian, such as totally liberal churches that deny miracle, the deity of Christ and his resurrection? Does this viewpoint not suggest that there is a parallel between universalism and the denial of the exclusivist claims of Christ, that universalists are denying that he alone is the only way to God (John 14:6)? At least this corollary of universalism and the denial of doctrine pertains to Jesus' claims to know the destiny of unbelievers. Universalism rejects his authority regarding the destiny of the wicked. It also obscures the great commission to make disciples of all nations—to enlist followers of Jesus identified by what they believe about him. Matthew says that Jesus "taught them to observe all things" that he had commanded them (Matt 28:20).

It is not surprising that in the modern history of universalism there is a united effort combining liberal churches with universalism to overcome the force of evangelical faith in America and in Europe. McLaren seems to have ambitions along this line. He professes that he honors the church in all

27. Young, *Shack*, 178. Young continues his anti-institutionalism in his *Lies*, chapter 12.
28. McLaren, *Last Word*, 197.
29. Robinson, *Unitarians*, 169.
30. Bell, *Love Wins*, 182–3.
31. In Young, *Lies*, chapter 2.

its forms yet advocates a "deep ecclesiology" (141). Whereas Young would simply reject the church, McLaren would construct something new around the world—the *emergence* of communities characterized by four things.

First, they are catholic, meaning that they are ecumenical and post-Protestant. Second, they are missional, meaning that they wish to join God in his "saving love for all creation," to be a blessing to the world, to pursue "a faith that seeks the good of God's whole world" (155). Third, they are monastic, meaning that they comprise an order or community where practice means to love everyone, where "the best way to get to good doctrine is through good practice, instead of the other way around" (156). Finally, such churches form a faith community (rather than a church), where the church is "wherever Jesus is at work." McLaren claims that he doesn't exclude other institutions (157), yet both he and Young criticize seminary training as obstacles to a better theology (Young, *The Shack*, 91; McLaren, 44). And seminaries form an arm of the church.

McLaren's new ecclesiology seems to have forgotten its moorings. Without the proclamation of the gospel, there is no reason for the church. Where is the church's responsibility to proclaim faith in Jesus Christ, and the good news about salvation in him and deliverance from judgment for sin? What about the role of the church to preserve the truth of Christ? Universalists have gone to the heart of the gospel and redefined it. It is a serious error when the omissions, what writers such as Young and McLaren do not say, reveal what they view the role of the church is in the world.

Why This Study Is Important

Every Christian should realize how significant this discussion of universal reconciliation is. There is the increasing promotion of universalism in film, books, articles, unpublished material and on the internet. The latter makes information readily available and apparently has been appropriated by these writers of fiction.

Universalists themselves clearly acknowledge how serious this discussion is. The two writers of fiction have asserted that the position of universal reconciliation is a break with the standard "paradigm" of evangelical belief (Young, UR, 32), that they are dealing with matters of "ultimate concerns."[32] Informed by their former background they are aware that to most evangelicals universalism is a "dangerous heresy" and "one step removed from

---

32. McLaren, *Last Word*, 199.

atheism";[33] it is one of the "worst heresies."[34] Similarly, Bell writes that evangelical preaching has distorted the gospel by emphasizing entrance into heaven over a relationship with God. Thus it distorts the nature of God, changing him into a "violent God" and "vicious tormenter."[35]

The evangelical church needs to recognize that the very heart and soul, the meaning, of evangelical faith is at stake. Evangelical faith and its doctrines, including the person of Christ and his view of hell, are under attack by universalism. Universalists have come to their convictions because they believe that the evangelical position on hell and other doctrines is responsible for all kinds of society's ills, including war and injustice. In *The Last Word* McLaren blames belief in the doctrine of original sin for the shift in focus away from injustice on earth (for example, racism) to individual salvation (135). The emphasis on individual sin makes people let social injustice continue (135). Like the Pharisees, evangelicals adopt a view of hell that "marginalizes the poor by shifting focus from their poverty on earth to their destination in heaven" (137). Conservatives twist the understanding of the gospel so that "their earthly plans won't be too inconvenienced" (137).

McLaren (141) embraces a "post-Protestant" church; his characters are "recovering fundamentalists" (143). He does not use the term "evangelical" because it has been captured by the "religious right" and "so is of little use to anyone else" (184). McLaren (176) and Young (*The Shack*, 182; *Lies*, chap. 5) are agreed in not liking the term "Christian" either, and prefer to be known as followers of Jesus. McLaren (194) identifies evangelicalism as really "neofundamentalism"; he prefers to be called (like Jim Wallis) a "postevangelical" or a "19th century evangelical." Bell attacks evangelicals as having a "shriveled imagination" (180). Young rejects his "modern evangelical Christian fundamentalism" roots (*Lies*, 236).

The Universalist "New Man"

All of these writers proclaim that embracing universalism has changed their lives and their preaching. Their new thinking about hell has transformed them into more loving people. They have a greater love for God and their neighbors (Young, UR, 32; *Lies*, chap. 28; McLaren, 175, 198). Their new theology affects all that they think. In particular the doctrines of salvation, Scripture, Christ, the atonement, the afterlife, the nature of the church, and most of all, the nature of God (Young, UR, 33; *Lies*, chap. 28; McLaren,

33. Ibid., 14.
34. Ibid., 30.
35. Bell, *Love Wins*, 173–4, 183.

186; Bell, 178–88). McLaren (18) and Young (UR, 32) acknowledge that they had departed first from the exclusivist view and had begun embracing universalism initially without any biblical basis for doing so. In effect, this means that something, such as emotion or logic, but not the Bible, led them to embrace new beliefs. This is a key point!

McLaren (195) is not satisfied with "either the conventional view or mild modifications of" the traditional view of hell. Thus it isn't incidental nor to be taken lightly that universalism declares that there is need to discover a new kind of Christian and a new kind of Christianity (note the title of the first book of McLaren's trilogy; more on this below), and a new kind of church. These writers demonstrate that the issue involved is more about the nature of God than it is about hell (Young, *The Shack*, 120, has "Papa" assert to Mack who has graduated from seminary: "I [God] am not who you think I am"; see also McLaren, xi–xii). Bell uses the parable of the prodigal son to assert that God's love "simply is" and that God has no "desire to inflict pain or agony on any one" (176). He indicts evangelicals as proclaiming a gospel that makes God "violent" (183) and a "vicious tormenter" (173-74), that they embrace the "toxic notion that God is a slave driver" (180). Young accuses the God of evangelicalism of being "the originator of evil, a distant deity who had a plan that included the torture of a child. One can't run to God if God is the perpetrator" (*Lies*, 238).

Universalism Not a Minor Threat to the Church

It is clear, then, that universal reconciliation is not a minor distortion of doctrine. It goes to the heart of evangelical faith—who God is; what he accomplished at the cross; what sin is; who Jesus is; how and when people are saved (or if they need to be saved!); what the nature of the judgment after death is; the witness of the history of the church; the meaning of the institutional church, and other matters.

Universalist authors seek to supplant evangelical theology with a different theology. Recently Young spoke of the collapse of evangelical faith and asserted that he stood on the cusp of a new "reformation"![36] His supporter, C. Baxter Kruger, suggests similarly that after 500 years Young is presenting a "large-scale challenge of Christianity," challenging "our fundamental notions of God," that the church needs a "reformation," and that Young may be the new Martin Luther![37]

---

36. Miller, "Controversial Book," last 4 sentences/paras.
37. Kruger, "Genius," paras. 12 and 14.

There is a long history of conflict between evangelical faith and universal reconciliation. In more recent years universalism joined with rationalism and liberalism in its acceptance of German higher criticism to undermine and almost destroy evangelical faith on the continent of Europe and in England in the 19th century (as universalism acknowledges and boasts). In early America, it opposed the evangelical Great Awakening under Edwards and Whitefield—an awakening that brought one out of every six people to personal faith, and strengthened the moral foundation for the new Republic. In later years, universalism joined with liberalism and Unitarianism to undermine evangelical faith. In 1960, the Unitarians (who are anti-trinitarian) and universalists joined together to form one "denomination."[38] What brought them together was their "liberal doctrine."[39]

The present writing of universalism, including its fiction, continues this conflict. It is more seductive than a direct assault on the evangelical understanding of hell would be. Universalism in the emergent church and its embrace until recent years in various organizations such as Young Life make this critique all the more urgent. From being on the sidelines of evangelical faith universalism is attempting to join the team.

The Procedure of This Study

In the first section of these pages I present the case for universalism as argued by universalists themselves, and I include my response to each of their points. I cite both nonfiction material and the fictional material in order to evaluate universalism from biblical and exegetical grounds, from history and theology, and from rational and emotive considerations. All of these areas are the same ones that universal reconciliation uses in its claims to be the truth.[40]

In the second section of this study I bring universalism under the spotlight of the Bible to show how Christians can deal with universalism in their churches and in their personal encounters. I discuss major texts of Scripture, from Jesus and the Apostles, that universalism for the most part ignores or inadequately discusses or distorts in light of the contexts. These texts oppose the position of universal reconciliation. In the next part of this second section I compose questions that raise theological obstacles

---

38. See Ahlstrom, *Theology in America*, 37-41; and Mead, *Denominations*, 212-3.

39. Robinson, *Unitarians and Universalists*, 169.

40. Where the claims of different authors are basically identical I will not distinguish among them and simply cite the material as "universalism" or give the names of the authors without page numbers.

to universalism's view of hell. I show why hell must be everlasting for Satan and unbelievers. Then I cite the fatal consequences inherent within universalism—the harm that comes to the church and its message of hope for the world. Then I show how universalism is subversive to the institutions of society including the church, marriage, and government. Finally, I make some concluding observations about how to deal with universal reconciliation in its many forms in contemporary society. I draw upon the witness of those who in the history of Christianity in America have had to deal with universalism in their day. In the Epilogue, I cite a powerful text dealing with the reality of sin and the consequences of dismissing or denying it, and make a final appeal to readers of this book.

The following pages show that universalism departs from the true and actual meaning of the Bible and from Christian faith and doctrine. It also distorts the record of the history of Christianity. I draw upon my many years of teaching the interpretation of the New Testament, the Greek language, the Greek Old Testament (called the Septuagint, or the LXX), and the early Apostolic Fathers of Christian history (who wrote in Greek). I also draw upon my personal acquaintance with Paul Young and his departure from evangelical faith.

Throughout, my concern is that the Spirit of God will guide us into the truth, as Jesus promised he would do (John 14:26). We need to have no fear in exposing falsehood in pursuing the truth. As Jesus promised, the truth will make us free (John 8:32). We also affirm the love of God as immeasurable and vast and unrelenting and unfailing, as also revealed "in Christ Jesus our Lord" (Romans 8:28–39).

Section 1

Refuting the Appeals of Universal Reconciliation

Introduction: The Four Appeals of Universal Reconciliation

I'VE DISCOVERED THAT UNIVERSALISTS present their case for universal reconciliation under four major considerations. Each of these comprises a separate part of this section one. The first appeal is to biblical language, seeking to redefine terms such as "age" or "eternal," "hell," "*gehenna*," "torment," "punishment," and others, so that there is no such thing as everlasting torment in hell.

The second appeal is to reason and emotion. Here the thrust of the argument is that it is unreasonable to believe that God could send to endless torment those who have either not heard the gospel or have heard it and rejected it. It is unfair and violates a sense of justice if a person must have to spend an eternity in hell for committing a sin over the short span of a human life. In addition, the appeal to emotion means that God is unloving, he is more inhuman than humans are, if he takes pleasure in hurting, in tormenting people and angels who have rejected him. This portrayal of God shows that he is an impotent, bully kind of deity. Universalists attribute this portrayal of God to evangelical theology.

The third appeal of universalism is to history. Universalism claims that it, not exclusivism (people must be saved by believing in Jesus as the only way to escape an eternity of suffering in hell), was the predominant belief of the early church for the first five hundred years. Politics and stupidity then took over, and the traditional view of hell prevailed until the Reformation. With the latter came a new freedom to discover again the doctrine of universalism. It has had its followers among the Anabaptists and among those who follow Arminian theology. In the centuries that followed universalism first opposed the rationalism that sought to destroy evangelical faith in Europe. But soon it found rationalism to be its ally and it came to prevail in Europe. Universalism was in America from the very beginning and continues to grow steadily. Several times universalism has defined its creed, and these declarations set the standard against which to recognize universal reconciliation. I cite all of these creeds.

The fourth and most serious appeal is to specific texts of Scripture. For Christians this is the most important source of doctrine. Universalism appeals to texts to teach that God wills all to repent and to be saved, that Jesus has died for all, that atonement and reconciliation have already been made for all, that all will confess Jesus as Lord. If all people do not realize this salvation before they die, then God will use the corrective fires of hell to convince people and fallen angels to repent. God's love to draw all people does not end with their dying. At some point in the future even hell and the lake of fire will cease to exist. Obviously the name "universal reconciliation" derives from these sorts of texts that incorporate the term "all" or "reconciliation."

Part 1

The Appeal to the Language of the Bible

Chapter 1

The Meaning of the Word "Age"

ONE OF THE FIRST appeals that universalism makes for its case is to define the terms used in Scripture that are associated with life after death. The arguments from the language of Scripture concentrate on redefining several sets of words: (1) *ōlam, aiōn, aiōnios;* (2) hell, *sheôl, hades, gehenna,* lake of fire; and (3) torment, punishment, burning, brimstone, judgment.

The proponents of universal reconciliation claim that the first (1) set of words, representing the Hebrew word for "eternity," and the two Greek words for the same, cannot mean "eternity" but are limited in their scope of time. They refer only to an "age" or "ages," an indefinite period, but not endless time or timelessness or eternity.

The Strategic Significance of Aiōn in the Defense of Universalism

The discussion regarding the meaning of *aiōn* is one of *the most serious and far-reaching.* This is witnessed by the fact that the universalist John Wesley Hanson devoted an entire book to this matter—to try to prove that the term cannot mean "eternal," especially in the three passages where "eternal torment" occurs.[1] Other universalists paved the way for his extended treatment as they too wrestled with this term.[2]

---

1. Hanson, *Aiōn—Aiōnios*. He devotes 162 pages to proving his points.

2. A hundred years before Hanson, Chauncy in his *Salvation of All Men* (1784), was apparently the first American to argue that *aiōn* "never should have been translated as 'forever' or 'everlasting.'" He argued that the word is "commonly, if not always, used in the sacred pages" in the sense of "age." See Cassara, *Universalism,* 79, 82.

Hanson's research laid the groundwork for many that have followed. Most recently, Rob Bell employs the same kind of arguments in his attempt to define *aiōn*, devoting several pages to the meaning of the word.[3]

To this day universalists cite Hanson's work as though he had proven his case.[4] His arguments are among the most persuasive on the meaning of *aiōn*. It is hard to imagine anyone improving on the thoroughness of his study.

Hanson's writing is exhaustive, comprehensive, and persuasive to the casual reader. But to the careful reader his work is unconvincing. In the end he fails to prove his points about the noun and the adjective forms of *aiōn*. His work is filled with special pleading, assumptions, and much argumentation from silence. While a large section is devoted to church fathers he misrepresents them and church history.

In the following paragraphs I will support my judgment of his work. I take up Hanson's arguments in detail as among the best defenses of universalism. While I cannot be exhaustive and touch on every point I want to be detailed enough to show that Hanson is far from proving his case. In devoting this kind of attention to his work I will have confronted the most exhaustive defense of the bedrock of universalism—the denial that the suffering of the wicked is eternal. On the definition of *aiōn* the whole case for universal reconciliation stands or falls, at least as far as Scripture is concerned.

For the reader who does not wish to wade through the following extended discussion there is a summary of the refutation of the arguments of universalism discussed in this chapter near the end of the chapter. It involves twelve points.

Hanson devotes the first half of his book to show that the OT literature, especially the Greek OT, and pagan sources prior to the NT used the term *aiōn* to mean not endlessness or eternity but an indefinite amount of time. In the second half of his work Hanson argues that when Jesus and the Apostles appeared they continued this meaning and, with no intimation that they were giving the term a new meaning, they must have meant the same thing. The Greek OT (known as the LXX or Septuagint) was their Bible.

---

3. Bell, *Love Wins*, 30ff., 57ff., 91ff.

4. As witnessed by discussion on web sites (see "universalism") and by universalist authors that reflect his influence, such as Talbott, in his *Inescapable Love*, Paul Young (in his UR paper), and others.

The Claims of Universalists Regarding "Age" and a Biblical Response

What are Hanson's claims for the OT era? Regarding the Hebrew word *ōlam*, Hanson claims that it is "manifestly incorrect" to render it by "eternal" or "everlasting" (12). Also, by its own intrinsic force the Greek word *aiōn* cannot denote "endless duration" (13); "interminable duration" does not reside in the word (14). On the basis of the history of the use of this word the doctrine of endless punishment cannot be found in the Bible (14). Rather the idea of "eternity" is a derived meaning (13, 28). The basic idea of the word is a period of "indefinite length," an age (13). Only because of what the term refers to could it mean "eternity."[5]

Hanson goes on to claim that when the term is applied to "life" it denotes not so much duration as the quality of "the blessed life "(94). He cites many references which, he thinks, support this (Matt 19:16, 29; 25:46; Luke 16:9; John 3:15, 16, 36; Rom 5:21; 6:23; Heb 5:9; 1 John 5:11, 13, 20; and many more). The phrase "eternal life" refers to a life of faith, regardless of its duration (95).

For Hanson it is permissible to find the sense of "endless" when *aiōn* describes "God, Christ, the Gospel, the good, the resurrection world." The idea of "endless" is "imputed to *aiōn* by the subject treated" (95).

Here I raise my first objection. Is Hanson not involved in a case of special pleading? Someone or something has already determined that the words listed, such as God or the good, are already endless. Why cannot the opposite—evil—be endless? Does not the "resurrection world" include the resurrection of the wicked (Rev 20:5, 11–15)? *If people are created and born with immortality*, does this not include both righteous people (those who are in Christ by virtue of their faith in him) and the unrighteous, the sheep and the goats respectively in the parable of Matthew 25?

Hanson identifies several translations that are "absurd"—unacceptable—to him. For example, to translate the double use of *aiōn* in Philippians 4:20, "to God be the glory forever and ever," makes no sense since "eternity" cannot be followed by eternity, by the very nature of the case. Yet, as I will show below, this phrase can be explained as an emphatic expression for eternity (so also in Rev 14:11).

---

5. Bell, *Love Wins*, says that *ōlam* is a "versatile, pliable word," with most occurrences referring to "a particular period of time" (92). He acknowledges that some uses of it that refer to God do come "much closer" to the concept of "forever as we think of if" (92). Strangely he uses this information from the OT to support a counter claim regarding Jesus' use—that Jesus may not be talking about forever "as we think of forever" (92).

Hanson asserts that of the 199 occurrences of the noun and the adjective of *aiōn*, more than 150 do not mean "endless." This is true; as with all adjectives the nouns they modify greatly influence the meaning of the adjective. But Hanson wants to use this statistic to claim that it cannot mean "eternal" when used with punishment (104). This claim is beside the point. Each text needs to be examined to find out what the context supports.

Hanson then claims that if the term means "endless" in the thirteen texts where it modifies punishment, it would have been used more frequently with this meaning. It is "preposterous, incredible" to believe that it means "endless" with such texts (104). Why, he asks, did not Luke, John, James, and the Johannine Epistles use it with this meaning?

Yet this opposition amounts to an argument from silence. On what basis are we the readers able to demand that an author should have used a term more frequently with a certain meaning? How many times would suffice to meet this demand? This argument could be used for all kinds of things only partially revealed in Scripture (such as the signs of Christ's coming, the nature of his rule, the forms of church order, the relations within the Trinity, the deity of Christ, and more). Again, it is context that determines meaning and apparently the other contexts call for a limited meaning. Unfortunately Hanson will make this argument from silence many times.

Hanson discounts the ten times that *aiōn* is used with the kingdom of Christ and his rule (for example, Luke 1:33, 35; Heb 6:20; 2 Pet 1:11; etc.). These texts cannot mean an endless kingdom for Christ's kingdom is to be delivered up to the Father and come to an end (so 1 Cor 15:24–25) so that "God may be all in all" (92). Yet, contrary to this universalist claim, Christ's reign will be forever. For the text may be interpreted to mean that Christ is co-ruler with the Father; or that the Father rules through the Son. At least the meaning of "God" here in the phrase, "that God may be all in all" (15:28), may refer to the divine nature or being, which both the Father and the Son share. It is noteworthy that the text doesn't say that Christ's kingdom ceases. Rather it is delivered to the Father. Thus the kingdom may well be forever in the service of the Father or as subject to him. Note how other texts point to Christ as reigning at the end of the age (including Matt 25:31). Hanson wants to read his interpretation from elsewhere into 1 Corinthians 15.

In addition, Revelation 22:1–5 pictures the final state, and the "throne (note the singular) of God and of the Lamb" is mentioned twice (vv. 1, 3), as though it is one throne but two persons (God as both Father and as Son, as together deity) occupy it, just as both divine persons of the Godhead are similarly designated the temple (21:22), and the lamp of the Holy City (21:23) (although later (22:5) only the "Lord God" is said to shine on people). Is it not possible that Jesus Christ as God reigns forever, but as Son there is ongoing subjection of the Son to the Father? It is also possible that this text means that there is not eternal subjection, but at a point of "time" in the future God as Father, Son, and Spirit is "all in all." I will return to the discussion of 1 Corinthians 15. The difficulty of comprehending the Trinity certainly contributes to the discussion on these texts.

Dealing with the Most Challenging Text for Universalism

Hanson and other universalists give much space to addressing the most difficult passage for universalists (namely Matt 25:46).[6] Hanson introduces this section of his work with words that leave no doubt as to where he stands and what the stakes are regarding universalism. He writes that the parable of the sheep and the goats is "the sheet-anchor of the great heresy of the partialist church [this is the evangelical church], the principal proof-text of an error hoary with antiquity, and not yet wholly abandoned—endless punishment" (106). It is equally significant for the evangelical position.

Matthew 25:46 reads: "Then these (the goats) will go away to eternal punishment, but the righteous (the sheep) to eternal life."

In this conclusion to the parable of the sheep and the goats, the goats are consigned to "eternal punishment" but the sheep are consigned to "eternal life." Hanson begins by giving six reasons why the meaning in the first clause cannot have the meaning of endless duration but why it does have it in the second clause. He then elaborates extensively on each of these points. He also cites additional arguments, including appeals to church fathers and Jewish usage, as I will show.

Answering the Six Claims That the Parable Supports Universalism

He succinctly lists the six reasons as follows and I take up each one in turn.

1. The whole account is a parable, and not to be taken literally. Yet, I respond, all the parables are meant to teach something. Is it not obvious that two different, opposite destinies are proposed, and if one is endless the other must be?

"2. The punishment is not for unbelief, but for not benefiting the needy." Heaven and hell are not the issue since faith and unbelief are not

---

6. Hanson, *Aiōn*, 106–32. Bell, *Love Wins*, appears to ignore the parable. But Young addresses it in his UR paper.

the issues. Rather, works are the issue, and since we all fail in regard to these then all are guilty and none are saved.

Yet, I respond, the parable is probably teaching that genuine faith is basic and that works demonstrate the reality of one's faith. Hence it is appropriate to speak of reward for some and judgment for others (as also in James 2). Note that the people designated "sheep" are said to be "blessed by my Father" and "righteous" (v. 37), not simply the doers of good deeds. They know God and they intrinsically bear the marks of their righteous Father (Matt 5:20, 48; 6:1, 33). So the punishment cannot be limited to failure to do good deeds. Further, Hanson's logic is defective, since obviously some people are saved. His use of the word "guilty" reflects the idea that contrasts "righteous," so all are not "guilty."

"3. The word *aiōnion* [eternal] denotes limited duration" because its "general antecedent usage" has a limited sense. Jesus cannot use a different sense from the Classics and OT usage, Hanson argues. However, I respond, there are some uses in the NT that even Hanson thinks have the meaning "endless" (when used of God and in other contexts, as shown above). Again, it is the context of each text that determines meaning. Thus his argument elsewhere contradicts what he says here.

"4. God's punishments are remedial." All come from a Father seeking the improvement of his children. Yet, I note that while this is true regarding the chastisement of his people (Heb 12:5, written to Christians), it is not true of all humanity. If God views all people as his children, why then does he show wrath toward some (Rom 1:18; 2:1–16)? In his great sermon to pagans in Acts 17:20–31, Paul clearly distinguishes in the same text between a general universal sense in which all are God's "offspring" (the word "children" is not used) by virtue of his creating them, and another sense in which only those who repent and believe the gospel are his "children."

Hanson's point here is classic liberalism, and is a reminder that universalism prides itself as being rational and in league with liberal theology and opposed to evangelical theology (recall the introduction above). The same objections against liberal theology work well with universalism.

"5. The events here described took place in this world, and must therefore be of limited duration." Hanson is arguing that the events Jesus is describing were fulfilled in the destruction of the temple and Jerusalem in AD 70. The context is the Olivet discourse (Matt 24–25), and Jesus tells his disciples that all the things prophesied will be accomplished within the life span of one generation. Hanson asserts that the return of Christ took place then, ending the Jewish age and ushering in the Christian age. Thus the "eternal punishment" warned in 25:46 is "age-lasting" and ceased in AD 70.

Yet this overlooks the parallel clause promising "eternal life" for the sheep. Did their "eternal life" cease in AD 70? This is the major hurdle to this interpretation. In addition, how is it that Jesus returned in AD 70? Where is he? Where is his victory over evil? Where is his kingdom in force? His coming is to break forth as lightning from the east to the west (24:27). Why are there no universal reports of his universal return (24:27–31)? Finally, the several parables at the end of the discourse teach that there will be delay before Christ returns (the faithful and wise servant, the ten virgins, and the talents). The final parable is that of the sheep and the goats and deals with the reward of Christ's people who persevere by good works to the end when he returns.

A final question is this. How is it that no early church father, living right after AD 70, affirms that Jesus Christ returned then? Unanimously they look for his yet future coming, as do most Christians today. The *Didache* (an early composite document dated from the AD 60's to 150) devotes its final chapter of eight verses to the second coming of Christ and the attendant events associated with it (*Didache* 16:1–8). Verse 1 begins: "'Watch' over your life: 'do not let your lamps go out, and do not be unprepared, but be ready, for you do not know the hour when our Lord is coming.'" Verse 8 reads: "Then the world 'will see the Lord coming upon the clouds of heaven.'"[7]

Clearly the *Didache* is following the wording of Matthew 24–25. Similarly 1 *Clement* 23:5 and 2 *Clement* 12:1–6 look forward to the return of Jesus Christ.

The parable itself still points to the future, to the end of this age. Hanson overlooks how the parable begins: "When the Son of Man comes in his glory and all the angels with him, then he will sit on his glorious throne. All the nations will be assembled before him, and he will separate people one from another like a shepherd separates the sheep from the goats" (25:31–32). How did this event take place in AD 70? Rather the parable looks to the last events of history and final judgment.

Thus Hanson's claim that the events have occurred in history is false, and false also is his inference, that the judgment is of limited duration.

"6. The Greek word *kolasin*, rendered punishment, should be translated chastisement, as reformation is implied in its meaning." To support this point Hanson cites the Latin equivalent and the Greek usage by Plato (yet Plato also wrote of death being the punishment for sins, and this could hardly be said to be remedial; see his *The Laws* 838b–c). Hanson himself acknowledges that some uses of the term in Jewish literature (Josephus)

---

7. Holmes, "Didache," 267–9.

did not have reformation in mind. While it may have a corrective idea in 1 John 4:18, in 2 Peter 2:9 and in this parable (Matt 25:46) it does not seem to have such. There is an air of finality to all three parables of Matthew 25 with no hint that somehow at his return Jesus is going to relent and not carry through the threatened judgment. For Hanson to say that "surely Divine inspiration will use it in its exact sense" (meaning that Scripture must have only one, "correct" meaning for the term) is to beg the question again. The point is that good exegesis must examine the context for the meaning, not impose on it some presupposed meaning that fits one's predetermined theology.

Hanson does allow for the term the idea of the "punishment" of people but only for the good purpose of purging them "because he loves us" (111). Endless suffering or revenge cannot be involved because such has no good end in view. Yet, Hanson again is allowing his presuppositions about the nature of God as love, not the context, to define the term. He says that we ought "to give God the benefit of the doubt and understand the word in a way to honor him" (118). Thus the prior commitment that Hanson has to the love of God as God's supreme attribute, not to the words of the text, lead him to disregard the relatively plain meaning of the text. Also, is it not honoring to the nature of God to punish evil since he is also just or holy (see 2 Thess 1:5–6)? Is this not a good end? Hanson's over-emphasis on the love of God leads him to a distorted, truncated view of God.

Something else must be said here. Another word for "punishment" (*basanizō*) occurs in Matthew 18:34–35. In the parable of the unforgiving servant, these verses conclude it: "And in anger his lord turned him over to the prison guards to *torture* him until he repaid all he owed. So also my heavenly Father will do to you, if each of you does not forgive your brother from your heart." Here Jesus predicts that, as people act in righteous indignation, so his *Father* (note the word) will act to "torture" people if the condition of forgiving others is not met. This parable and that of the sheep and the goats are remarkably parallel, both involving judgment for failure to do righteous (note v. 46) deeds. It is not an impossible picture for Jesus to depict the loving Father as "torturing" people who reject him and his forgiveness. One loses God's forgiveness if one fails to exercise forgiveness of others (so in the "Lord's Prayer"; Matt 6:12, 14–15).

Hanson's Other Arguments against "Eternal Punishment"

Hanson makes several other attempts to justify his commitment to finding only limited reformation, not eternal punishment, in Matthew 25:46. He attacks scholars such as Trench (114) who disagrees with Hanson's definition, and the scholarly ability of Augustine the church father of the fifth century (126). This approach constitutes an *ad hominem* argument—attacking the person rather than his reasons (often the sign of a desperate position).

He appeals to the fact that the ideas of the "worm dying not" and the "fire not being quenched" (Mark 9:48) picture not destruction but the transmutation into a "higher form" of existence: burning destroys in order to produce ash which becomes fertilizer for new life (115). But is this what the biblical picture means, being drawn from Isaiah 66:24? It is the last verse of Isaiah and describes those who are in a state of existence that contrasts the state of those who are in the new heavens and new earth—a picture of finality if there ever was one!

Hanson appeals to the Jewish historical setting, to the idea that an oriental shepherd regarded his goats "as nearly as valuable as his sheep" and this is validated by Jesus placing them in the "next best place to his right hand, namely, his left hand" (115). In addition, Hanson asserts that Jesus speaks to the goats tenderly by calling them "kids" (115). Yet the text makes it clear that "second best" is totally worst—there is no good in it. It is judgment, rejection, and punishment away from the presence of the great Shepherd. Here Hanson is grasping at straws. He is desperate to find answers.

While Hanson can cite a text where "eternal" is used in parallel clauses with a different meaning ("the everlasting mountains . . . his ways are everlasting"; Hab 3:6), the idea is not parallel with Matthew 25. In this OT text mountains and God are clearly not equal. But the text of Matthew 25:46 speaks of people in both clauses, with some going to endless life and the others to endless suffering (116–7). People do live eternally, just in different destinies.

Hanson makes other appeals. He asserts that "eternal" modifying "life" and "punishment" is qualitative, not quantitative (118). This is an argument still being made today by universalists such as Thomas Talbot and Rob Bell (it is a term of "quality and vitality of life"; so Bell, 58–59). But if this is so, why has Hanson made such an effort to argue that the term modifying "punishment" cannot mean "endless" but the opposite? In addition, I observe that even should the terms have a qualitative force, are they not qualitatively different? Hanson next cites Kingsley who claims that *aiōn* never means "endlessness," since then the plural forms ("eons of eons") become meaningless (there cannot be several eternities) (119).

Now it is correct for universalists to assert that "usage determines meaning" [or, perhaps it should be more accurately stated: context determines meaning], but the preceding discussion of Hanson shows that universalism often does not follow this principle. While universalists build a substantial case for proving that *aiōn* and *aiōnios* do not always mean "eternal" (with which everyone would agree), it is incorrect for them to assert that *aiōn* "is never used in Scripture or anywhere else in the sense of endlessness" or "eternity," that it always meant "a period of time" (119), "*an age*." Kingsley's claim is based on the plural forms, but these may be explained otherwise (see below).

Hanson then appeals to the fact that the NT could have used other terms that clearly, intrinsically mean "endlessness," such as the Greek terms for "imperishable," "unfading," "immortal," "eternal, perpetual" (119–22). Again, this is an argument from silence and assumes the prerogative belonging to the author. Interestingly, one of these terms (*aidiois*, "eternal") describes the chains of the fallen angels (Jude 6). There seems to be no hope for them, but universalists affirm that God's love is so great that it will conquer the fallen angels and bring them to heaven. By this way of thinking, universalists become more compassionate than God, and are not afraid to suggest this (so Young, UR, 31–32). This is blasphemy!

And if appeals are going to be made for what terminology should have been used, I can also make this claim. If "correction" or "improvement" is the idea involved in the word "punishment," why wasn't the term *paideia* used which the lexicons identify as clearly signifying "punishment with a view to correction"? The noun and the verb are clearly used this way in every verse of Hebrews 12:7–11. It is translated by all as "discipline." Why wasn't "discipline" used in Matthew 25:46 if this is what the verse means?

Hanson makes the emotive appeal when he quotes Farrar as saying that he would rather die as a "beast that perishes" than that his "worst enemy should endure for one year the kind of hell described by" evangelicals such as Jonathan Edwards, E. B. Pusey, D. L. Moody, or Charles Spurgeon (126). He says that Jesus and the Apostles avoided charging "God with being the author of so cruel a calamity" (130). Thus Hanson assumes a standard of love by which he would measure both God's love and his justice. But the Scriptures themselves make no such statements. Is it not arrogant that there is an assumption here that they but not evangelicals have a better understanding of the nature of God? And recall Matthew 18:34–35 cited above, where Jesus "charges" his Father with torturing.

Then Hanson appeals to the idea that even "everlasting life" for the sheep is not everlasting but only a limited duration, since in many texts believers may lose this life—thus how could it be eternal (129)? It is a reward earned by works and not dependent on faith (128). Again he argues that it has the sense of moral quality rather than perpetuity (129); it is spiritual regeneration, the life of the gospel, spiritual life, the Christian life. Thus Hanson appeals again to the idea that the word is qualitative not quantitative.

Hanson's Oversight

Hanson makes one great omission as he treats the parable of the sheep and the goats. He overlooks the verse in the middle (v. 41) where Jesus identifies those on his left, the goats, as to be separated from him, under the curse of the Father, and destined for "the eternal fire that has been prepared for the devil and his angels." These three characterizations are the opposite of the way that the sheep are characterized (righteous, blessed by the Father, inheritors of the kingdom prepared for them, destined for eternal life). What is more, here the destiny is not simply punishment but "eternal" or "everlasting fire." Thus in one parable Jesus says three times that something is "everlasting"—fire and punishment for the wicked and life for the righteous. Finally, the destiny of the goats—those not righteous—is the same as that of the devil and his (not God's) angels (also v. 41).

Evangelicals often wonder, no doubt, why it is that universalists insist not only on the rescue of wicked people from hell but also on the rescue of the devil and his angels. In light of this parable it makes perfect sense. Universalists insist on consistency in God's love: his love is not limited by anything (such as his justice is limited by love) nor by anyone or any creature.

A final observation about Matthew 25:41 needs to be made, as revealed by the Greek text. It is remarkable that Jesus uses two participles to describe the righteous as "blessed" by the Father to inherit a kingdom "prepared" for them, and two participles to describe the wicked as "cursed" by the Father (supplying "the Father" is demanded by the parallelism) and destined for the fire "prepared" for the devil. All four participles are in the perfect passive form. This special syntax (of the four words in quotes) means that the words describe permanent states. That is, the verbal ideas express ongoing results, lasting results, in the present from actions taken in the past. Hence, at the future judgment the righteous experience the lasting effects of being blessed and prepared for the kingdom; and the wicked experience both the lasting effects of being cursed and destined for the prepared eternal fire. The grammar argues that these are unalterable states and judgments and destinies.

One could hardly make a stronger rebuttal to the claims of universalism! This grammatical point goes unrecognized by universalists.

This then is the extended argumentation that Hanson representing universalism makes to deny the reality of everlasting torment in Matthew 25:46. I will return to this parable in the second major section of this book when I discuss the teaching of Jesus regarding hell and punishment.

Further Universalist Defense of the Limited Meaning of Aiōn

But Hanson is not done with his case for a limited meaning for *aiōn*. For many more pages he argues that the term means only for "an age." For example, he discusses (132ff.) Jesus' warning that the one who blasphemes against the Holy Spirit shall not be forgiven in this age or in the age to come (Matt 12:32), that such a person will never have forgiveness (Mark 3:29; Luke 12:10). Hanson argues that such people will be redeemed in the age to come. Yet Matthew's words include the reference to the "age to come" and denies forgiveness then as well! Also, the Apostle Paul, living within the eon inaugurated by the death of Christ, says that Christians are living in the final age, in the last days, in the "consummation" or "the ends of the ages" (1 Cor 10:11; so Col 1:26; Heb 1:1–2; 9:26—Jesus "has appeared once for all at the consummation of the ages to put away sin by his sacrifice"; cf. Matt 13:39, 40, 49). There is no age after the present one except the era of fulfillment, of reckoning and judgment, in which the wicked are still seen as wicked (Isa 66:24).

Hanson discusses virtually all these texts and insists that the "age" of the OT has been replaced by the age of the NT (Matt 12:31, 32). But these texts assert that the final age has already been inaugurated. There is not a future age wherein people will be able to live out a life of obedience after repenting.

Hanson takes up other passages difficult for universalists (e.g., 2 Thess 1:9, "punished with everlasting destruction from the presence of the Lord"; 2 Pet 2:7, "for whom the mist of darkness is reserved for ever"; Heb 6:2, "eternal judgment") and makes the same argument that suffering is only for an age or that the desolation is only for a prolonged time, not for ever. He offers no new reasons to believe this, no doubt relying on his earlier claims. The rebuttal to him lies also in what I've said above.

Christ's Descent to Hell?

Hanson appeals to Christ's going to preach salvation between his death and resurrection (138) (1 Pet 3:18–22). I deal with this text, the "descent of Christ to hell," in the following pages. For now, suffice it to say that even if this is the meaning of the text, it does not say that Christ proclaimed *salvation* at this time. The text implies that it was a preaching of judgment. While this descent of Christ occurs in later forms of the Apostles' Creed, it was not in the earliest forms and it was never interpreted to refer to a second chance to believe and escape hell. It was always an act of triumph and victory and judgment. Again, I further discuss this creed below.

A Different Philosophy of Translation

Universalists commonly address the philosophy of biblical translation and argue for a better way. Like the others, Hanson argues that *aiōn* should have always been translated by "age" or the English "eon" in order to avoid all confusion (138–9). He appeals to Webster's dictionary but acknowledges that the definition "eternity" also occurs there. But this appeal to uniformity in translation is a significant blunder. The Concordant Version of the Bible was a failed attempt to practice this approach. It is doubtful that any linguist today espouses the idea that the same Greek word should always be translated by the same English word. This idea rejects the basic principle that different contexts call for different English words. A simple illustration proves this. The word *logos* (commonly rendered "word") has fifty-two English definitions listed in the standard Classical Greek lexicon by Liddell and Scott. Because of its occurrence in so many different contexts fifty-two English words are needed to convey the different nuances. Thus Hanson advocates something completely contrary to good linguistics and even disregards his own English dictionary (which still today has "eternity" as one of the definitions for eon).

For several pages Hanson addresses the idea that with the preposition *eis* used with *aiōn* (as in "for the ages" or "for eternity" and "forever and ever") the meaning is always absolute eternity (139). This phrase occurs in several places (Rev 14:11; 19:3; 20:10). Hanson argues that the meaning still remains "for the ages of the ages," meaning a time of long, but limited duration. For if one term means a limited time, Hanson argues, the use of double terms must still mean a limited time. "Eternities of eternities" is "absurd," "ridiculous" and "nonsense," Hanson says (139–40, 143). Yet the words may be rendered as "forever and ever" as an emphatic way of speaking of endless duration probably derived (as Hanson acknowledges, 141) from the OT way of speaking (see my further discussion of this below). While Hanson is correct to point out that the phrase "for ever" is often limited in scope (Exod 21:6; 1 Cor 8:13; etc.) he is wrong to find that this is the only meaning, even when it is used to describe God's reign, the reign of his people, and the torment of the wicked (Rev 14:11; 19:3; 20:10). Since this phrase occurs only twice of the destiny of the wicked, Hanson argues that if it the phrase were so important it would have been used more often. Instead it is not used by Jesus and much of the rest of the NT. Again this is an argument from silence and of little merit in determining meaning in a specific context.

Hanson gives sixteen points (141–5) to prove that the phrase "for ever and ever" always means a long but limited time. For the most part this list makes no new arguments. One new point is easily answered. He argues that the language in the clause, "they have no rest day nor night," restricts the application to this world (Rev 14:11). Yet Hanson cannot really believe this. For he has said already that the text refers to a very long but limited duration. Does this not carry the application beyond this world, beyond anyone's lifetime, into the next world—the realm of hell? Thus even he must acknowledge that such phrases are using phenomenological language derived from what humans can experience to describe something beyond their experience. It is figurative language. Thus "to affirm that it always implies duration without end, is as contrary to the fact as to affirm that it never does." This statement that Hanson cites from a Dr. Whiton (143) states it correctly since it implies acknowledgment that context determines meaning. And no evangelical affirms that the term always means duration without end.

An Inconsistent Hermeneutic

Yet Hanson, citing Canon Farrar, insists that while the literal meaning of texts leads to universal restoration and the final annihilation of the wicked, the texts dealing with the endless torment of the wicked cannot be taken literally but figuratively. But on what basis can such an inconsistent approach to interpretation exist? There is only one basis—on the assumed presumption that God is love and cannot judge with endless torment. Such a hermeneutical approach should be laughed out of existence, for if it were applied to the rest of the NT we would have no understanding of the NT about any crucial doctrines. And this is an apt description of how liberalism has arisen and exists: it discounts a consistent interpretative method because it has made a prior commitment to a theology that accepts only what agrees with human reasoning or rationalism. In subsequent chapters I will make this clear.

Hanson reinforces my point by citing favorably for his position (145) one of the greatest proponents of liberal theology and destructive higher criticism, De Wette. Hanson terms him "one of Germany's greatest theologians" (145). Hanson wraps up this section of his book by again making an argument from silence: why is such a "momentous doctrine" (the "eternal" punishment of the wicked) only cited fourteen times if it is true (145)? I reply that while this doctrine may be lacking in numbers it is not lacking in sternness or severity. Just one mention would have made it a doctrine with which to reckon, just like the doctrine of the "rapture" or the "snatching away" of the church (termed this way only once, in 1 Thess 4:13–18).

The Assertion That the Early Church Was Universalist

In the remainder of his book, Hanson argues for his limited meaning of *aiōn* by appealing to the "early Christians" (146–59). He argues that the first five hundred years of church history show that limited punishment, not eternal punishment, was the view of the majority of the church. He wrote another book devoted entirely to this argument. Universalists commonly state this view as fact. I devote several chapters to this historical issue in the coming pages (see chaps. 6, 7, 8). I find that this claim is patently false and I prove it in these chapters.

Suffice it to say here that Hanson is totally correct to say that the early church fathers, for the first five hundred years, illuminate what the NT means on the issue of the suffering of the wicked. They continue the teaching of the NT. But Hanson is wrong in thinking that they continue a view of the suffering as limited in duration. Rather, as I've just written to show how Hanson and universalists misinterpret the NT, he is wrong also in claiming that his view that *aiōn* is limited in duration was the view of the early church fathers.

I take up Hanson's arguments from both of his books on church history in my chapter on early church history. I encourage the reader to turn there for the refutation of universalism's claim that the church for the first five hundred years was universalist. If nothing else convinces one about what the church should believe today based on what it believed then, this section will.

Hanson's Revealing Conclusion

Hanson completes his book and defense of a limited meaning for *aiōn* by making an extended statement that reveals just what is the most important reason behind his position. He writes:

> Should any reader of this volume ask, "Why all this labor to establish the meaning of one word?" the author would answer that such a labor should seem unnecessary. Men ought to refuse to credit such a doctrine as that of endless punishment on higher grounds than those of verbal definition. Reverence, not to say respect, for God, the fact that he is the Father of mankind, should compel all to reject the doctrine of endless torment, though the weight of argument were a thousandfold to one in favor of the popular definition of this word. But there are those who disregard the moral argument against the doctrine which is unanswerable; who violate the noblest instincts of the heart and soul, which plead trumpet-tongued against that horrible nightmare of doubt and unbelief; who cling to the mere letter of the word, which kills, and ignore the spirit, which gives life; who insist that all the voices of reason and sentiment should be disregarded because the Bible declares the doctrine of endless punishment for sinners. It is for such that these facts have been gathered, and this essay written, that no shred nor vestige even of verbal probability should exist to mislead the mind, and so seem to sanction the doctrine that defames God and distresses men; that it might be seen that the letter and the spirit of the word agree, and are in perfect accord with the dictates of reason, the instincts of the heart, and the impulse of the soul, in rejecting the worst error that ever yet was invented,—the monstrous falsehood that represents God as consigning the souls he has created in his own image to interminable torment. It is because the word under examination is the foundation-stone of that evil structure, that this monograph has been written.

The statement is extremely revealing. The greatest argument against the torment of the wicked is not the witness of Scripture but one's view of God. Scripture *must* be in accord with reason and emotion: the "dictates of reason, the instincts of the heart, and the impulse of the soul." Even if the odds against the restoration of the wicked were a thousand to one, it should be embraced. *The weight of the statement is that one's belief should be fashioned finally not by the authority of Scripture but by emotional ("sentiment") and rational ("reason") concerns.* This perspective still shows up in the fictions and nonfictions of Young, McLaren, and Rob Bell. It is distinctive of evangelical faith that the final authority for belief is the Bible plainly interpreted, not emotions or reasons—not subjective thoughts about God. If evangelical faith based in the assertions of the Bible is not the correct approach, then competing subjective understandings of who God is become determinative. Yet we do not know God correctly apart from the teaching of Scripture. *How can one profess to believe correctly in and about the God of the Bible if one rejects what the Bible says of him?*

Hanson completes his defense of the limited meaning of *aiōn* by confidently declaring that he has woven an unbreakable rope of arguments (162). Yet I think I have raised enough questions about each of his arguments to make his conclusion at least implausible if not impossible. If the evangelical view has been strengthened then this long and somewhat laborious effort in addressing Hanson's defense has not been in vain. Universalist claims about "age" form not an "unbreakable rope" but a weak, shredded cord which is incapable of final persuasion. It will fail all who trust it for salvation.

Updating the Universalist Claims about Aiōn in More Recent Literature

Is Hanson's effort to redefine *aiōn* still pertinent today? Do contemporary universalists support his efforts? The answer to both is "yes." The writers of universalist fiction are in stride with Hanson. McLaren defines "eternal life" as the life of the ages—across the ages; and this means the kingdom of God.[8] It means to live a new way, "in a new reality" (78). While this is partially true, it fails to recognize many clear texts in which *aiōn* means "eternal." To claim that *aiōn* never means "eternal" goes too far.

Also the claim proves too much, even for universalism. If *aiōn* never refers to "eternal," what of those places where the term describes God or the life of Christians (where "eternal" means "everlasting")? Is God not eternal? Is heaven not eternal?

Other errors include the claim that *aiōn* should always be translated "age" and not "world" in some contexts (yet note Heb 1:2); and that the singular form cannot have the same meaning as the plural. Yet the singular and plural might mean the same if the context has a collective idea, or if the author seeks to make a point of emphasis, to reinforce the idea of eternity. This meaning is acknowledged by Greek language resources (as in *EDNT*).[9]

Universalists also claim that the KJV (King James Version) translators did not accurately follow the Greek and Hebrew texts in translating *aiōn*

---

8. McLaren, *Last Word*, 77.
9. See Holtz, "*aiōn*," 44–46 and Balz, "*aiōnios*," 46–48.

because they in 1611 were bowing to an "ecclesiastical doctrinal mandate" so as not to disturb the church. As a matter of fact, however, the translators were the best scholars of the day; and modern translations validate in many places their choices of translation. Further, there is no proof that the translators of the KJV had an ecclesiastical motive to avoid any allowance for universalism. In any case, one must ask: Why is universalism concerned so much about the translation of the KJV, a translation that has clearly been improved on during the last more than 400 years?

Next, universalism claims that "eternity is absolute timelessness," and thus it is wrong to use "eternity" to translate *aiōn*. Yet eternity may include time or a different kind of time. Even the English dictionary acknowledges that "eternity" may refer, as does "everlasting," to "continuance without end" and "a long period of time that seems endless."[10] How else can the Bible, which seeks to accommodate itself to how mortal human beings think, express a reality beyond them? I deal again with this matter below.

Since context determines meaning there are places where *aiōn* must have the meaning "eternity."[11] In answering Hanson above, I've sought to show that the context of Matthew 25:46 demands the idea of endless punishment. Another example of where *aiōn* must mean "everlasting" or "eternal" is a text that uses "eternal" in contrast to what is "temporal" in the same verse (2 Cor 4:18). Paul would have his readers concentrate on eternal rather than temporal things. Thus "eternal things" cannot mean things that "endure for an age," for the words are put in contrast to what are "temporal things." The phrase "for an age" is still a temporal period. There are several other texts where the meaning is "eternal" or "everlasting" (Matt 18:8; 25:41; Mark 3:29; 2 Thess 1:9; Jude 6, 7, 13; Rev 14:11).

What about the nonfiction of Rob Bell? He is clearly in league with universalists in his various pronouncements on the meaning of "age." Indeed, in his book, *Love Wins*, he devotes portions of chapters 2 and 3 to this matter. Like others cited above, he declares that "age" has a limited meaning, that it doesn't mean "forever" (31), that "eternal" in the Bible is not a category or measure of time (58) but a term of "quality and vitality of life" (59). Yet as shown above, "eternal" is both things. But this partial truth allows Bell to develop his view that hell is not forever but at least present in the experience of many now and in the future. For hell again is more an intensity of feeling than a period of everlasting suffering (chapter 3). In

---

10. Neufeldt and Guralnik, eds., "eternity," 466.

11. Buis, "Punishment, Everlasting," 955, stresses the importance of context. He quotes F. von Huegel as saying that "the essence of hell lies assuredly above all in its endlessness" (955).

Lies Young argues similarly against an everlasting hell (in chap. 15: "Hell is separation from God").

Use of Modern Scholarly Resources

Finally, universalists fail to cite the standard Greek lexicons of our day, such as *BDAG*.[12] The latter gives four definitions (determined by context) for the term *aiōn,* with many references for each: (1) very long time, eternity (which is a time to come that has no end) [esp. in doxologies that praise God (see Matt 6:13; Rom 9:5; 11:36; etc.; note Heb 13:8)]; (2) a segment of time, age; (3) the world as a spatial concept; (4) the Aeon as a person. The adjective has the meanings of (1) without beginning; (2) without beginning or end [esp. of God]; and (3) without end.

Clearly scholars affirm several meanings for these cognates including "forever" regarding the destiny of people (cf. John 6:51, 58). For this lexicon all three perspectives of time (backward, the present, and forward) can be labeled "eternal" (where we might prefer "everlasting" for the forward life of the believer who has "everlasting life"; so John 3:16). This lexicon also cites secular Greek sources (Plato used it of the Eternal Being compared to time; etc.) where "eternity" is an appropriate meaning.

The dictionary for *The Greek New Testament*, a standard text widely used today, cites these definitions for the noun *aiōn*: age; world order; very long time, eternity (and with the preposition *eis*, always, forever); Aeon (personified as an evil force); existence, the present life. The entry for the adjective cites eternal (primarily of quality rather than of time); unending, everlasting, for all time.[13]

Even more complete is the longer entry for *aiōn* and *aiōnios* in the major source, *TDNT*.[14] Paralleling much of the discussion in *BDAG*, some of the pertinent statements include the following. "Only in the light of the context can it be said whether *aiōn* means 'eternity' in the strict sense or simply 'remote' or 'extended' or 'uninterrupted time'" (1:198–9). The "plur. use is simply designed to emphasize the idea of eternity which is contained but often blurred in the sing, aiwn" (1:199). Finally, these "formulae contain nothing peculiar to the NT. From the time of the LXX they form part of the common usage of Hellenistic Judaism" (1:199). Even *ōlam* begins in Isaiah

---

12. "*aiōn,*" 27–8. BDAG stands for *A Greek-English Lexicon of the New Testament and Other Early Christian Literature*.

13. "*aiōn,*" "*aiōnios,*" 6.

14. Sasse, "*aiōn,*" "*aiōnios,*" 197–209. This is the *Theological Dictionary of the New Testament*.

"to have the sense of endless time or eternity in the true sense" (1:200).[15] The "usage of the NT is distinguished from that of the LXX only by an intensification of the tendency already displayed in the LXX to replace the simple formulae by more complicated" (1:200).[16] The word "has the full significance of eternity when it is linked with the concept of God" (1:200). "Eternity is thought of as unending time—for how else can human thought picture it?—and the eternal being of God is represented as pre-existence and post-existence" (1:201–2).

These statements refer to the OT concept that the NT took over and extended to Christ (1:202). The *TDNT* goes on to discuss the noun as the time of the world and as personified (1:202–8), and the adjectival form, that it has similar ideas (1:208–9). Other lexicons agree with these meanings.[17]

For universalism to fail to use any of the current standard Greek lexicons and dictionaries on this issue is similar to an English person failing to utilize Webster's dictionary or the Oxford Dictionary giving the history of the English language. This failure makes any claims that universalism asserts regarding the meaning of *aiōn* suspect and unconvincing. Universalists might claim that these sources are engaged in a conspiracy to oppose universalism but such a claim is without credulity. As shown above, even non-Christian sources recognize the meaning of "eternity" for *aiōn*.

Summary of Universalism's Claim Regarding "Age," "Ages," and "Forever"

Since universalism tries to be scholarly, it often cites a multitude of sources (older dictionaries and lexicons, commentaries, authors) for its idea of "age" rather than "eternal" for *aiōn*. Yet this attempt to be scholarly fails. The majority of sources support the meaning "eternal" or "everlastingly" in at least one Scripture text. In addition, there is no citation of several recent theological dictionaries nor of a recent edition of *BDAG* (as noted above), nor of any recent commentaries (of which there are scores available). Even Ellicott, of the 19th century, is aware of the options and uses "eternal" when necessary.[18]

---

15. Bell, *Love Wins*, 92, fails to give adequate treatment to this use of *ōlam*.

16. These statements about the Greek OT contradict those of Hanson in the discussion above.

17. Greek dictionaries (*BDAG*, *EDNT*, *TDNT*, *DNTT*, and *NIDNTTE*) agree virtually unanimously about these meanings.

18. Ellicott, *Commentary*, 37. He translates the word as "eternal life" in 1 Tim 1:16. On 1 Tim 1:17 ("to the king of the ages"), Ellicott notes that the word has the "usual

Still, universalism insists that all the Greek occurrences should be translated by "eon." It maintains that to refer to times in the past as "eternal" is mistaken; and time in the future is "eons" rather than "eternal." Universalism cites a host of texts (Matt 12:32; Luke 20:34; Heb 1:2; 9:26; Eph 2:7; 3:11 and other verses; 1 Cor 2:7; 10:11; 2 Tim 1:9; Tit 1:2) where, universalism asserts, the KJV especially and other translations are wrong to have the translation "eternal." But here universalism reveals again its faulty methodology.

Summary of Universalism's Faults Regarding Aiōn

After studying universalism's position dealing with "age" and "forever" several far-reaching observations summarize the preceding discussion. (1) Universalism is basically uninformed on how to do word studies, since by and large it neglects context as the determiner of meaning. Also, there is the unscholarly assumption that the same Greek word should always be translated by the same English word (the idea behind the Concordant version, often cited). This is the error called "root fallacy." *No reputable linguist or biblical interpreter affirms this approach.*

Actually, words in Greek and English have multiple meanings or a wide field of meaning, and there are no true synonyms and no exact equivalents between languages. Hence one context may call for a different translation as compared to another context. For example, the Greek word *logos* has fifty-two English translations (including "repute," "show," as well as the familiar idea of "word"). To argue that *aiōn* should have the same translation, "eon" or "age," everywhere is not credible. It must always be context, context, context as the determiner of meaning.

Proving Too Much

(2) As pointed out above, universalism's insistence on translating *aiōn* by "age" and not "eternal" proves too much, for then neither God, nor heaven, nor the saint's life is "eternal." Universalism's treatment of *aiōn* as describing the glory of God in various doxologies (Rom 11:36; 16:26) avoids the obvious: since God is eternal, his glory will be. To deny "eternal" here, on the basis of an erroneous concept that a word always carries its root idea (here "age") is to commit the "root fallacy" I've just described. Context determines

---

temporal meaning" but here the plural form means that the temporal periods "adumbrate the conception of eternity" (37). He has similar discussions in his comments on Gal 6:8; Eph 1:21; 2 Thess 1:9; 2:16.

meaning, and here the context demands the concept of timelessness (*BDAG* agrees). Because universalism proves too much, it violates logic; for "what proves too much proves nothing."[19]

Indeed, the whole concept of "eternity" derives not so much from the vocabulary but from our understanding of the nature of God. The nature of God must be immutable, eternal, and almighty for all his attributes, including mercy and righteousness, to exist.[20]

Universalism does acknowledge that believers do have endless life and that God is eternal, when other terms are employed, but it denies that the term *aiōn* when applied to believers (John 3:16) or to God (Rom 16:26) can mean everlasting or eternal. For universalists to translate this word always as "life of the eons" avoids the obvious meaning. God is described as "the one who is and who was and who is to come" (Rev 1:4), and this assertion of eternality is then used for Jesus Christ (Rev 1:8). Then almost immediately in the context Jesus Christ describes himself as the "first and the last, and the one who is alive, and I became dead and behold, I am living for ever and ever" (Rev 1:17-18). The last words involving *aiōn* clearly point to the nature of God and of Christ as eternal and everlasting; and the same terms occur at the end of the Revelation to describe Jesus Christ again: "I am the Alpha and the Omega, the first and the last, the beginning and the end" (Rev 22:13).

Universalism's insistence that the final age has not yet dawned, that there are yet future ages, contradicts the statements of Hebrews 9:26 (that Christ has suffered at the conclusion of the *aiōns*) and 1 Corinthians 10:11 (that believers live in the consummation of the *aiōns*). Modern translations (NIV, NET, RSV, NASV, ESV, Beck, Jerusalem, NAB, GNB, Kingdom, etc.) correctly and consistently use "eternal" or "forever" scores of times.

One final observation is pertinent. The earliest church fathers clearly support the idea of eternity for forms of *aiōn*. I devote below a whole chapter to this matter. But one example is worth citing here. As far as I know the most elaborate use of *aiōn* occurs in *1 Clement* 65:2, in the final words of the letter. In his benediction the author wishes that God be glorified through Christ, that there would be "glory, honor, power, majesty, and eternal dominion to him, from everlasting to everlasting of everlasting." Here *aiōn* occurs four times; and it hardly makes sense to find here that the term refers to a defined limit of time.

(3) Universalism cites scholars who agree with its doctrines and fails to interact with scholars who disagree. In my study I've discovered that

---

19. See Campbell and Skinner, *Endless Salvation*, 14.
20. So Clark, "Eternity," 384. See all of 381-4.

universalism often fails to cite a single recent, modern evangelical commentator or theologian.

Misrepresentation

(4) Universalism misrepresents the opposing side, claiming that evangelicals want to translate *aiōn* as "unlimited" time because God is "unlimited" in time. Rather, the truth is that evangelicals want context to determine meaning in any given place. (5) In its citation of sources universalism argues that the preposition *eis* shows that *aiōn* cannot mean an unlimited time ("for the ages"), since *aiōn* has the thrust of goal, and "eternal" cannot have an end or goal. This assumes that *eis* can only have one idea, when actually prepositions are quite flexible. Also this again proves too much, for then even God would be described as having an end or goal—something that even universalists would not want to embrace. Romans 11:36 says: "For of him and through him and for (*eis*) him are all things. To him be glory for ever (*eis tous aiōnas*)." Finally, to say that "eternal" cannot have an end or goal misses the point. (6) The point is that Scripture takes human limitations of thinking about time into view and is simply asserting that whatever eternity means this is "how long" God and his people will endure. It is time without a limit, or beyond time.

Additional Errors in Understanding Aiōn

(7) Universalism faults the KJV for its multiple translations of *aiōn* including "eternity." Yet such variety is justified because of differing contexts. (8) Universalism claims that the phrase, "for the ages of the ages," speaks about temporal periods lying in the future. Yet most sources view the plurals as simply being emphatic, as actually stronger ways of affirming everlastingness or eternity than the singular forms would convey. (9) Universalism argues that while the kingdom of Christ is said not to have an end (Luke 1:33; etc.), his kingdom "for the ages of the ages" will end when he delivers it up to the Father. This produces an unnecessary contradiction because universalist authors continue the error of "root fallacy" (meaning that a word in all its settings always has the same root idea) cited above. The same kind of error is evident when universalists want to render other texts (Rev 22:5; 1 Cor 10:11; Heb 9:26), in which *aiōn* occurs, so as to limit them to time and to deny "eternity." (10) Universalists expend much effort in their interpretation to justify the claims of universalism rather than to take the obvious meaning of Scripture as the best one. (11) Universalists assert that

"orthodox scholars" who do translation work often contradict themselves and are inconsistent by using different translations of *aiōn*. Yet this variety in translations simply shows that such translations are using synonyms and variety and trying to avoid the error of "root fallacy." They are trying to be good linguists first before they jump into theology.

Rejecting Consensus

(12) Finally, an important question begs for an answer. If so many translations and scholars reject the interpretation of universalism, why isn't this consensus persuasive, to cause universalism to change its view? *Universalism seems oblivious to the obvious.* Universalism is pursuing its own independent path contrary to the vast number of scholars and translations. And pride and independence form the greatest sin.[21]

In summary, universalism engages in several faults regarding word studies. A major fault is failure to interact with scholarly commentaries that most evangelicals use in their understanding of these texts. I will engage such sources in Section Two of this book.

This has been a lengthy chapter. But the argument that universalists make about the meaning of "eternal" is the most foundational one in the whole edifice of universalism. If I have chiseled some big cracks in this foundation then the whole ediface of universalism built upon it is in danger of collapsing.

Now I turn to other terminology that universalism questions. Universalism seeks to redefine, not only *aiōn* but several other terms associated with the afterlife.

---

21. As even Young, *Shack*, 136–7, 146, acknowledges.

Chapter 2

The Meaning of Hell

UNIVERSALISM HAS A SPECIAL interest in interpreting the meaning of hell and other terms pertaining to the afterlife. Again there is failure to use *BDAG* (153) and other linguistic sources which note that the term "hell" in the gospels "is the place of punishment in the next life." *EDNT* (1:239–40) says that gehenna designates the "place of eternal punishing fire." The logic that leads Young as a universalist to conclude that because hell "is so twisted and warped it cannot obtain lasting fulfillment, being tormented by the fires of its own unsatisfied passions" is perplexing and confused. If in this age we have seen what horrible forms evil can take, and take for a very long time, why could not other forms, even more perverse, develop in the coming era?

The Meaning of Sheôl

Evangelicals agree that the OT word *sheôl* means the place or state of the dead, the grave, rather than a place of "endless punishment." They agree that *sheôl* also has a figurative sense referring to a state of degradation or calamity arising from "any cause" including the "judgment of God" (which Young and McLaren also admit; cf. Bell, 66). Thus it means both "the grave and netherworld, particularly the latter."[1] *BDB* reflects these same ideas and allows for a difference of destinies.[2] Evangelicals also affirm that this

---

1. Merrill, "*sheôl*," 6. He cites the ideas of a place beneath the earth, a personification of a fearsome enemy, God's being able to deliver from it, and the more elaborate descriptions of it in Isaiah and Ezekiel, including a place of judgment and God's deliverance from it (6–7). This is from a standard, multivolume Hebrew theological dictionary.

2. Brown, Driver, Briggs (BDB), "*sheôl*," 982–3, agrees. This source cites these ideas: underworld, distinguishing the condition of the righteous and wicked, a later distinction of places, and figurative for "extreme degradation in sin" such as a place of

figurative sense is the foundation for the NT's belief in endless punishment: what happened in time reflects a deeper sense of reality beyond time that comes more clearly to the foreground in the NT. In the next chapter I cite additional evidence in the OT for the belief in life after death.

The Meaning of Hades

Universalism then seeks to show that in the NT the words "hades" (eleven times), "tartarus" (once), and "gehenna" (twelve times) never mean endless punishment. Several texts are cited. As with its claim about *sheôl* in the OT, universalism claims that the word "hades" may mean "grave" or the "state of the dead" but never "hell." Yet it also has the figurative meaning that *sheôl* has in the OT. Evangelicals again would agree with this latter idea. *BDAG* (16–17) points out that the word is understood as the "underworld, the place of the dead" (Acts 2:27, 31; Ps 15:10), and, as "the depths," it is contrasted with the "heaven" (Matt 11:25; etc.). It is also personified (Rev 6:8; 20:13–14). Additional texts allow it to have the idea of "hell" in certain places, as in the parable of the rich man and Lazarus (Luke 16). The former is in torment in hades in contrast to where Lazarus is (I discuss this further in chapter 12). The senses of the NT are quite parallel to those for *sheôl* in the OT.

The Meaning of Tartarus

"Tartarus" (occurring only in 2 Peter 2:4) is dismissed as pointing also to the use of a pagan story to represent destruction but not endless punishment. Yet *BDAG* (805) says that the verb was used by the Greeks and in Jewish apocalyptic to refer to a place lower than hades "where divine punishment was meted out." Could not Peter adopt the word to point to a common belief that he and his readers held regarding the judgment to come in the afterlife, without accepting all the embellishments that the Greeks associated with it and which he omits? It seems that this is consistent with uses of other terms regarding the afterlife.

The Meaning of Gehenna

The fourth and most important word is "gehenna," a word carried over into Greek from the Hebrew. This word connotes suffering and takes its meaning

---

exile. This is the standard Hebrew dictionary.

from the place, the valley of Hinnom, where the bodies of the worst criminals were thrown and burned to prevent putrefaction; and worms always fed on the remains. It has antecedents in Jeremiah 19 and in Isaiah 66:23, 24, which Jesus uses or alludes to in Matthew 5:29, 30 (the "undying worm and the unquenchable fire"). It is invariably translated "hell" in the NT. Universalism denies that endless punishment defines the term anywhere, but what I have said above regarding Jesus' mention of judgment coming in the next life clarifies that indeed suffering after death is contemplated. Jesus warns that it is into gehenna that God is able to cast both the body and soul *after death* (Matt 10:28; Luke 12:5).

Universalism argues that just because Jesus said that God is *able* to cast such into hell doesn't mean that he actually *will* (so McLaren). *BDAG* (153) notes that in the gospels it is the "place of punishment in the next life." It does have a symbolic meaning also, pointing to what is foul and repulsive and to dreadful judgments, which universalism admits. Yet such judgments extend beyond the physical in light of Jesus' belief in and teaching about the afterlife.

The Influence of Jesus

I point out here how significant it is that Jesus uses OT terminology to describe endless suffering. Previously, before the coming of Christ, the OT words seemed to refer only to the grave and physical death (as in Isa 66:23, 24). But Jesus infuses these texts with a deeper, additional meaning. The physical judgment to come typifies or points to spiritual suffering in an afterlife. Jesus gives greater clarity to the meaning of the OT text.

Universalism, however, is not quick to abandon its denial of an afterlife meaning for gehenna. It argues that if it really meant "endless suffering" why didn't Jesus use it more often and make his meaning clear the first time he used it? It also seems entirely out of proportion to link it to the judgments of the judge and the Sanhedrin (Matt 5:22–30). The first argument is an argument from silence and has little merit. The second argument perhaps fails to comprehend the seriousness of what it means to call someone a "fool." Such a vocabulary betrays a lifestyle totally void of appreciating the dignity of a person made in the image of God. Universalism finally asks why the word is lacking everywhere else in the NT outside of Jesus and James? This is another argument from silence. And this argument about Jesus' infrequent use is blunted by the fact of the weight of Jesus' use. As I pointed out above, no one else in the Bible uses language ("eternal torment" and "hell" from gehenna [except James 3:6]) as strong as Jesus does. *Universalists may find Jesus' language sparse but it is not sparing.*

It seems that the traditional view, that "hell" is endless punishment, finds justification in the terms used by Jesus and his teaching. For universalism to profess such concern for the love of God and reject the witness of Jesus is a serious breach of theology and logic, and belief.

The Meaning of Torment and Punishment

Universalism's view of a third group of words, "torment, punishment, burning, etc.," is particularly disturbing. It goes to the very heart of evangelical faith. There is misrepresentation of the character of Christ. Universalists claim that Jesus is the lamb who would never afflict harm or torment, that his "desire is entirely redemptive." Yet this claim overlooks his being also the one who in the temple became angry and beat the money changers, his being the Lion of The Revelation (chap. 5), the one who is the "Lamb of wrath" (Rev 6:16–17), and the one who is worthy to inflict all the wrath of the seal, trump, and bowl judgments (Rev 5:9). He is the one who at the end of the age returns to punish with his sword all the wicked of the nations including the antichrist gathered against him. He is the one who at the final judgment inflicts God's wrath (19:15; cf. also Rom 2:6). And there are other texts (discussed in coming pages) that associate Jesus with the coming wrath of God.

Thus universalism's picture of Jesus Christ is distorted by ignoring several texts. Revelation 14:10 shows that the wicked are "tormented" in the "presence of" or "before" the Lamb, which also suggests that such "torment" has the Lamb's approval. It seems to stretch the text to read this as internal torment, as referring to the conscience (since elsewhere it includes physical suffering [9:5; 18:10, 15]). Revelation 19 reveals that at his return Jesus smites the nations with his sword and will reign with a "rod of iron" (v. 15); he "treads the vat of the wine of the wrath of the anger of God almighty" (v. 15); and he actually puts to death the wicked with his sword (v. 21). Even in his relationship to the present-day church (Rev 1:16), and in his relationship to the church of Pergamum (2:16), he appears with a large, punishing sword.

Thus it is not true that the picture of Jesus is such that he would never inflict harm. The Jesus of universalism is not the Jesus of the Bible. While much of this language may employ symbols, it does cast Jesus in the role of Judge who will carry out a sentence of judgment. He is the agent of judgment for the nations, as Paul the Apostle affirms in Acts 17:31 (cf. Ps 2:12: "Do homage to the Son lest he be angry and you perish in the way").

The text of Matthew 25:46 is one of the most crucial for the issue of "punishment" or "torment." As noted in the pages above, the verse is the conclusion of the parable of the judgment of the nations divided into the sheep and the goats. The verse asserts that the goats will "go away into eternal punishment, but the righteous into eternal life." As pointed out above, universalists claim that the two phrases "eternal punishment" and "eternal life" mean respectively "punishment of the ages" and "life of the ages" (Matt 25:46). Yet this view does not do justice to the text (see my discussion below). Does universalism mean to say that there is not a single promise of believers' having eternal life in heaven (because of the use of *aiōn*)? Universalism cannot take this view, and be consistent, for its whole thesis is that the wicked are going to be chastised in hell until they are worthy of living forever in heaven. But what kind of heaven is it if it cannot promise eternal life, a final unchangeable destiny?

Finally, the attempt to limit here the meaning of "punishment" *(kolasis)* to "correcting," "chastising," or "pruning" seems to neglect the context (cf. 1 John 4:18) and the several uses in the Apostolic Fathers where it means "punishment." Again *BDAG* (440) defines it as "punishment." This particular word occurs only in two places: 1 John 4:18 (which does not pertain to the suffering of the wicked) and Matthew 25:46.

Universalists argue that if Jesus intended the meaning of "torment" or "punishment" he would have used *timoria*, since this term is used by Josephus to describe the Essenes' belief that the penalty of sin was torment without end (*timorion adialeipton*).³ But again, this claim means virtually nothing. Checking again the standard Christian lexicon (*BDAG*, 826) on the usage of this term shows that this noun occurs only once in the NT, appearing in a text that warns of punishment by God (Heb 10:29)! In verses 30 and 31 the text clarifies what "punishment" from God will mean. God is the one who exercises "vengeance" who "will repay," who "will judge his people" (v. 30). The author concludes: "It is a fearful thing to fall into the hands of the living God" (v. 31).

The word *timoria* also occurs several times in the Apostolic Fathers, namely Barnabas, the Shepherd of Hermas, Papias, and the Martyrdom of Polycarp. I take up the discussion of many of these references in chapter 6 on the history of eternal punishment as found in the early church fathers. In addition, the use of the verb (*timoreō*) occurs in the NT only in Acts where Paul uses it to describe his "punishment" of early Christians prior to his conversion (Acts 22:5; 26:11). Like the noun, the verb also occurs in the Shepherd of Hermas. The point is that context must determine meaning.

3. So writes Hanson, *Universalism*, 27.

Obviously Paul's "punishment" of Christians could not be forever, but God's punishment of the wicked could be (and is, in the light of the context of Heb 10).

A couple other observations are in order. Universalists assert that since Jesus doesn't use the term *timoria* he did not teach endless suffering. Yet to expect Jesus to use the term if he meant eternal punishment is basically an argument from silence. The fact is that only the author of Hebrews uses the term and it occurs in no one else nor in any other biblical book. Another fact is that Jesus uses other terms (such as "torment") that may mean eternal suffering if the term is modified by "eternal" (which happens in Matt 25:46). The duration of punishment itself is determined by modifiers.

Further research uncovers other significant details about the words for suffering. A lexicon specializing in "semantic domains"—it groups words together that have similar fields of meaning—lists several words meaning "punishment."[4] These include the words *krisis* ("judgment"); *kolasis* ("punishment", with the "implication of resulting severe suffering"); *paideia* ("punishment for the purpose of improved behavior"); *timoria* ("punishment, with the implication of causing people to suffer what they deserve"); *ekdikesis* ("punishment on the basis of what is rightly deserved"); *orgē* ("divine punishment based on God's angry judgment against someone"); *mastigoō* (a verb meaning "to punish severely"; Heb 12:6); and the verbs *basanizō* and *tympanizō* ("to punish by physical torture or torment"; Matt 8:29; Heb 11:35). The repeated claim by universalists is that all suffering from any of the pivotal terms (*kolasis, basanos*) is only chastisement and correction. But this lexicon shows that none of these terms in dispute has this limitation.

Yet this lexicon shows something that is even more significant. There is a term in this list which does have the meaning, "punishment for the purpose of improved behavior," namely *paideia*. The word and its cognate forms occur with this sense—of a father's chastening—eight times in the seven verses of Hebrews 12:5–11. But this term is never used to refer to suffering after death! We would expect this term to be used if the contexts referring to judgment had this force. These contexts never employ this term. *This is a serious blow to universalists' view of the Greek terms used in Scripture.*[5]

The other word for "torment" comes from cognates of *basanos* (occurring in Rev 9:5; 14:11; 18:10, 15; Luke 16:23, 28). The last reference is to the parable of the rich man and Lazarus (which I discuss extensively below).

---

4. Louw and Nida, *Greek-Lexicon*, 489–91.

5. Of course, this is my counter appeal to the argument from silence. But it underscores how empty are such claims—that an author should have used some particular word.

It also occurs in reference to the suffering caused by demons (Matt 4:24). The verb form *(basanizō)* occurs with the following meanings (from *BDAG*, 134): (1) literally of judicial examination (not in the NT); (2) of any severe distress, usually physical, as in diseases (Matt 8:6; Rev 12:2; Matt 8:29—the demons ask Jesus whether he had come to torment them "before the time"; Rev 9:5; 11:10; 14:10; 20:10); or essentially mental (2 Pet 2:8); and (3) generally, to harass (Matt 14:24; cf. Mark 6:48—the storm harassed the disciples). These various uses show that (1) torment was often physical; (2) that most of the references refer to God or Jesus tormenting the wicked or demons; or describe the wicked as suffering torment in hell. *BDAG* cites the noun *basanos* as meaning "torture, torment" with the idea "to be in torment" (Luke 16:23) and of hell as "the place of torment" (Luke 16:28).

Jesus' Use of "Torment"

The most interesting observation about these terms is that no one but Jesus uses the only two terms for the torment of the wicked in hell (Matt 25:46; Luke 16; except Rev 20:10, which implies that God torments the wicked in the lake of fire—but this may also be Jesus Christ). It is in his, the Lord's, presence that the wicked are "tormented forever" in Revelation 14:10. No one else—not John, Paul, Peter, etc.—uses these terms in this way in the NT. This is a telling bit of information that should temper all attempts to think of Jesus only with regards to love. Surely this represents his sense of justice and anger toward sin. To this evidence must be added the statements of Jesus that his home town of Capernaum and its neighbors would suffer worse in the day of judgment than the wicked cities of Sodom and Gomorrah (Matt 10:15; 15:23–24; cf. Luke 17:29—where Sodom itself is a picture of the judgment at the return of Christ). Jesus made this pronouncement during his earthly ministry of teaching and working miracles.

The claim of universalism that there are only two "right" reasons for punishing a criminal (to protect society and to restore the criminal to society after being improved by the punishment) overlooks the reason for punishment as a goal in itself, the idea of retribution. This idea finds expression in the government's exercise of the sword (in war and in the death penalty, as taught in Rom 13:1–7), in the OT's (and the NT's) sense of judgment on various nations, and as one of the purposes of Christ's return. "With flaming fire he will mete out punishment on those who do not know God and on those who disobey the gospel of our Lord Jesus. They will undergo the penalty of eternal destruction away from the presence of the Lord and from the glory of his strength" (2 Thess 1:8–9) (I expand on this and other texts in Section 2 of this book).

The Wrath of God

The suggestion of universalism that those who commit the "unpardonable sin" (Matt 12:31–32) will be pardoned in the coming age, that a way opens up for forgiving such sinners, is reading into Scripture something it never says and runs counter to the finality of Jesus' words. Jesus says that the one who slanders the Holy Spirit not only will not be forgiven in this age; he also will not be forgiven in the "coming age." *In light of this text, universalism amounts to wishful thinking.*

The universalists' idea that the judgment of wrath in Romans 2:5–9 is only remedial and temporary, that it continues only until the wicked are broken and call upon God for mercy, and are delivered, again adds to the text what is not there. This interpretation also overlooks the principle involved in the context of Romans 2: all will be recompensed by God according to their works (v. 6). What "good works" that mark the righteous (vv. 7, 10) will the wicked be able to do in hell to prove that they are saved and change their destiny? One must do good works one hundred per cent of the time and never commit a sin. The text gives every appearance of addressing people of the present age. The Apostle is not addressing those in hell. In spite of claims that spokespeople for universalism make to the contrary, universalism really does "minimize" the wrath of God.

One serious concern surfaces in reading a defense of universalism. Throughout much of this discussion very little is said of the need for unbelievers, the lost, to believe in Christ as their Savior (Rom 10:9–10). Little is said of the role of faith. Instead, there is wording to the effect that the wicked are chastened to call out for mercy. Yet this is not saving faith in Jesus Christ, and saving faith alone gives entrance into "eternal" life. As James says: "the demons believe but tremble" (Jam 2:19).

Universalists engage in much argument from silence, and they make a great appeal to what God must do as the God of love, but virtually nothing is said of the finality and permanence of God's justice and judgment on those who do not believe. John 3:16 makes faith the defining issue (cf. vv. 17–18, 36). The words that follow, that the one who does not believe "has been judged already" (3:18), suggest a definitive final judgment and a finality to the state of the unbeliever.

The Rich Man and Lazarus

It is particularly instructive to review universalism's treatment of the story of Lazarus and the rich man, who died and "was in torment" (Luke 16). Universalism points out that the story as a whole is drawn from the Greeks and others, and is a parable and not history. Yet it admits that there are additional elements in Jesus' account that are not found elsewhere. Nevertheless, universalism dismisses the mention of endless and irreversible suffering as part of a pagan story, of Greek mythology, that Jesus did not really believe or teach. He simply uses a story his listeners knew to illustrate the judgment that awaited the Jews. It is similar to his using other material which is not true, such as the story of Beelzebul (Matt 10:25; 12:24). It is like using a fable to teach some lesson.

This is a strange claim for followers of universal reconciliation. While Jesus is the great pattern for love, universal reconciliation rejects Jesus' authority when he teaches about hell!

Yet if Jesus uses this material to warn of judgment, does not the "judgment" suggest something both physical and spiritual, since the setting is after death? Jesus clearly believed in life after death (John 11:26) and warned of a pathway to destruction in contrast to that leading to life (Matt 7:13–14). He spoke of a day of judgment coming for the unrepentant (Matt 11:20–24) and for careless speech (12:36). He said that in this age and in the age to come there is no forgiveness for slandering the Holy Spirit (12:31–32), that his generation would experience judgment (12:41–45). He said that judgment will come to the tares at the end of the age when the lawless will experience harsh treatment after death but the righteous will be blessed (13:40–43). He warned that stumbling blocks could lead to eternal fire (18:7–9). Many more texts could be cited. Thus if Jesus believed in actual suffering after death, of judgment, why cannot that be seen beyond the metaphors in Luke 16? In light of the larger context of Scripture it cannot be excluded.

I take up the account of the rich man and Lazarus in the last section of this book, in greater detail, to show what it does tell us about the afterlife. Suffice it now to say that the story of the rich man and Lazarus is a major hurdle for universalism.

Other Descriptions of Torment and Everlasting Suffering

In addition to the terms just discussed, universalism deals with other descriptions that seem to describe endless suffering (see Young in UR and

McLaren). It considers such phrases as "tormented with burning sulfur" and "the smoke of their torments rises for ever and ever" found in Revelation 14:9-11. Similar words are used of the wicked and the devil's judgment. Satan is "thrown into the lake of fire and tormented for ever" (Rev 20:10, 15). Universalism argues that (1) the torment is in the "presence of Jesus" (not in hell); (2) the torment is a "city type" (Sodom, Edom), not individual; (3) the "eternal" idea comes from the smoke ascending, but this smoke is used elsewhere of finite judgments (as in Isa 34 and Jer 49).

Smoke Rising Forever

This passage presents the suffering of the wicked in the strongest terms possible (Rev 14:9-11). As noted above, the figure of smoke from the OT is a symbol of something greater in the NT. It is judgment. The time of it as taking place after death and its nature as being everlasting come from the context which describes the saints as on Mount Zion (v. 1), as "purchased from the earth" (vv. 3-4), that the hour of judgment had come (v. 7), that those who die in the Lord are blessed (v. 13), that the time for the harvest of the earth had arrived (vv. 15-18), and that the time of God's full wrath had arrived (vv. 10, 19-20). Surely the context points to a time of unprecedented and final judgment.

The Lake of Fire

Universalism also takes up the terms, "the lake of fire" and "the second death." Here there is an attempt to deny that endless suffering is involved because this judgment only applies, it is claimed, to death (hades), the beast, and the false prophet. Since these are not human beings, universalism claims, they cannot suffer. They are entities that are destroyed by the lake of fire. The second death cannot be endless death because Scripture says death is to be destroyed, to cease (1 Cor 15).

Yet the text (Rev 19:20) says that the two, the beast and his false prophet, are cast *alive* into this lake of fire. This suggests, along with the rest of Revelation, that these two are both individuals and systems they lead. As individuals they experience everlasting separation from God, because a thousand years later they are still there (20:10). In addition, the unbelieving and the devil are put there. In regard to death being destroyed, this must refer to the first, physical death which for believers and unbelievers is only temporary, not everlasting (20:5-6). Only unbelievers experience the second death (v. 6). Believers experience eternal life and never experience a second death. This fact reflects a qualitative difference between the two groups of humanity. The wicked enter a state of existence qualitatively different from the righteous, and Scripture offers no hope of escape.

Universalism's discussion regarding the lake of fire is quite confusing. Universalism constantly makes the point that punishment and suffering are intended to cleanse the wicked. It spills much ink to make the lake of fire an experience of purification and to give it the meaning that it ends death. Yet this seems directly opposed by the context. It seems, rather, to be the final disposition of the wicked who are in hell and already dead. The text does not say that hell brings an end to sin, since sin still exists outside the Holy City (so Revelation 22:11, 15); and hell is not used to purify the wicked to make them suitable for the new Jerusalem, for they are still outside the city in 22:15. These are crucial hurdles for universalism to overcome.

The more obvious meaning for the words that death and hell are cast into the lake of fire, and that there is a second death (Revelation 20), is that the wicked who are in hell experience a resurrection from hades or hell to be judged before the "great white throne." Their final judgment is that they are cast into the lake of fire to experience another death (in addition to their earlier natural death) which is unending suffering (20:14–15; 21:8).

The Bible does not say anything regarding the change of this destiny. The text does not say that the lake of fire destroys death (as universalists claim), or that it undoes all the work of the first death so as to purge away sin. It simply says that the lake of fire *is* the second death (20:15); and having a part in the lake of fire is the second death (21:8). Rather than purging away sin, the lake of fire validates the enormity of sin. It is a final destiny beyond natural death. Nowhere does the text even hint that the lake of fire has a cleansing, chastising, disciplining function. In addition, the lake of fire continues to exist (21:8) after God makes *all things* new (21:5). It continues on forever.[6]

The Apostle Paul's claim that death is the last enemy to be abolished (1 Cor 15:26) probably does not refer to the second death of Revelation (as universalism would have it), but speaks to the believers' hope of resurrection, that natural death is conquered. The wicked are resurrected, not to life but to another level or kind of death after judgment. They "will rise to be condemned" (John 5:28–29). And if the wicked experience what is called a "second death" there is the suggestion that it is a different kind unlike their first death. On what basis can a universalist say that this second death can be reversed, since its nature is unknown? The words suggest a final, irrevocable

---

6. Everyone wonders how and why the lake of fire can keep existing when all things are made new. In Section 2 of this study I suggest how this might be resolved.

death that suits the wicked for a realm outside the "new heavens and new earth." Also, the wicked are not considered in the context of 1 Corinthians 15. Believers are the "all" who, after "falling asleep in Christ" (vv. 17–18), are "made alive" (v. 22), who are raised in their turn after Christ returns (v. 23).

Finally, in contrast to universalism's use of Revelation 2:11, the promise to the overcomer is that he will be totally free of the lake of fire, not that he will not be "hurt" by it as though he experiences part of it. It is totally unacceptable to compare the lake of fire judgment for the wicked with the Christian's purification and destiny. Believers never stand at the great white throne judgment where the wicked stand (as Rev 20 shows). Believers are resurrected immediately into the presence of God as recipients of eternal life.

The Unrighteous Will Never Change

Universalists then claim that for sentient beings the lake of fire, the second death, is "temporal, or timely suffering," since they are tormented "day and night" (20:10). The gates of the heavenly city are left open (21:25) that it might be accessible to those in the lake of fire who "upon their faith and reformation" may enter it from the lake of fire. The second death is a process of punishment. [7]

But this is false interpretation. The text never says that anyone from the lake of fire ever gets out in order to enter the city. There is no statement that the two realms, the holy city and the lake of fire, are in near proximity to each other or even in the same realm. Regarding the open gates, Jesus the revealer (22:16) shows that the gates are open to admit the nations and the kings of the earth (21:24–26), but the "unclean and no one who practices abomination and lying, *shall ever come into it*, but only those whose names are written in the Lamb's book of life" (asserts the very next verse, v. 27). The words seem to be quite final. This book of life is also that book which determined who was thrown into the lake of fire earlier, after the great judgment (20:11–15).

Finally, the very last picture that John gives us of the new heavens and new earth and the holy city reveals that the wicked are still outside (22:15). Indeed, verse 11 probably means that people will never change from this time forward. It asserts that the righteous and holy continue to be such, and those who do wrong continue to do wrong and the filthy continue to be such. *This verse is a powerful testimony to eternal, unchanging destinies. It*

---

7. Bell, *Love Wins*, 115, appeals to this text

directly opposes the claims of universal reconciliation, including the idea that the "open gates" allow for all to change their destiny.

This last statement is reinforced by the description of the wicked (v. 15) that employs the present tense to describe their continuing pursuit of evil even in the lake of fire. None seeks to repent. This explains why they must endure an eternity of suffering separation from God (note that they are "outside") because of a choice they made to disbelieve in a short life time. *In the everlasting state they continue to sin.* Again, there is no Scripture to support the idea that the second death is a "process of punishment." Instead, there is an air of finality to it.

Chapter 3

The Reality of the Belief in the Afterlife

IN ADDITION TO THE attempt to reinterpret passages dealing with an eternal destiny in hell, the supporters of universal reconciliation move on to a much more serious matter—the existence of an afterlife itself. In the attempt to deny the eternal consequences associated with the term "hell" universalists attack the existence of an afterlife in hell altogether. This approach enables them to trivialize Jesus' use of the term. This is a very interesting approach. Universalists pursue this trivializing approach in different ways.

For example, universalism creates an interesting apology for Jesus' use of the language of hell. Jesus did not, universalists claim, originate nor endorse the belief in hell. Instead, the teaching about the afterlife arises from four pagan sources (Babylonian, Egyptian, Zoroastrian, and Greek).[1] The OT has only hints of belief in an afterlife which later Jewish writers developed. Universalism apparently uses this information to shift blame from Jesus as the one who created the teaching of hell. Instead he borrowed it from pagan sources and uses it for rhetorical purposes only.

Yet McLaren's acknowledgment (189) that there are glimpses of belief in the afterlife in the OT (Isa 26:19; Dan 12:3) is problematic. One must ask: if other ancient peoples believed in an afterlife, why didn't the Jews? Where did the pagans get it? Could they have derived it from the Jews and corrupted it? Are the "hints" in the OT of an afterlife evidence of a far greater depth of teaching? Indeed, it is, as shown in the following pages.

There is another serious obstacle to overcome. If Paul the Apostle can say that people have consciences that call them to account lest they suffer for sin at the judgment after death (Romans chap. 2, vv. 14–16), did not people always have consciences? If so, then doesn't Paul assume that people have

---

1. McLaren, *Last Word*, chaps. 8–9. See also Hanson, *Universalism*.

always been accountable to a judgment after death? If in the NT an afterlife is revealed, doesn't this demand that it always existed?

Another thing needs to be said. Just because the Christian understanding of hell may have precursors, such precursors do not make it a human construction that humans can tear down. Jesus embraced the teaching on hell more so than anyone else in the whole biblical canon. Our knowledge of hell comes almost exclusively from his teachings.[2] If universalists are going to "deconstruct hell," what will they do with Jesus' teaching? Will they "deconstruct" Jesus?

A parallel thought reinforces just how convincing this observation is. Jesus brings all kinds of issues and doctrines to the forefront, to clarity, or to revelation for the first time, and to fulfillment, that were never before known or known only in part. These include not only our understanding of hell and heaven, but our understanding of the resurrection, the trinity (the greatest revelation of all), the Holy Spirit, sin, human beings, Satan, the kingdom, the future course of history, the judgments to come, God's love for Gentiles, the meaning of the law, how to interpret the OT, and others. Virtually every doctrine that evangelicals embrace derives from the teaching of Jesus that advances over anything previously known. All these truths and doctrines derive from a shadowy or incomplete expression in the OT, just like his teaching regarding hell. It took the coming and teaching of Jesus to inform us more fully on all these matters.

The Evidence of Afterlife in the OT

Yet there is greater evidence in the OT for the belief in an afterlife than is usually granted by universalists.[3] Recent works point convincingly to it as embedded in the OT.[4] It begins with God's creating human beings in

---

2. See Buis, "Hell," 114–17.

3. See extended discussions in Collins, "Eschatologies," 330-7; Charles, "Pagan Sources," 756—63, who cites examples of common concepts, common convention, expansion, reminiscence, parallel, borrowing, transposition, adaptation, imitation, allusion or citation, and a multitude of examples.

4. For the idea of resurrection embedded in the OT, see Osborne, "Resurrection," 931-6. He cites the following references: Gen 5:24; 2 Kgs 2:9-11; 1 Sam 28:1-25; Job 14:7-19; 19:25-27; 26:5-6; Ps 16:10; 49:13-15; 73:18-26; 86:10-13; Prov 9:18; Isa 24:1—27:13; 26:14, 19-21; 53:9-10—prophecies of Christ; 66:24; Ezek 32:21; 37:1-14; Dan 12:1-3; Hos 6:1-3; 13:14; perhaps Deut 32:39; 1 Sam 2:6. Osborne points out that the OT does not deny belief in an afterlife. Resurrection became even more affirmed in Second Temple Judaism (932-3). It occurs in Josephus, *Antiquities* 18.1.4 par. 16. I've discovered it in his *Against Apion* (2.32) as a reward for the righteous. Whiston, *Josephus*, 377, 633.

his image and likeness (Gen 1) and his putting his divine breath into them (Gen 2). It is reflected in the Devil's lie that Adam and Eve "would not die" (Gen 3). It is reflected in the assumption that Satan is both created and has everlasting existence (3:15), the statement that Eve is the mother of all living (3:20), that the "tree of life" is the source of living "forever" (3:22), that Enoch "walked with God and was not for God took him" (5:24), and that Abraham "was gathered to his people" (25:8). At the burning bush, God declared to Moses, "I am the God of Abraham, Isaac, and Jacob" (Exod 3). Jesus understood this to mean that the three patriarchs were still alive (Matt 22:32). He was amazed that religious leaders of his day did not understand or believe this truth. He intends that we believe this truth as well.

By the time of Jesus, the Jews had developed a significant understanding of the nature of the afterlife. The people he spoke to clearly believed in eternal punishment.[5]

Jesus' Unique Role in Teaching about an Afterlife

In the end, it doesn't matter where Jesus got what. He is the greatest interpreter of the OT ever to live, and he found it there. If he affirms it as something that his followers should believe, they believe it. By raising Jesus from the dead God proved that Jesus is worthy to be the judge of all humanity (Acts 17:31). He also claimed to be wiser than Solomon (Matt 12:42), and proved that he was.

Jesus' resurrection to an afterlife is proof that an afterlife exists, and validates all his other teaching about an afterlife. His resurrection is essential to the gospel (1 Cor 15:1–11), and is the reason we believe everything else he said (15:12–19). He promises to his followers everlasting life and escape from judgment (John 5:24; 11:24–25). His resurrection became the catalyst both for his followers to expand on his teaching in various apocalypses and for his opponents to develop heresies to remake his teaching (as in Gnosticism).[6]

The issue is not the source of Jesus' teaching but its truthfulness. The truth of his teaching does not reside in its originality or novelty. Rather it resides in "what he chose and what he omitted from his culture, and in the relative importance each teaching was given in his overall hierarchy of

---

See also Jewett, "Eschatology," 342–58; Powell, "Hell," 953–4.
Other references touching upon the afterlife are Gen 42:38; Deut 18:11; Job 7:7–10; Ps 6:6; 88:1–18; 115:17; 139:8; 146:4; Eccl 9:2–5; 12:7; Isa 8:19; 29:4; 38:10–11; 39:18.

5. See the Appendix on Jewish understanding, in Morey, *Death*, 267–72.
6. See Collins, "Eschatologies," 336.

values."[7] *And Jesus gives a significance to the meaning and nature of hell that exceeds his instruction about heaven.* Why was this so? Perhaps because the concept of hell needed reinforcing in light of people's inclination to ignore it or deny it or to distort it—the very things we see happening today, and what has occupied the attention of the church for almost two thousand years.

In light of this it is both unscholarly and anti-Christian to label hell "a human construction" that can be "deconstructed." This is the language of postmodernism but it is offensive to the person of our Lord Jesus.

We accept Jesus' teaching, whatever it may be, because he is, after all, the only, unique resurrected God-man and the "pioneer and perfecter" of our faith (Heb 12:1–2). To be a Christian is to follow Jesus as revealed through the teaching of the Apostles wherever that may lead. *We don't contest with our Leader; we comply with him.*

Indeed, one must ask: if there is a positive realm to the afterlife (i.e., heaven), which evangelicals and universalists alike confess, where did this belief come from? Why isn't belief in heaven discounted as rhetorical language, so that heaven has no real existence, and is employed simply to raise the hopes of a better world in order to cope with this fallen one? *If heaven has always existed, then hell must have also.* I write more about this in the excursus after chapter 5 and in chapter 13.

Jesus' Use of the Language of Hell

Yet it is important to give further consideration to show how universalists virtually deny the authority of Jesus on the matter of hell. McLaren (60) and Bell (chap. 3) claim that Jesus didn't endorse the beliefs about hell. The language came into his ministry because of the Pharisees. Prior to his time the Pharisees wanted to blame others (scapegoats) for the nation's sins, so they used the pagan teaching about hell and the afterlife to frighten people to repent. They taught a self-made righteousness. Jesus takes up their language of hell for a specific purpose: to protect the scapegoats and to alter the Pharisees' understanding of righteousness. Jesus, then, isn't endorsing the ideas of hell; he is only using them to turn the Pharisees' methods and their concepts of hell back on themselves. This is "persuasive rhetoric" to

---

7. See Talbert, *Sermon*, 78, who writes these words of Jesus' teaching in the Sermon on the Mount, but they are applicable to all the NT. In fact, he is referring to the statements of Klauck, *The Religious Context*, 2-6, who is addressing the contents of the NT as a whole. He quotes him as saying that "the specific characteristic of Christianity" is often to be "found less in the details and the individual aspects than in the total pattern and in the unifying centre-point, which gives structure to the Christian universe of meaning" (5).

reinforce good behavior (62). The words do not matter; their force or purpose does (81). Thus in the Sermon on the Mount Jesus seeks to redefine God's righteousness as a compassionate, kind, and merciful righteousness (63), contrary to the harshness of the Pharisees' definition.

McLaren uses this construction to argue that Christians' traditional use of hell parallels the Pharisees' use, and needs to be abandoned. Hell is neither real, nor should it be used to manipulate people by threatening certain scapegoats—people who are marginalized, etc.—that they will go there. Young (both in UR and in *Lies*, chap. 15) similarly disparages hell by rejecting it as a place of punishing sin. Bell (64–73) ties hell to the present evil in the heart and society-wide chaos.

This construction of Jesus' use of the language of hell falls seriously short. For in the Sermon on the Mount (Matt 5–7) Jesus is speaking to the ordinary people, and "threatening them with hell" (to use McLaren's words). In addition, *there is a serious moral issue if Jesus uses language about a reality (hell) he doesn't really believe*. Finally, *universalists themselves don't believe this, for they use all kinds of arguments against suffering eternally in a real hell, when hell (by their reconstruction) does not exist anyway*.

The other, greater problem is how to explain and understand the other side of afterlife—heaven. Is this not a reality either? How can Jesus speak rhetorically about hell, but truthfully about heaven? How can anyone trust his words about the borrowed concepts of heaven if he didn't take as true or actual the words about the borrowed concept of hell? Is it possible that heaven doesn't really exist but that Jesus uses the rhetoric of heaven because he wants people simply to live like saints wanting to go there (*although people actually have no place to go to*)?

Finally, what of those who do not wish to repent? If there is no hell, and yet some wish to go there because they do not want to repent, what happens to them? How does God respect their choice—their choice not to believe? *If all are going to heaven anyway, how does heaven differ from hell? Does God coerce all to go to heaven anyway?*[8] McLaren is aware of the need to address free will and admits that "freedom of choice" is not a good gift to humans (102). Does he have a better way to construct a human being? *Is he charging God with malpractice—creating defective human beings*? It is little wonder that most have not followed this reconstruction of hell.

Also, there is the matter of the rest of the NT which uses terminology other than "hell" but still speaks of everlasting judgment. There are words

---

8. Indeed, if people in hell can repent and go to heaven, nothing prevents the idea of their rebelling again; and the whole cycle of repentance-rebellion-repentance goes on and on. Thus heaven is not a safe haven after all. This is impossible. The supposed early universalist, Origen, was aware of this problem. See my excursus after chapter 5.

such as "wrath and fury" (Rom 2:3–9); "sudden destruction" (1 Thess 5:3); "eternal destruction" (2 Thess 1:6–9); "eternal judgment" (Heb 6:1–2; and other phrases); "set on fire by hell" (Jam 3:6); "unrighteous under punishment" and "same destruction" (2 Pet 2:4–9, 12); "eternal chains in nether gloom" (Jude 6–7); "torment . . . forever and ever"(Rev 14:11); and others.[9] This language is an obstacle to universalists.

Belief in Hell Brought on Hitler and the Holocaust (of All Things!)

Just how extreme universalism can be in its faulty view of the afterlife is shown when universalists suggest *that the holocaust under Hitler can be blamed on the belief in hell (McLaren) or when they make Hitler look better than the evangelical view of Jesus (Young)*. Regarding the former, the argument is that the Christians of Germany, the Catholics and the Lutherans, who believed in hell didn't have to fear going there, and viewed outsiders (scapegoats, such as the Jews) as "hell-bound" anyway. The lives of the "scapegoats" were more easily disposed of then because God "will consider them disposable later" (83). McLaren (84) also suggests that the present war on terrorism creates an environment where the church fails to break rank with the state and speak out prophetically.[10] Such is McLaren's perverse reasoning.

This idea lacks all merit for any serious consideration. It ignores the fact that many evangelicals, such as Dietrich Bonhoffer, did speak out, and were killed by Hitler. It is far more likely that the failure of the church in the 1940's resulted from the fact that a hundred years earlier German rationalism abetted by universalism (as universalist historians acknowledge) invaded the church and *produced a society that no longer believed in hell or in heaven and had lost its moral compass*. I will demonstrate the persuasiveness of this view in Section 2.

Universalists blame the belief in hell for other things. Preoccupation with individual salvation from hell distracts people from addressing injustice in our world today (McLaren, 84), including the holocaust of the past and those holocausts of the present. Belief in hell focuses all the attention on whether one has believed in Jesus in a "certain prescribed way" (85; Young, *Lies*, chap. 13, and Bell, chap. 2, write in a similar vein) and thus minimizes human injustice. It is blamed for apartheid in South Africa (see 166–7). Speaking about a woman whose Jewish father suffered at the hands of the

---

9. See Buis, "Hell," 116.
10. In common Young (UR, 123; *Lies*, chap. 11) and McLaren (84) oppose war.

Nazis, McLaren asks: "What kind of God would add his own eternal torture to the obscenity of human torture her father suffered?" People are just not "lucky enough to believe the right things" (85). He concludes that people "burn in hell forever, eternally tortured, because [they] didn't believe in Jesus" (85).

But why does McLaren here take all the metaphorical language of hell as literal? *His language about God and right belief rises to blasphemy here.*[11]

Bell (183) claims that the preaching of hell makes God "violent" and in turn people become violent. Apparently he would make all the extreme, mass murders of our times the result of evangelical preaching!

It appears that it is not evangelicals who have created scapegoats. Universalists make those who believe in hell the scapegoats for the most vile behavior on earth. Such talk appears quite unloving for universalists who are quick to indict evangelicals for being unloving.

Universalists Trivialize Hell

There are other ways by which universalists trivialize hell. They deny it as being central to Christian teaching. Instead, it is compared to anti-Semitism, or to the belief that God is impassible (unfeeling), and "we were wrong about that" (McLaren, 93). Tradition is "living," not static, McLaren (93) affirms.

Here universalists commit the sin of the Pharisees, as shown in Scripture (see Matt 15:1–9). Like them, they make a crucial doctrine into something merely traditional which can be disbelieved and disobeyed. Instead they should consider it the authoritative teaching of Scripture which should be obeyed.

The doctrine of hell is also minimized by treating it as a topic of debate, that powerful people argue both sides (this is the approach of Bell, 64–73). Yet the evidence is not there. The people who support the elimination of hell are few, and include those who are on the edge of evangelical belief for other reasons (J. Sanders; Clark Pinnock; NT Wright, who actually supports the idea of everlasting hell; and others).

To help bolster his case for his interpretation of the biblical text, McLaren (99) cites several supposed sources. But at the end of his fiction he admits that he invented these sources, that they are fictitious! *Apparently*

---

11. Indeed, Young (*Lies*, 238) similarly slanders God when he writes: "The God I grew up with was of little comfort. In fact, that God was considered the originator of evil, a distant deity who had a plan that included the torture of a child. One can't run to God if God is the perpetrator."

theological fiction allows one to invent sources to support one's theology, and to present them as respectable, when outnumbered by the vast majority! This is a serious ethical matter. It leads to the question: *What else in his writing is McLaren inventing?*

McLaren suggests other ways by which to minimize hell. He compares it to the genre of parable with all its symbolism. He emphasizes that hell is rarely preached these days (xiii). He subjects it to public opinion polls (104). He claims that it is used wrongly to motivate evangelism (101). He asserts that people use it to scare evil out of people (101; Young writes similarly in *Lies*, chap. 2; cf. Bell, 173–83). McLaren compares it to what other world religions teach about the afterlife (104–5). Finally, he deconstructs it as a human construction borrowed from other religions so that something better, a better understanding of justice and grace, may come along (this is McLaren's choice; xvii–xviii). Yet what is the *better* thing to come along—universalism's view of hell? *But Jesus has already given us the best.*

Universalists Pit God's Justice Against His Love

Perhaps the most disturbing way to trivialize hell is to minimize it in comparison to God's love. While McLaren makes several references to the grace and justice of God (112), it becomes clear that for him justice is predominately social justice. His submitting justice to love is witnessed by his words that hell cannot "have the last word"; "always grace" must be the last word (101). Similarly, Young in his novel, *The Shack*, has wisdom affirm that "mercy triumphs over justice because of love" (164). Bell's way of putting it (64) is to assert that God ceases to be loving if hell is eternal. In light of what universalists have publicly affirmed in the past (the Boston ministers in 1878), that God's justice is limited by his love, it is clear that *universalists consistently subject God's holiness to his love.*

In summary, universalism's claims regarding the limited nature of hell, gehenna, the "smoke that rises forever" (Rev 14:10), and "the lake of fire" and "second death" often involve red herrings, misrepresentation of what the texts say, omission of texts, and failure to accept the symbolic nature of much in Revelation. Universalism's discussion of the story of the rich man and Lazarus (Luke 16) proceeds to dismiss it as simply Jesus' use of a pagan story that he didn't believe, to teach Gentile acceptance and Jewish rejection. Jesus' terms for hell are meant only to say that truth will come at the judgment, that fraud will be "burned away." In this way Jesus' teaching is abrogated.

What Does Hell Mean?

So what is the meaning of hell? Much of universalism's appeal for acceptance is to quote emotive language such as "the smoke goes up forever" (Rev 14), "tormented for ever and ever" (Matt 25:46; Luke 16); "hell where their worm does not die, and the fire is not quenched" (Mark 9:47–48; quoting Isa 66:24); and "the outer darkness; in that place there shall be weeping and gnashing of teeth" (Luke 22:13). Universalists cite these words in order to provoke abhorrence on the part of their readers.

Yet all of these descriptions might be figurative and metaphors employed by the Bible to cast the nature of hell in such a way that no one would want to go there. Yet whatever hell actually is we can be sure that it is separation from God.[12]

For when Jesus died on the cross, he did not scream out because of the pain of fire or darkness or the torment, but because he was separated *everlastingly* for a brief time or moment from God. "My God, my God, Why have you forsaken me?" (Matt 27:46), he said from the cross. The absolutely holy One became sin for us (2 Cor 5:21). It was this separation that made his dying so far reaching in its scope, so conclusive in its depth, that he could be said to bear the sins for all people, past, present, and future. Justice and love were both served. Hell is separation from God. This is the worst kind of punishment.[13]

---

12. Yet Young, *Lies*, chapter 15, rejects hell as separation from God.

13. Powell, "Hell," 953. He points out that the "complete and deserved separation from God" involves also separation from and enmity with people, and being at odds with oneself because of conscience. Thus there is "total conflict: with God, one's neighbors, and oneself. This is hell! If the descriptions of hell are figurative or symbolic, the conditions they represent are more intense and real than the figures of speech in which they are expressed."

Part 2

The Appeal to Emotion and Reason

Chapter 4

Reason Makes Hell and Judgment Unacceptable

"God is a bully."

THE SECOND MAJOR APPEAL that universalism makes for its case is its appeal to reason and emotion. McLaren, Young, and Bell all employ emotive arguments to bolster their affirmation of universalism. These arguments for universalism parallel some already used to redefine biblical terms in the pages above. Yet now they are used to argue for universalism from the standpoint of love or logic. Several arguments are used.

McLaren appeals to the logic that the teaching of eternal punishment leads to greater violence on earth. He blames those who believe in hell for the evil of Nazism (83) and apparently for the apartheid in South Africa (166–7). *By believing in the end of the world Christians are a worse influence than are atheists who believe in the salvation of the world* (152). Why? Because Christians who believe in an afterlife "evade justice [on earth] so they can go to heaven" (153).

Bell (173–5) goes so far as to assert that the evangelical proclamation of the reality of hell as a future judgment turns God from a loving being into a violent and vicious tormenter. Evangelical preaching changes the nature of God so that he cannot be trusted; he becomes terrible. In turn people become violent (179–83).

Apparently the old saw that I heard in my youth, that "Christians are so heavenly minded that they are no earthly good," has become: "Christians are so hellishly minded that they are no earthly good."

Yet the truth is just the opposite of this. Keller cites Miroslav Volf, who lived through the violence of the Balkans, as asserting that it is *"the lack of belief in a God of vengeance that 'secretly nourishes violence.'*"[1] The best way to prevent personal retaliation and blood vengeance is "belief in the concept of God's divine justice."[2] People can trust God to right their wrongs so that they do not have to. This is precisely what Paul argues in Romans 12:17–21, that Christians do not have to take up personal vengeance but leave it to God, including his appointed servant, the state. *When universalists such as Young and McLaren become anti-government, they doom the very hope of judgment, and this leads to violence.* The curtailing of divinely appointed government (Rom. 13:1–7) will not bring greater relationship with God and social justice; it dooms it. It brings anarchy. What Young and McLaren wish for is only an *idle wish and an idol wish*—seeking to establish some other way to achieve God's purposes instead of the institutions he has ordered by which to do so.

Keller also cites Czeslaw Milosz of Poland who critiques Marx who labeled religion as the "opiate of the people" because the promise of an afterlife led the poor and the working class to put up with unjust social conditions.[3] This is very much the view of McLaren. But Milosz says that the "true opium of the people is a belief in nothingness after death"—that our evil deeds are not going to be judged, contrary to what religion teaches.[4] Milosz has seen that a loss of belief in a God of judgment can lead to brutality, such as Nazism and Communism. Thus the critique of history that McLaren makes is false. Perhaps his American inoculation from the brutal ideologies of the world has blinded him.

---

1. Keller, *Reason*, 74.
2. Ibid., 75.
3. McLaren follows and cites Carl Marx in this criticism of the evangelical church.
4. Keller, *Reason*, 75. These quotes come from Keller's chapter (68–83) titled, "How Can a Loving God Send People to Hell?" It is a powerful apology for hell that refutes the universalist's (such as Young, McLaren, and Bell) message that love must take priority in our understanding of God. Keller argues that a God of judgment must exist; that God must be a God of judgment and of love (here he argues that anger toward sin is necessary; anger is not the opposite of love; rather, hate is, and the final form of hate is indifference); that a loving God would allow hell; that believing that some people go to hell does not make people unequal; that we learn that a God of love exists only from the Bible—not from history, other religions, or daily life—and this God is also revealed to be a God of judgment. Thus Keller observes: "Hell is simply one's freely chosen identity apart from God on a trajectory into infinity" (78); and: "No one ever asks to leave hell. The very idea of heaven seems to them a sham" (78). It is then "a travesty to picture God casting people into a pit who are crying 'I'm sorry! Let me out!'" (79). "All God does in the end with people is give them what they most want, including freedom from himself. What could be more fair than that?" (79). As shown in the parable of the rich man and Lazarus, those in hell have become totally absorbed in an identity that excludes God (see on Luke 16 below).

Universalism divides its arguments from reason and emotion into several categories. The first section concerns argument from concept. I must say that I find this section particularly disturbing. I believe that universalism oversteps the bounds of critique and argumentation and ends up slandering God, Jesus Christ, and every true Christian. I base my claim on the statements that universalists make in reaction to the traditional Christian belief in the eternal suffering of the wicked.

Universalists' statements include the following from Paul Young.[5] "Jesus is fundamentally involved" in the torture of billions of people; the universalist's own compassion appears to be greater than God's; God in the end is "grossly unjust"; in comparison to Pharaoh, Nero, and Hitler, "the doctrine of eternal torture makes Jesus a million times more vicious and vindictive than these three put together." Can you the reader believe that anyone once an evangelical could say such things?

It goes without saying that the vast majority of Christians must somehow be able to believe what they do about eternal suffering without becoming slanderous of the nature of God and the nature of Jesus. The resolution lies in a fuller understanding of the meaning of the death of Christ, the manner of his death, the seriousness of sin, how humanity fell into sin in Adam, the incarnation, and the nature of God himself as one who is both just and love.

In his most recent, nonfiction, work, Young writes that the God of his "modern evangelical Christian fundamentalism" was of little help and comfort to him. "In fact," he says, "that God was considered the originator of evil, a distant deity who had a plan that included the torture of a child. One can't run to God if God is the perpetrator."[6]

McLaren writes similarly. He declares that the traditional view of hell is "sadistic" (30). He makes comparison to Abraham Lincoln's words in his Second Inaugural Address ("with malice toward none and charity toward all"). By the traditional teaching of hell God is less magnanimous than Lincoln, for God is represented as "with malice toward many and charity toward a few" (68). McLaren has one of his characters say that God will treat people with "a cruelty no human father has ever been guilty of—eternal conscious torture" (75). He continues: "No wonder Christianity is a dying religion in so many places in the world" (75).[7]

---

5. These statements come from William P. Young after he had publicly embraced universalism in his 2004 UR paper, 22–23. They are representative of much more.

6. Young, *Lies*, 236, 238.

7. Similarly Young, in "Orthodox Novelist," in response to C. Baxter Kruger's 5th question, rejects "eternal conscious torment." Also similarly he claims that the evangelical church is crumbling (Miller, "Controversial Book," last 4 sentences/paras.). Bell

This last statement is patently false. By conversion Christianity is the fastest growing religion in the world. Christianity is dying only in Europe where universalism coupled with rationalism has led to its decline! *The same thing will happen in America as universal reconciliation demolishes the fear of God in the nation as a whole and among God's people.*

McLaren makes a comparison. As he would treat his children without punishment for their bad behavior, so God will deal with his at the judgment. There will be no punishment, only God's acceptance of confession (80). Similarly, Young devotes several pages to show in his novel *The Shack* that Mack's love for his children could not let him send any to hell; and thus God cannot do so (161–3). The movie communicates the same. God as Judge is a metaphor, as in the OT (McLaren, 40).

Jesus' Use of the Language of Hell

What about the language of "hell"? Hell is "a humanly constructed idea" (BM, 71). The point is not whether Jesus confirms hell's existence, but his purpose for using the language of hell (71). Jesus uses the best available model of hell but it isn't completely true for hell is "incomprehensible" (72–73). As pointed out above, Jesus uses the language of hell to reverse the Pharisees' rhetoric of hell to show that God's righteousness was compassionate and merciful.

Yet what do Jesus' models point to? His own experience of judgment at the cross shows that hell is at least separation from a holy God for his bearing sin.[8] In the Sermon on the Mount Jesus shows that God expects a greater righteousness in personal behavior than the people—not the Pharisees—could ever imagine (Matt 5:6, 20, 48; 6:1–21, 24, 33; 7:13–14, 20–21, 24–27, 29). Throughout the Sermon it is the people who are in danger of the judgment of hell. Jesus taught as one "having authority," not as having love.

McLaren continues. Jesus used the language of hell to threaten the exclusivists (the Pharisees) to show that God's righteousness was compassionate and merciful, "that for God there was no out-group" (74). Jesus used the "power of the language of hell to disempower the injustice of the powerful and to empower the disempowered to seek justice" (136; yet this is not true of the Sermon on the Mount where the poor are addressed). Contemporary Christians, McLaren claims, are followers of the Pharisees not Jesus in their

---

(64), too, questions eternal torment.

8. In his *Lies*, chapters 15, 27, Young asserts that neither hell nor sin separates anyone from God.

use of the language of hell to "instill compliance through fear" (163; so also Young and Bell, 69–70).

According to McLaren, Jesus "deconstructs hell—he uses the language but "sows seeds for its own demise and replacement" (75). Similar to his understanding of Jesus, McLaren would deconstruct conventional concepts of hell in the sincere hope that "a better vision of the gospel" will appear (xvii). Jesus "fulfills the language of hell" just like he fulfills (deconstructs) the law of Moses by replacing it with the new covenant (76). The uses of "hell" in the Sermon on the Mount are not to be taken literally but convey accountability. The road to destruction (Matt 7:21–24) is not to hell; and the road to heaven is the road to true life (76–77).

Yet Jesus did distinguish an out-group (Matt 7:21). It is those on the broad way to destruction. *Thus universalism is more inclusive than Jesus is for he would exclude the Pharisees but universalism would include them! And Jesus never claimed to fulfill or deconstruct hell. It is never said that there is a "new hell" to replace the "old hell" as there is a "new covenant" to replace the "old covenant."* He never said that he came to "fulfill" hell, but only to fulfill the law (Matt 5:17).

Does Dan, McLaren's fictitious pastor, believe in hell? While he admits that judgment and accountability are real, there is no confession of hell as real (137). Indeed hell is part of Dan's past, a "sinking ship," and he needs to leave hell behind (143). The destiny of all is not "heaven or hell, which aren't the ultimate reality, but in relation to God . . . whose will is peace and justice for all" (164). From the kingdom of God "no one who wants to come home will ever be turned away" (173).

Thus for universalists hell is only a warning, a threat. It is not a destiny (McLaren, 26). As a warning hell issues from love, from wisdom, from better judgment, whether it be God's or people's. It does not matter from what it comes, for its purpose, not its substance, is the point (26).

The Pragmatic Argument: "Christians Don't Believe What They Profess"

Next, universalism attacks Christians who say that they believe in the eternal suffering of the wicked but they don't really believe it. If they did believe it they would go from door to door warning the wicked to repent.[9]

I respond that how we are to conduct ourselves in light of the eternal suffering of the wicked should be dictated by how Jesus lived, and how the greatest apostle, Paul, conducted himself. I don't think that even Jesus and

---

9. Young, UR, 23–24.

Paul would meet universalism's *ad hominem* argument—"either those who teach eternal torture are extremely and brutally calloused or they do not truly believe what they teach." [10]

The Evangelistic Argument: Scaring People Away from Hell

As far as the "Evangelistic Argument" is concerned, universalism indicts Christians for using the torments of hell to evangelize the lost, whereas Jesus and the Apostle Paul did not do so.

Yet universalism overlooks some other considerations. These include trusting in the purpose of God (Rom 8:28); or, framing what universalists call the evangelistic argument in other terms. Moreover, the Apostle Paul was highly motivated by the love of God—the love of God revealed in Christ and the consequences for those who did not place faith in him and his atoning work. Paul was constrained by love to reach all people (cf. Rom 1:14–16; 1 Cor 5:14–21), but he was also constrained to warn of God's condemnation and wrath (Romans chaps. 2; 11) and a coming day of retribution and eternal destruction (2 Thess 1:8–10). In addition, Jesus himself warned of hell four times more frequently than he spoke of heaven (note Matt 5–7). Peter's first sermon on the Day of Pentecost has overtones of judgment to come (Acts 2). In his message on "Mars Hill" Paul explicitly warns of a day coming when God will judge the world in righteousness by the resurrected Christ (Acts 17:30–31; cf. Rom 3:21–26). In the end, evangelicals follow the practice of the Apostles for the content of their preaching.

The Just Punishment Argument: "Eternal Judgment Is Unjust"

Universalism also appeals to the issue of "a just punishment for the crime." Universalism claims that eternal judgment is "unreasonable, illogical. . . wicked and unjust" for a temporal sin committed within time. Bell

---

10. Ibid., 24. Moreover, universalists thereby indict the shortcoming of universalism and themselves. I don't know of any universalist running door to door, pounding and warning people to turn from sin and to believe in Christ before they die. I'm sure that universalists do not live the way that they condemn others for failing to live. Why is this the case? Could it be that universalists can care less about winning the lost to Christ in the present since they believe that the wicked will have a second chance after death? And it's not just a chance that they will be saved after death but, by their teaching, a certainty. Unbelievers *must* come to faith. Truly this is deterministic and coercive.

uses this argument at least four times (2, 102, 110, 175). He identifies it as one of the main reasons for writing his book.

In the pages that follow I give a full answer to this objection to biblical doctrine. For now I point out that universalism links this argument to the culpability of human sin. It argues that humans are going to be punished, by the traditional view, for a sin that is inherent in their nature; they cannot help but sin. Yet it is not biblical to claim that a sinner commits a "crime which is inherent in his own nature" (Young), in order to deflect the culpability that humans have for rejecting God. The Scriptures show that people were not created with a sin nature. Their original nature was sinless.

In addition, universalism is incorrect to say that people have no choice but to sin, that they are "slaves" to sin; that Adam already made the choice for each person. This sounds very much like the objections raised to the Apostle Paul's teaching in Romans. Some objectors would advocate that people ought to sin to make grace abound (Rom 6:1, 15); others would insist that God should not fault anyone for failing to obey him, for no one can resist his will (9:19).

Instead, a better, biblical theology affirms that we all made the choice corporately, together, when Adam chose, and our daily sinning confirms that we would repeat our sin in Adam's. This corporate identity in Adam has inherently the seed of a promise within it—it enables a corresponding identity of deliverance from sin in Christ for those who believe (see further below). Further, God holds all responsible for their choices to sin (note Rom 2; Jam 1:12–18), just as he holds all responsible for their choice in Adam (Rom 5). We are hardly to be described as "victims" of the inheritance of sin. Certainly Scripture does not so describe humanity in general, nor believers.

The Destiny of Infants

In regard to the matter of "unborn or infant children," universalism faults the church for creating a way for infants to be saved. Whether this doctrine be right or not, the problem exists for universalism as well, but even more so. For universalism would hold that the infants go to hell for a time rather than to heaven! The church's concern for fairness or justice leads to infant salvation; but universalism's concern for the same seemingly leads to the torment of infants and to a far greater perversion of justice—the salvation of even Satan and his angels apart from the death of Christ (see below). Jesus did not, could not, die for fallen angels or for Satan. Jesus came to help humanity alone, as Hebrews 2:16 asserts. Yet, according to universalism, they are somehow, by some unexplained means, going to be saved.

The Inadequacy of General Revelation

Universalism addresses the matter of general revelation, that God reveals himself to every person. Universalists generally accept the traditional view that natural revelation is not sufficient to bring salvation to any person. I would observe, however, that general revelation holds the potential of leading to faith in the true God.[11] It was possible for people in the times of ignorance before Jesus' death to be saved apart from faith placed explicitly in Jesus Christ (Acts 17:27–29; Rom 3:21–26). However, according to Romans 1:18–32, the usual response of people to general revelation is to reject it and become idolaters—to worship willfully the creation instead of the Creator. But now that Christ has come the earlier times of "ignorance" no longer exist, says the Apostle (Acts 17:31; Rom 3:24–25). People are held accountable to believe the gospel in order to escape the judgment of God.

The Number in Heaven Will Exceed the Number in Hell

One of the great assumptions that universalists fault evangelicals for believing is that there will be billions more in hell undergoing torment than the few in heaven enjoying bliss. They use this argument to gain sympathy for universalism. But this is a faulty argument. It is more likely that just the opposite is true. When we consider that throughout history forty percent of all conceptions are lost as misconceptions, that many infants died before the ages of five or six (perhaps as many as thirty to forty percent of all those born), and the number of those who on the basis of general revelation seek after God, as well as the many who believe the gospel, then there is a basis to believe that the number in heaven will far exceed the number in hell. Some reformers (Calvin, Zwingli) and some modern theologians (Edwards, Hodge, William Shedd) affirm such.[12] If this is true then a lot of the air in the universalists' "balloon" about the number in hell is lost.

---

11. See my paper, "Meaning of 'the Law.'"
12. See my article, "Number in Heaven." Also, Shedd, *Endless Punishment*, 107–17.

Chapter 5

"A Loving God Cannot Punish Anyone"

The "Wages of Sin" Is Not Death

THE ADVOCATES OF UNIVERSAL reconciliation continue their rational and emotive appeals by addressing the meaning of "death." In its interpretation of the text that the "wages of sin = death" (Rom 6:23) universalism makes one of its most far reaching and aberrant, blasphemous claims. Universalists challenge the fact that the wages of sin is death, at least if "death" is defined as "eternal torment" or "eternal death." *They deny that the evangelical view can maintain that Christ ever atoned for sin*, because he never suffered eternal torment—he never suffered eternally in hell to pay the debt of sin. Young is especially slanderous in his claims about this.[1]

Universalists are correct to challenge the idea that eternal torment occurs in Romans 6:23. The word "torment" doesn't occur there. I don't know of any worthy commentary that says this. "Torment" occurs only in a few

---

1. Young (UR, 29) writes: "If eternal torment is the punishment for sin, it then seems that Calvary was nothing but a farce, a burlesque, a travesty, and a sham. Then Jesus died a failure and in vain, and never redeemed anyone from anything. If eternal torment were the penalty for sin, then Jesus is not the Savior of men, for He failed to take our place, and pay our debt, by being eternally tormented. And if He is not the Savior of men, then He is not even a good man, but a liar, and therefore a rogue and a deceiving rascal. And therefore, if eternal torment is the penalty for sin, then salvation is a mere myth, and the Bible the world's most abominable maze of evil imaginings; for it then merely leads men to trust for deliverance to a concept which will lead to everlasting sorrow . . . If the wages of sin is eternal torment, then we must re-write the Bible from Genesis to Revelation." Young (UR, 30) seeks to define "death" as the following. It is "dead in trespasses and in sins. It is a sad and most horrible fact that there are billions of people going about this earth dead in their spirits. Dead to God. Dead to virtue. Dead to truth. Dead to purity. Dead to righteousness. DEAD." Bell (64) opposes eternal torment in hell as contrary to God's nature.

places (see the references above). But what does universalism do with these few places, especially since it is Jesus himself, and he alone, who uses the terms, "eternal torment"?

So what does Romans 6:23 mean? In the vast majority of places the single term "death" occurs (as in Romans 6:23) which by the various contexts must include a spiritual significance and is said to be "eternal." Here "death" is in contrast to the second part of the verse where "eternal life" is affirmed. This suggests that the death is also "eternal." Also, in light of the fact that God is just, there are various degrees of suffering in hell; and some will suffer more than others. In brief, orthodox theology asserts that the unrighteous go to a realm of eternal separation from God which is apart from the realm of bliss that the righteous inhabit. The word "torment" and similar words (such as "lake of fire," "outer darkness," "weeping and gnashing of teeth") may be metaphors to picture for our limited understanding what eternal separation from God may be like. But the correct understanding of the word "torment" is not necessary to the understanding of the everlasting destiny of unbelievers.

What Kind of Death Did Jesus Die?

In contrast, universalism seems to say that Jesus died as only a man, not as the God-man. When Jesus atoned for sins, he actually abolished death. To abolish is to do away with entirely. Death is no more. In this way universalism interprets the "death" of Romans 6:23.

The real sticky point for universalism is the word "eternal," whether or not it be "eternal *torment*." There is no "eternal death" in the view of universalism. The latter rejects the idea that there is eternal judgment or eternal suffering of any kind. It has to reject the idea that Christ's death was an eternal death; otherwise, by its logic, Christ would have had to die eternally (or be separated from God eternally). Yet in asserting that the "wages of sin is death," if there is no eternal death then Christ only abolished temporal or physical death or a spiritual death that has no everlasting consequences.

There are significant objections to universalism's view of the death of Christ. First, there are all kinds of texts that say that Jesus died to achieve eternal, everlasting significance and consequence. For example, the second part of Romans 6:23 (which universalists usually do not quote) affirms that "the gift of God is *eternal life* through Jesus Christ our Lord." If the last part of the verse pertains to eternal life achieved by Christ, then the earlier part must refer, in parallel to and as a sufficient contrast to, eternal death. Also, the verse just before affirms that *eternal life* is the outcome for the believer:

"you have your fruit in holiness, and the end, eternal life." Thus the burden is on the universalist to prove somehow that the death in Romans 6:23 is also not eternal.

Second, a casual reading through Romans 1-6 reveals a magnificent host of facts about the eternal impact and significance of Christ's death. It shows that Christ died not only as a man but as the Son of God as proven by the resurrection (1:3); that he secured salvation (1:16; 5:10–11), righteousness (1:17; 3:22, 26; 5:17, 19), propitiation (3:25), justification (4:25; 5:1, 9, 16, 18), reconciliation (5:10), the grace of God (5:15, 20, 21), reigning in life (5:17), eternal life (5:21; 6:8, 11, 22, 23), newness of life (6:4), victory over sin (6:14, 18), and sanctification (6:19); and that he saves the sinner from wrath (5:9). He provided atonement for sins both past and present and future (3:25–26). Colossians 1:14 adds that Christ secured "redemption, the forgiveness of sins." Only a divine person could forgive all sins by his sacrificial act. These verses demonstrate that the death of Christ was not just physical but had spiritual significance for the believer; and that this significance is eternal to offset the eternal or everlasting separation the sinner would otherwise experience. Jesus died as a sacrifice for sins.

How does the evangelical Christian answer the problem that Christ did not suffer eternally or everlastingly, but he should have if the wages of sin is eternal death? The answer is that Jesus' death was that of the God-man. He accomplished things by his death (such as those enumerated just above) that only God could do. In his separation from God at the point of dying for sin he the sinless one "became sin for us that we might become the righteousness of God in him" (2 Cor 5:21). "He died for (or, "on behalf of" or "instead of") all" (v. 15; cf. v. 19). The Scriptures simply state that these eternal consequences were secured by him at his moment of dying on the cross once for all. Hebrews 9:26, 28 is especially clear on this. ". . . He has appeared once for all at the culmination of the ages to do away with sin by the sacrifice of himself . . . So Christ was sacrificed once to take away the sins of many." Hebrews 9:10–14 continues this thought: "And by that will, we have been made holy through the sacrifice of the body of Jesus Christ once for all . . . But when this priest had offered for all time one sacrifice for sins, he sat down at the right hand of God . . . For by one sacrifice he has made perfect forever those who are being made holy."

Only a divine-human being (note John 10:30: "I and the Father are one essence") could accomplish total forgiveness of sins at the moment of his death on the cross. The one who possesses the same essence of being or nature as God made cleansing of sins (Heb 1:2–3). He cried out that God had forsaken him as he became sin for us (2 Cor 5:21; Ps 22:1). Then before he released his spirit he claimed that his atoning work was finished (John 19:30).

Thus Romans 6:23 must mean that there is not only physical death involved but also spiritual death or separation from God. The "death" is spiritual (everlasting) and also physical (as a sign of the spiritual). Thus, in opposition to universalism, the death of Christ was esteemed by God to be eternal in its weight and substance even though it was brief in its duration. It is not surprising that most commentators on this verse affirm that this is "eternal death" but they don't use the words "eternal torment." In effect, universalists raise a straw man by accusing evangelicals of finding "eternal torment" here.

Yet even here there is a problem with universalism. For their continuous opposition to *eternal* death assumes that time is counted the same in the future after life, for both believers and unbelievers. But it is probably better to assume that time in the future life is more qualitative than quantitative. In addition, the term "everlasting" might be more precise than "eternal," but this meaning universalism also rejects.

Again universalists are in error when they affirm that Jesus' death abolished death for all (Young, UR, 30), for Scripture clearly witnesses that only those who believe in Christ, who place faith in him as their Savior, receive eternal life—that they are alive spiritually (Rom 6:22–23; John 3:16; 11:25–26). The rest of humanity abide in spiritual death and never experience life. Apparently universalists are here implicitly acknowledging that Romans 6:22–23 is a case where "eternal life" must be "*eternal* life."

In summary, while there is mystery in the concept of Jesus Christ's death (since he also died as the God-man), God viewed Christ's death as *sufficient* for the wages or payoff for the sin of all for all time. His death took care of sins which before the cross were not fully dealt with in the scope of the *justice* of God (Rom 3:22–26). Whatever the penalty of sin is, including eternal torment, the death of Christ for sin, by which he was separated from God, is *sufficient* payment for sin. His death was the redemption, the payment required, to bring freedom from sin's penalty and power (Rom 3:24; Col 1:14). The rest of humanity that reject Jesus Christ reject deliverance from sin and are still in bondage to it and to death (Rom 6:19–23). This is the fuller meaning of the disobedience, the fall of Adam and Eve. The consequences of their sin were both physical death and estrangement or separation from God (witnessed by their shame).

Universalists Assert that the "Good News" Is Not

Universalism objects to the meaning of the "good news" as used in Luke 2:16 and elsewhere, that it is not good news at all if it warns of a destiny of hell for unbelievers unless they believe. To the unbeliever it is "very bad news." Instead the "good news" is how the world, not just individuals, will be saved (McLaren, 69). Salvation is "deliverance by God's just intervention to stop oppressors of people" (70). The "good news" is that God is even "better than we thought" (68). McLaren asserts: "No thought of God that you can ever have is too good . . . Nothing about God is too good to be true" (68). Thus the point is not whether hell exists; the point is [social] justice (70). Yet what if our thoughts about God are in error? If we deny thoughts about the justice of God our good thoughts of God will be distorted.

At one point McLaren explicitly defines the gospel as the following. "All who have confidence in Jesus will not perish but will have life in God's kingdom for ever, beginning now" (111). While use of the word "confidence" appears admirable at first, one wonders why the words "believe" or "place faith in" were not used. Biblically speaking, there is a Greek term meaning "put confidence in" but it occurs infrequently. Instead the Bible uses "believe" and its cognates over 600 times. Is universalism reluctant to affirm "faith" because the term is a hall mark of evangelical teaching? Does not modern universal reconciliation still follow the old universalism by saying nothing in its tenets about "exercising faith in Jesus Christ"? Does it seem appropriate that those in hell will really "believe" the gospel? It seems that it would be best to use the terminology of the Bible, unless one is indeed attempting to construct a "new kind of Christianity" (as universalism asserts). It is also interesting that the need to "believe the gospel" is not given as determining one's eternal destiny (McLaren, 112; Young, 192; Bell, 188-9).

McLaren says that the gospel is not good news about how to get to heaven but "to tell people God loves them, accepts them, doesn't hold sins against them . . . that Christ died for their sins . . . I tell them they truly can be transformed" (165; also Young, 182). In regard to justification, McLaren (165-6) asserts that it equals forgiveness, that the forgiveness of others leads to reconciliation which leads to social justice. It is to be noted that faith goes unmentioned by McLaren. Young says that God is reconciled to the whole world, not just to those who have faith (*The Shack*, 192).

McLaren also affirms that the gospel is not about being ready to meet God but about becoming the right kind of person and about creating the right kind of world—"a good and beautiful world" (171), not more religious and more conservative (176). Yet the last chapter of Revelation is filled with exhortations to get ready for Jesus' return, and promises of it (Rev 22:7-20;

so also Heb 10:37; 2 Tim 4:1–8; Tit 2:13; 1 Thess 1:10; 1 Cor 16:22; and many more texts). The Bible warns about the destruction of the present world (2 Pet chap. 3; Rev chaps. 19–20), and commands Christians not to love it (1 John 2:15–17).

In his more recent nonfiction, Young has become much more outspoken in opposing the Christian understanding of the "good news." He asserts that all people are already saved, that there is "universal reconciliation." The gospel then is not offering people the opportunity to believe but it is announcing to people that they are already the children of God *whether they believe or not*.[2]

This universalist aversion to "good news" misrepresents the biblical use of the phrase. The gospel is "good news" because it is the message of deliverance from the penalty and power of sin for those who believe (Rom 1:16). The rest who reject the message reject the forgiveness and deliverance and life offered freely in Christ. Unbelief rejects the good news; and those who fail to exercise faith are held responsible for their decision (Rom 10:14–21). Retribution comes to those who "do not obey the gospel" (2 Thess 1:8).

It is as though the good news which universal reconciliation proclaims is a beautiful young woman who appeals as a prostitute to passersby. Universalists like McLaren, Bell, and Young think that she is attractive but they don't realize that if they actually embrace her and sleep with her the consequences are everlastingly destructive and damning.

Universalist Assert That People Are More Loving Than God

At the center of universalism is its argument regarding the love of God. It struggles with the command that Jesus gives us, that we should love our enemies, while God himself, in the traditional view, hates the wicked and torments them forever in hell. "Are we required to be more loving than God?" universalists ask (Young, UR, 7).

A proper response here seems to be that there need be no contradiction. God is omniscient, knows infinitely far more than we, mercies some and hardens others (Rom 9), and is both hated by people and is hostile toward human beings (Col 1:21; Rom 9:14–24). Again universalism has neglected a substantial body of truth—that God is not only love but also holy and just, who will not, and cannot, overlook sin but pours out his wrath both *now* (Rom 1:18–32) and in the judgment to come (Rom 2:5, 8; 3:5). He will exercise judgment (Rom 2:2, 3, 5; 3:6). If God's people can provoke

---

2. See Young, *Lies*, chapter 13, especially 118. So also Bell, *Love Wins*, 134, 157.

him to anger (Heb 3:7–11), certainly the wicked can do so. God can be both merciful and harsh (Rom 11:22, 28). Jesus' death was not only an act of the love of God (Rom 5:6–11) but an act that satisfied his justice—that he "might be just and justify the one who believes" (Rom 3:26), as the Apostle Paul makes clear.

Jesus himself demonstrated that justice toward sin was necessary, including the suffering of torment. His opponents who were worthy of hell included not only Pharisees (which universalism admits) but all those in his home town of Capernaum (and the neighboring towns) and Jerusalem—including women, children, and people who perhaps had never seriously considered his claims. Moreover, at the end of this age God will judge in wrath by Jesus Christ (Rom 2:16).

Finally, *who has a truncated view of God's love*—the evangelical who affirms that sin cost God so much as evidenced by the fact that it led to his giving in love his only Son to be an atonement for it? Or, the universalist who devalues the death of Christ by allowing Satan and his angels to skirt the accomplishments of the death of Christ on the cross and get to heaven by some other way?

Note that at his passion, Jesus only promised paradise to the one thief, who expressed a measure of repentance and faith. He did not "out of love" promise the other thief, who rejected his claims, such a destiny. Apparently Jesus' own love did not extend so far as to violate his sense of justice and holiness when it was violated by the one who refused to repent. He respected his freedom to reject him. Yet universalism is not content to respect both Jesus' decision and the thief's choice, and asserts that Jesus' love will finally win him over to repentance after he is punished a while in hell. *This is not love winning him over but the pain of punishment crushing him.* It is as though Jesus says to one thief, "Today you will be with me in paradise"; and to the other he says, "Tomorrow you will be with me in paradise after I've punished you awhile to bring about repentance." The only caveat that universalism would offer is that the word "punished" should be read as "chastised."

When it comes to the conduct of Christians, they are to be as loving as much and as often as they can, by divine enablement. Yet they are also to "pursue holiness" (Heb 12:14), and justice as citizens of a state (Rom 13:1–7) (which suggests that "love your enemies" may have a limit before the state). The first commandment, to love God, has priority to the second, that of loving our neighbors (Matt 22:34–40).

Universalists Claim That Universalism Makes Them More Loving

Universalists also appeal to their personal experience. This is their "existential argument." Near the beginning of this study I dealt with the claims of both Young and McLaren that they have become more loving people since embracing universal reconciliation. Both affirm that their change has affected much of their theology. If this is so, we should come to expect that everything that they write (including their fiction), and what they believe and do, will reflect this new perspective.[3]

Universalists Assert That Death Does Not Fix A Person's Destiny

One of the key doctrines of universalism is its assertion that death does not fix the final destiny of people. Universalists devote much attention to defending the idea that there is not an eternity of separation from God.

First, they appeal to Scripture. They claim that there is "not one text" in Scripture that limits God's grace to physical life (Young, UR, 33). If God's grace were limited to physical life, it would mean that God has no will and no power to save a spirit without a body. They argue that it is the spirit of man that is of central importance to God, and there is no reason why God can't provide salvation after one's body has died.[4]

The only problem with this argument, an argument from silence, is that there is "not one text" that supports the claim of universalism. And there are texts, such as Hebrews 9:27 ("It is appointed for men once to die but after this comes the judgment") that strongly support the view that the order of one's entire existence is life, then death, then judgment with nothing intervening or following. While universalism points out that this verse does not say that after death there is eternal damnation, they are remiss to recognize that "judgment" refers to a finality of something and it isn't pleasure or joy or bliss. Judgment means a determination of an everlasting, adverse consequence.

---

3. See my review of *The Shack* at burningdowntheshackbook.com. Young makes this point about his personal transformation in UR, 32–33. His conversion to UR, he says, affected his personality and his theology. In *Lies*, chapter 28, he states that the God of his "modern evangelical Christian fundamentalism" failed him (236-8).

4. Young, *Lies*, 181–7, devotes a whole chapter (21) to argue that God can save people after they die. Bell, *Love Wins*, 105–7, supports this idea.

Also, Luke 16 makes it clear that one cannot pass over from one realm (suffering) to another (bliss) (see my discussion in chap. 12). *Indeed, if universalism is correct, then there should be allowance for some to pass the other direction, from heaven to hell, perhaps to evangelize there.* After all, isn't God's power able to accomplish this? Why not assert this also? And if heaven becomes populated with the former wicked, why does it have to exist at all? Why cannot the present existence or place suffice? Finally, the future state of the new heavens and new earth still has the existence of the wicked outside the holy city (Rev 21:8, 27; 22:14–15), and this is the final picture drawn in Scripture. However symbolic this picture may be, one thing is clear: there are two different categories of people, two different locations or realities, and two different destinies that exist everlastingly.

Universalism Has an Impoverished View of Grace and Mercy

There is one more thing. Universalism's understanding that grace and mercy are by the traditional view limited to physical life (and not also extended into hell) is a paltry view of grace and mercy. For all eternity into the future the saints will be experiencing the grace and mercy of God and its results. Are these not among the things for which the saints will forever give to God "glory and honor and *thanks*" (so Rev 4:9)? Believers receive joy forever for having made a decision during their brief lives!

Universalists (Young, UR, 33) go on to claim that the "church system" limits God's "mercy and power" so as to deny that he could save a non-breathing person. Yet if they want no limits to these attributes, why do they not mention the attribute of holiness or justice and give it full strength? The answer is that then these attributes must balance each other so that God cannot violate his mercy or power or holiness. He cannot abrogate justice or mercy in the exercise of his power. No matter how powerful he is he cannot do an unholy act nor an unloving act. What greater mercy could God display than that at the cross where God incarnate chose to end his life for sinners, in their place? Is it unworthy of God to judge those who refuse the offer of his gift of eternal life found in Christ? What more could God have done?

Think of it this way. If I should offer to my poverty-stricken adult child a wonderful gift, such as a new house, but my child rejects the gift and continues as a consequence to live in poverty, am I to blame if I do not force my child into the new house? Is it a loving thing to begin beating my child until she changes her mind and accepts the gift? Has not my gift now become the earned reward, a thing purchased by her suffering which forced the changing of her mind? I think the parallels are clear. In comparison to love, the attribute of holiness goes virtually unmentioned by universalism in general.

Finally, universalists commonly indict the "church system." Evangelicals submit to the authority of Scripture; whatever it teaches we embrace. There is no superior "church system" to invoke. This language appears to be a subtle attack on the institutional church—something universalism is not averse to doing often (Young, *The Shack*, 122–4; *Lies*, chap. 12; McLaren, 155, 197).[5] Evangelicals oppose the idea that God saves anyone after death, not because the "system" is sinister or something but because the Bible is silent on such an idea and actually teaches the opposite belief.

Universalists Claim That God Is Indifferent and Unloving

But universalism has only begun to argue its case for wholesale repentance after correcting the sinner with the fires of hell. Universalism falls back again to the appeal to emotions. It is unimaginable, universalists say, that God could allow those in hell to suffer such torments without intervening to rescue them. They are "tortured and tormented while the ages roll, and roll, and roll . . . without mercy and without remedy" (Young, UR, 34). At great length universalism goes on:

> If the above scenario be true then something horrid must have happened to both God and his saints in heaven. Before the death of these people God loved them all, and in many instances they loved each other, saved and unsaved alike, and would have performed a great number of kindnesses for one another . . . But now that both saint and sinner are out in "eternity," God and all the saints in heaven have either lost their love and compassion for their lost loved ones, or else God has brainwashed all the saints so that they have erased from their memory the fact that their beloved . . . are suffering the most terrible pain and hideous torture for all eternity.
>
> So we must conclude this: there is more love and compassion in the natural world than there is in the spirit world. Furthermore, there is more love for sinners while they have bodies than there is for sinners without bodies. What has happened to cause God and the saints to turn from love and pity for the lost, to a feeling that the lost are now getting what they deserve

---

5. I have said more on this near the beginning of this study.

and should suffer the torments of the damned for all eternity? . . . Can we believe that God, having created *all things for his pleasure*, having *so loved* his creation that he freely gave heaven's most precious gift, after a few paltry years, the brief span of a man's mortal existence, throws up his hands in futility and disgust, saying that he has done all he can and men would not respond, so he must cease all effort, seat himself upon his golden throne, and consign his creation to everlasting hell?[6]

The answer to the last, blasphemous question, is "yes." It is "yes" because God honors human beings as made in his image with the power to choose. The answer to the first question is that they refuse to believe and accept the gift of life in Christ (as John 3:16–18 makes so clear). God will not force his gift on anyone, for this would be a *denial* of love. Love allows freedom to choose and receive. Coercion is not love. C.S. Lewis remarked (in *The Great Divorce*): "There are only two kinds of people in the end: those who say to God, 'Thy will be done,' and those to whom God says, in the end, 'thy will be done.'"[7] And on love Alister McGrath (*Justification by Faith*) has said: "Universalism perverts the love of God into an obscene scene of theological rape quite unworthy of the God whom we encounter in the face of Jesus Christ."[8]

Has Not God Always Been Loving?

Another answer to the statements of universalists is this. If God's love and justice cannot allow anyone to suffer endlessly in hell in the future, then why did not his love and justice prevent suffering for sin in the first place? God was as righteous and loving on the day that sin was born as he will be at the end of this age and the commencement of eternal suffering. Why did not his love and justice prevent sin and all the resultant suffering from arising at all? It is not for us to speculate on what God could or should have done.[9]

---

6. Young, UR, 34. Bell, *Love Wins*, 64, asserts that God ceases to be loving if hell is eternal.

7. In Lewis and Demarest, "Spirit-Given Life," 498.

8 Ibid., 163.

9. See the similar argument in Campbell and Skinner, *Discussion*, 427.

What Is Enough Knowledge to Escape Hell?

Universalism appeals to the teaching of Jesus that Tyre and Sidon would have repented had they witnessed his deeds that he had done in Israel where there was no repentance. All they needed was more knowledge and information. From this statement universalism concludes that those in hell need only more knowledge and information and then they will repent. Universalists state what must be an important principle for them: "God will not inflict punishment on men who have not had ultimate knowledge" (Young, UR, 34). Universalism then appeals to certain texts (1 Tim 2:3–4).

Yet who defines what ultimate knowledge is? Believers aren't saved on this basis, but on the basis of an *adequate* and correct knowledge of who Christ is, on the basis of which they believe in him. Knowledge is important, and the content of truth to be believed is crucial, but *acting by faith* on the basis of the knowledge one has is what saves (Rom 10:14–21). Adequate and correct, but not complete, knowledge is essential. Failure to act on one's knowledge will leave one apart from God. The 1 Timothy passage indicates what God's purpose is, that all be saved, that all come to a knowledge of the truth; but God's will is also accomplished when he also wills that people have a choice to refuse the offer of salvation if they wish, and they exercise it. A purpose is not the same as a result. God may purpose all to be saved, to exercise their will, but not all *will* to be saved.

Universalism's View of Suffering and Knowledge Is Inconsistent and Unbiblical

In addition, universalism makes an illogical argument here. As stated earlier, it makes the case for remedial suffering as the cause why people in hell will repent and believe. Now it says that God will not inflict suffering where the knowledge is not "ultimate." In effect, this means that there will be *no* affliction in hell, for who there has "ultimate knowledge"? If they had ultimate knowledge they probably would not be in hell! So what is the belief of universalism? Is there suffering and affliction in hell or is there not? It cannot be both ways. Universalism is terribly inconsistent here. In addition, the preference in universalism for the love of God over the justice of God has run amok, for now God will not even chastise people for their refusing to believe! Even the unrighteous can perceive the fallacy of this position.

The Bible gives significant insight about the relationship of knowledge and faith. Rather than these two being in a complementary relationship (more knowledge means more faith or ability to believe) the relationship is much more close than this. 1 John 4:16a is an example of a text that shows that belief and knowledge are virtually one and the same: "And we have come to know and to believe the love that God has in us. God is love, and the one who resides in love resides in God, and God resides in him." John is dealing with the marks of a Christian, namely loving other believers, in contrast to the deceived secessionists who do not love believers. The words, "to know and to believe," form, according to most interpreters, a hendiadys, a figure of speech where the two words do not form two ideas but one idea. "To know" is the same thing as "to believe." If this is the case, then knowledge or the extent of it is not the issue, but believing knowledge is. It is not a matter of how much knowledge one has but whether one believes as an expression of whatever correct knowledge about Christ one has. To defend the idea that God is love by insisting that one must have both absolute knowledge and then reject such knowledge to be worthy of an eternity in hell is without biblical support. It is no more biblical to insist on absolute faith than it is to insist on absolute knowledge.

Further, the Apostle Paul shows that the knowledge that saves comes from God by the Holy Spirit. First Corinthians chapters 1–2 are helpful on this point. In Christ Christians are made rich "in every kind of knowledge" (1:5); the wisdom of the world is foolishness and does not lead people to "know God" (1:20-21); "God was pleased to save those who believe by the foolishness of preaching" (1:21); "not many wise by human standards" are among Christians (1:26); Christ "became for us wisdom from God" (1:30) lest people boast about their wisdom.

In 1 Corinthians 2 Paul expands this thought. His ministry among the Corinthians was not "with persuasive words of wisdom but with a demonstration of the Spirit and of power, so that your faith would not be based on human wisdom but on the power of God" (2:5). It is the Spirit who reveals the things of God to Christians (2:12).

In contrast to universalism's claim that absolute knowledge is necessary in order for one to be culpable of unbelief and deserving of everlasting judgment, Paul says that no such knowledge is possible till *after* one comes to salvation by faith. In other words faith precedes full knowledge; it is not the other way around. People are incapable of correct and full knowledge prior to conversion. Paul's concluding remarks make this clear (2:13–16):

> And we speak about these things, not with words taught us by human wisdom, but with those taught by the Spirit, explaining spiritual things to spiritual people. (14) The unbeliever [note: Paul does not say, the uninformed person] does not receive the things of the Spirit of God, for they are foolishness to him.

And he cannot understand them, because they are spiritually discerned. (15) The one who is spiritual discerns all things, yet he himself is understood by no one. (16) *For who has known the mind of the Lord, so as to advise him?* (citing Isa 40:13). But we have the mind of Christ.

The problem is not knowledge and the amount of it, but faith. Faith "as small as a grain of mustard seed" is all that is necessary to move mountains and to bring about regeneration and salvation. Universalists "put the cart [knowledge] before the horse [faith]."

Have There Been Multiple Visits to Hell?

As another way to hold out hope for conversion after death, universalism insists that there are past examples of someone going to hell to offer salvation to the lost there. Universalism argues that Christ descended to hell after his death and resurrection to proclaim the gospel to the lost. Appeal is made to the fact that Jesus has the keys of death and hades (Rev 1:17–18), and that Scripture teaches (1 Pet 3:18—4:6; Eph 4:7–10; Col 2:15) that he went to hell to preach the gospel so that the disobedient there might be led by him in a triumphant conquest out of hell because they trusted in him (so Young, UR, 35–37).

Yet these texts can be otherwise interpreted so that no such descent of Christ occurred. Most evangelicals hold that the 1 Peter text is referring to the preaching of Noah by the Spirit to the wicked of his day, who failed to repent and subsequently perished. It does not concern those of later times. Regarding the texts of Ephesians and Colossians, those conquered are unseen spiritual forces and authorities (probably fallen angels) which most certainly have not already been brought into heaven. This must be the case since Ephesians 6 describes people as still opposing God and his people.

In the opinion of most interpreters Ephesians 4:9 ("the lower parts of the earth") should be understood such that the "lower parts" are the "earth" (it is a genitive of apposition). Thus Christ came to the lower parts, to earth, in contrast to heaven. The "lower parts" are not part of the earth nor do they belong to the earth, such as its lower regions, i.e., hell (this latter meaning would be the impact of a partitive genitive or a genitive of possession). Again, the "lower parts" *are* the earth.

In addition, in Ephesians 4:9–13, the Apostle does not apply the words of the OT, "leading captivity captive" (reflecting Ps 68:18) to Christians. Only the giving of gifts is applied to them. The conquest of unseen spiritual forces took place at the cross. It is a conquest leading to judgment and forms part of the judgment; it is not a saving from judgment. Universalism's appeal to the example from Roman times that shows the emperor returning from his battle with captives demonstrates a hostile conquest, not a saving embrace based in love! Most assuredly the emperor did not love his conquered (if he did, he would not have conquered them); and the captives did not love the emperor for conquering them! Colossians 2:15 describes Christ as "triumphing" over his captives.

For universalism to link these texts with the triumph of Christ in the Apostle Paul's life is impossible, for Paul was a living human who placed faith in Christ, and became his willing slave, whereas those referred to in Ephesians are either dead humans or fallen angels who are "militarily" conquered.

Having decided that Christ has already once gone to hell to save or deliver people, universalists suggest that Christ could go a thousand times to hell to repeat his "leading captivity captive" (Young, UR, 37). They believe that this would be fitting today. They reason that many have never heard the name of Jesus, or if at all only profanely or in some empty religious platitude. People know nothing of his word or his power. The churches too often have cared nothing for them, and cares next to nothing for them today. So goes the argument of universalists (Young, UR, 37).

However, to suggest multiple visits of Jesus to hell is without biblical support. In fact it contradicts the many statements regarding Christ—that during the present era he is enthroned in the place of honor at the right side of God and dwells by the Spirit within his people. Finally, the tenor of Christ's triumph in these texts (1 Pet 3; Eph 4; Col 2:15) is one of a king conquering by force, which runs directly counter to all Scripture describing how people are brought into personal relationship with him. The picture of "leading captivity captive" describes a conquest, a subjugation or pacification of rebellious forces that Christ accomplished by his death on the cross. He sealed the fate of all opponents, visible and invisible, and their destiny is settled. The decision has been made. All that remains is the carrying out of the sentence at the end of this era. It is conquest *de jure,* but not yet *de facto.* Revelation 20:10 presents the carrying out of the sentence: all those who rebel against God, along with the devil, the beast, and the false prophet are consigned to the lake of fire forever.

Universalists Claim That Evangelical Teaching Is "Sadistic Humbug"

The universalist George Hawtin identifies the traditional exegetical interpretation of these texts as "sadistic humbug" (from Young, UR, 37). Similarly McLaren labels evangelical belief as sadistic (30). He even goes further and says that evangelical preachers deny every attribute of God, including wisdom, love, omnipotence, and justice. It is contrary to the nature of God and to the Word of God. Hawtin concludes with these words (cited by Young, UR, 37):

> Some will immediately ask me whether I do not believe in hell. My answer is very definite on this point. I most certainly do believe in hell, but the hell of the Bible and the hell of human tradition are not the same thing at all. The hell of tradition is hopeless and eternal, while the hell of the Scripture, like every judgment of God, is corrective, remedial, and restorative.

It is not surprising that universalists do not give any texts to support their idea of hell to refute the "sadistic humbug" of evangelical belief. There are none.[10]

The Bible Affirms That Hell Is Not Corrective Nor Restorative

There are many reasons why the universalists' view of hell's punishment is wrong. First, many biblical cases can be cited to show that hell is neither corrective nor restorative, contrary to the beliefs of universalists (Bell, 86–88). Let me give two. In the OT, Korah, Dathan, and Abiram led a rebellion against the leadership of Moses and Aaron (Num. 16). An additional 250 "well-known community leaders who had been appointed members of the council" joined in the rebellion (vv. 1–3). To prove that he had chosen Moses and Aaron as Israel's leaders God brought about a unique form of judgment (v. 30): the three leaders were swallowed up by the earth and went "alive to

---

10 As far as belief in hell being sadistic, Jonathan Edwards answered (as cited by Gerstner, *Heaven and Hell*, 38) that it is not sadistic if the suffering is deserved. "Not a cruel man but a good man rejoices in just punishment. It is sadism not to rejoice in just misery . . . The seeming 'sentimentalist' is therefore the true sadist, and the rejoicer in just punishment is the true lover of the souls of men." Yet these thoughts should not be confused with that behavior or speech that brings reaction against the teaching of hell because hell is taught in "crudely literalistic terms" or with "exultant glee or other unloving attitudes held by some" (Buis, "Hell," 116).

the grave" (vv. 31–33). God also killed the 250 others. Here the judgment of death serves to prefigure eternal death. This temporal judgment failed to be "corrective, remedial, and restorative" for the rebellious and the rest. Those who died were not restored. And on the very next day the whole Israelite community (v. 41) complained to Moses that he had killed "the Lord's people." At this God started a plague among the people that killed 14,700 people before Moses' intervention and Aaron's atonement halted it. This is an earthly example of people who have witnessed God's judgment against sin but deliberately persist in rebellion. Indeed, there is no record that those who began dying began repenting. It illustrates the fact that those bent on rebellion against God do not turn back when they undergo suffering. Here punishment was not corrective, remedial, and restorative.

Similarly, let's look at the other end of the spectrum, where people became fearful when they witnessed the judgment of God. Why should they fear if they know the teaching of Scripture is that "every judgment of God" is corrective, remedial, and restorative? In the NT, the deaths of Ananias and Sapphira in the early church (Acts 5) sparked "great fear that seized the whole church" (vv. 5, 11) among those who witnessed their judgment for lying to the Holy Spirit. Why did such a great fear come to those who observed these events if they believed what universalists believe they did—that judgment is only "corrective, remedial, and restorative"? Is it not the opposite, that the rest were convinced that God's judgment is punitive and final for those who lie to God? How is judgment corrective here for those who experienced it? Similarly, the warnings of judgment scattered throughout the NT (from Jesus, Paul, Hebrews and the Revelation) are never conveyed as corrective but punitive. Is this corrective meaning of judgment a secret about punishment and hell that only universalists are privy to? Why do not biblical writers use these words ("corrective," "restorative") for the suffering of the dead in hell?

Finally, would universalism use these words to characterize the death of Christ and his experiencing judgment for all humanity? Was it not punitive, instead of "corrective, remedial, and restorative"? First, Jesus did not have need to be corrected or restored. But universalism will reply: "But he took upon himself our sins and became liable for such treatment." Yet if his suffering was only remedial, why does it seem so much like severe, irreversible judgment? God forsook him on the cross, but universalism would have us believe that no one in hell has been forsaken by God.[11] And if his suffering was only remedial, does this not cheapen the meaning of the death

---

11. Young, *Lies*, chapter 15 (131–7) directly asserts that hell is not separation from God.

of Christ as the incarnate Deity? Does not his atoning sacrifice become insufficient? Is not the example of Jesus' death meant to illustrate the nature of "suffering" for sin, that it is punitive and penal and not corrective? *Note that in response to his suffering Jesus did not say, "I repent," but "It is finished."*

Somehow universal reconciliation moves from the punitive, penal nature of the judgment that Jesus endured and redefines it as remedial and corrective for those in hell. Yet those in hell have rejected Christ's death. Should not the penal suffering that Jesus bore follow those who reject his suffering to and beyond the grave? Those in hell continue to suffer penal punishment because they continue to sin and because they have rejected the forgiveness of their guilt and sin offered in the atonement of Christ.[12]

But universalists actually do not hold to the view of the death of Christ as penal substitution. Paul Young has publicly stated that he rejects such a view of the death of Christ.[13] This view, at least, makes him more consistent with the corrective idea of suffering that universalism espouses and outside the mainstream of evangelical belief. But it denies the full weight of the meaning of Christ's death—that in his suffering eternal death Christ took our place and bore the penalty that we deserve.

In his most recent nonfiction Young makes explicitly clear his views that the cross did not mean that God's judgment was being fulfilled. Instead, the cross, the death of Christ, was not God's idea but man's idea. Human beings interpreted Christ's death to be divinely ordained (he here cites Isa 53), but God had not planned it or ordained it. Instead, God took man's idea and used it for better ends.[14] This twisted logic is the result of thinking that denies the holiness of God that requires judgment for sin.

---

12. See the similar argument by Powell, "Hell," 954.

13. His rejection of penal substitution lies in the background of his making the cross "man's idea" rather than God's idea, in *Lies*, chapter 17.

14. Young, *Lies*, chapter 17 (147–53). Indeed, Young has recently gone so far as to say that penal substitution is "one of the most diabolical doctrines ever" (on the BadChristian podcast, #347, Jan., 2017). He says that the doctrine is "just nuts."

Excursus

Even Reason Demands That Hell Must Be Everlasting

I WISH TO CONSIDER here the nature of hell from another standpoint. If universalism doesn't want to take Scripture's teaching on the everlasting nature of hell let's consider logic and rational thinking. *On the basis of the reasoning of universalism hell is necessary and must be permanent.*

According to universalism, hell is not permanent because its fires are therapeutic not punitive, and all people and the devil and his angels will repent and will escape it. Yet wait a minute. If the fires of hell are only therapeutic, and limited in their length, would not the unrighteous and the devil in particular only have to wait long enough and the fires would cease? Yet the universalist would say: "The devil doesn't know this." But the devil would know this. He knows biblical teaching. If universalism is correct he knows that the torments in hell are limited in their duration. Yet, the universalist would answer: "Well, the fires go on as long as anyone or any angel refuses to repent." But the devil could reason: "God is so loving that he could not 'correct' me with the ultimate fires of hell; he could not destroy me if I hold out. Eventually God's love will overwhelm his sense of doing justice, and he will relent. Mercy will triumph over justice because of love." The universalist might reply: "But this is not so with the devil and the most wicked."

Yet this is precisely the logic of what universalism argues. If God's love trumps his justice at the end, why may it not trump justice along the way before the end? Why wait till the very end of the fires and allow them to get so intense?

The devil could appeal to the incident of the rebellion at the giving of the Ten Commandments when God relented out of faithfulness to keep his promise to Abraham and out of his compassion for the people. He did not destroy them all, only a few.

So the only thing that makes hell's fires threatening enough is to know that they are unending. It is only the weight of this reality that is strong enough to bring the unrighteous and the devil to repentance. For they would know and understand the Bible's teaching to this effect. But if it takes the teaching that the fires are eternal to cause repentance, then it is necessary that the unrighteous and the devil must be there permanently. For why should there be everlasting fires if there is no one there everlastingly?

This argument also means that there cannot be a reversal of destinies for any one after one dies. If the destiny of one can be changed then the destiny of all (in light of God's love *and* justice) can and must be changed.

There is another difficulty with the idea that the wicked, the devil, and fallen angels may one day repent ("change their minds"), get out of hell, and go to heaven. The fallen angels and the devil in a future heaven may rebel again against God. Universal reconciliation may reply that once repentant they are confirmed in their choice. But universalism cannot affirm this view. For universalism already rejects the existing evangelical belief that fallen angels are already confirmed in their choice, and cannot repent. Rather universalism affirms that they can repent. And if this is so they cannot be confirmed in their choice. Thus by the doctrine of universalism they can and will repent; and they may make the choice again to rebel at some future time in a future heaven; and repeat this process over and over.[1] The cycle of repentance, rebellion, repentance goes on *ad infinitum*.

The implications of this point are staggering. Ultimately they deconstruct the universalist view of hell. Consider the following consequences of such a belief.

---

1. Some universalists have anticipated my argument here. Reitan, "Human Freedom," 137–8, writes that those who "finally accept God's offer of salvation" are confirmed in bliss. Why, we may ask? He answers that there "simply is no possible world" in which people "could fall away and become unsaved." He goes on to assert that once people are united to God in love "libertarian freedom has *served its purpose*." It is no longer needed. Yet I may ask: Were not Adam and Eve in such a world and united to God in love, and they exercised freedom to choose contrary to God? There is simply no biblical nor rational argument that counters the recurring cycle of repentance-rebellion-repentance-rebellion once one denies the evangelical belief that the devil and his angels are already confirmed in their evil choice and cannot change. Reitan acknowledges that if his view is wrong, so that freedom to choose after death is possible, then the whole notion of salvation itself is threatened and one is never truly saved (138). This is just what I have concluded above. It is a scenario beyond all revelation and reason. Origen also discovered this problem; see the chapter on church history.

1. Heaven is not a place or state of final peace, rest, and security. The possibility of fallen-then-repentant angels rebelling again makes heaven a scary, insecure place. Strife and war may break out—will break out—again.
2. Should fallen angels rebel again their rebellion will be far more devastating in its effects than the first rebellion. Why? Because the fallen angels will have gained experience from their first rebellion to make their second more effective.
3. Jesus' work at the cross becomes impotent and incomplete. Jesus' first coming was meant to undo the rebellion of the angels (including the devil) and to end the effects of their fall as expressed in the temptation and fall of humanity. The potential of a future rebellion again becomes an assault on the omnipotence and omniscience of God.
4. Jesus' work at his second coming ends up being incomplete and impotent—for a final disposal of the evil, fallen angels has not taken place if they can repent and then rebel again.
5. The potential of a second rebellion holds God and all the inhabitants of heaven hostage.
6. It means that people also are not confirmed in their choice. They are susceptible to the deceit of a rebellious devil and may be persuaded to follow him again.
7. A second rebellion means that God is not finally "all in all" and glorified.

A second rebellion is a horrendous thought. It is also impossible for several reasons. These same reasons make impossible an initial repentance of the devil and his angels.

1. A second rebellion means also the potential of a third, a fourth, indeed, an unlimited number of rebellions. But this potential means that heaven and repentance and forgiveness really have no meaning. But this cannot be since God has declared that such do have meaning. Thus there can be only one rebellion of the angels and the devil and they cannot change their position.
2. A second rebellion also leads to the idea of a second fall of humanity, and the need for a Redeemer to die again. But this is impossible. Hebrews 9 and 10 assert that Jesus died once for all for all time.
3. A second rebellion allows for the idea of an earlier rebellion of which we are unaware. That is, the rebellion in Scripture may have been

preceded by an earlier rebellion and subsequent history that goes unrecorded in Scripture. If there can be a cycle in the future of rebellion-repentance-rebellion there is nothing to prohibit a past cycle that happened prior to the present one, or even several of them. Yet Christ entered only our time to die once for all (Heb 9:12; 10:26–28).

4. A second rebellion means that universal reconciliation itself is in conflict with itself. It is inherently contradictory. Why? If the fallen angels and evil people are not confirmed in their choice, and may repent and then may rebel again, then there is no such thing as "universal reconciliation." These terms assume a final, good disposition of everything and everyone that, by this scenario, never occurs. The preceding shows that the reconciliation is only potential, even unlikely. *There is no final reconciliation and it is not universal. Universal reconciliation is neither universal nor reconciliation.*

Thus universal reconciliation implodes upon itself. It never happens.

The permanency of hell also demands that heaven be everlasting (this is a more precise word than "eternal," since "eternal" leads some to think both backwards and forwards, but only God is "eternal"). If the believer is in Christ and he can never be severed from this standing (so Rom 8:28–39), as even universalists would claim, then there must be a permanent place to accommodate the righteous whose standing, their essential reality, can never be altered. Also this observation argues that, in parallel to heaven, hell must abide permanently. There must exist a place for the unrighteous. If heaven is permanent, then hell is (so Matt 25:46).

That an evil realm may exist forever in the future state is a serious concern, and I suggest below a way to deal with this. One does not have to take the path of universalism or annihilationism.

The permanency of hell also gives strength to the argument that "all" is limited in meaning. The permanency of hell argues that the statements that God has reconciled all (Col 1:19–20), redeemed and forgiven and atoned for all (1 John 2:2), mean that these great accomplishments of the cross are only potential for all but never realized for all. For if hell is indeed everlasting, as I have just argued, then some must be there permanently, and the expressions that say that all are reconciled, redeemed, forgiven, and more, are not meant to mean that these matters are actual or realized for all. As long as there is a single individual being (including the devil by the reckoning of universalism) still undergoing suffering, then hell continues to exist and not everyone is reconciled, redeemed, forgiven, and atoned for. The "all" is not "all."

The above process of thinking reveals why universal reconciliation is impossible. The most significant consequence of universalism, already pointed out in the pages above, is that God ceases to be God. He is a being who is neither almighty, nor loving, nor just. And significantly, universalism makes the death of Christ on the cross for the sins of all a great sham.

There is no final reconciliation and it is not universal.

The above logic also means that there cannot be a reversal of destinies for any one after one dies. If the destiny of one can be changed then the destiny of all (in light of God's love *and* justice) can and must be changed. And if there is a single being whose destiny cannot be changed, then no one's destiny can be changed. It's all or nothing (no one).

The consequences of all of the above considerations are clear.

1. There is no possibility of repentance for either evil humanity or the fallen angels (and the devil) when once they arrive in hell/the lake of fire.
2. There is no change of destiny for these.
3. Hell is a reality.
4. Hell must exist for all eternity.
5. Heaven must exist for all eternity.

Any other view than the evangelical view destroys the meaning of the gospel and doctrinal truth. *God is not so loving that he will not allow people to make a final choice to reject him.*

In the end, if the universalism view is correct, that God is so loving that he can have none existing apart from him, then the work of the cross is ultimately unnecessary and meaningless. If God is so loving, why not rescue all apart from the cross? If God is so loving, why does he allow suffering in this life? If God is so loving, why did he allow his Son to die in judgment for the sin of all? The truth is that the cross is the great definer of the nature of God, where *justice* demanded a sacrifice for sin and *love* provided the Son (as Rom 3:26 affirms). The suffering of Jesus Christ on the cross explains why there is any suffering for anyone. It is because of sin.

Universal reconciliation not only fails to persuade from the position of the clear teaching of Scripture but it fails to persuade from the viewpoint of logic and reason. *By its own logic universal reconciliation is neither universal nor reconciling.*

Part 3

The Appeal to Church History

Overview

THE THIRD MAJOR APPEAL that universalism makes is to arguments from church history. The basic assertion is that universalism was the view of the church for the first five centuries before Augustine corrupted Christian theology. Universalists go to great lengths to try to prove this claim. In addition, universalists seek to give a rationale for universalism's decline in the subsequent centuries, and for its resurgence after the Reformation. Universalism boasts of its conquest of Europe and its significant advance in America.

Whole books are devoted to defend the first claim, that universalism was the majority view of Christians for the first five centuries. For example, J. W. Hanson gives thirty-one points to defend universalism.[1] He builds on the earlier work by Hosea Ballou.[2] J.M. Austin, another universalist, wrote an earlier, similar defense, in 1855.[3]

---

1. Hanson, *Universalism: The Prevailing Doctrine of the Christian Church During Its First Five Hundred Years*. As will be shown, his thirty-one points are filled with half-truths (points #5, 13–18, 31), overstatements (#8, 9), assumptions (#1, part b of #3), falsehoods (#4, 6, 7, 10–12, 23–24), and totally irrelevant points or arguments from silence (#19–22, 25–26, 29, 30). Hanson is indebted not only to Ballou but to subsequent works by E. Beecher (1878), Farrar (1878, 1881), T. Allen (although he only "hoped" that universalism was correct). In his book, *Aiōn—Aiōnios* that I dealt with in chapter one, Hanson devotes a major section to proving that the early church fathers did not use the terms with the meaning of "everlasting" or "eternal." This is his earlier work which he has enlarged in the present work. I will take up the more narrow focus of the earlier work later in this chapter.

2. Hosea Ballou, *Ancient History of Universalism*. Others (Frank S. Mead, Morwenna Ludlow) point out that Ballou moved the universalist movement toward Unitarianism.

3. To my knowledge Austin's work is unavailable and I can cite it only from

The Earliest Christians Followed Jesus

Hanson makes several interesting admissions, including the statement that the earliest Christians followed Jesus' terminology of "endless torment." While universalists choose to redefine this terminology as neither "endless" nor "torment," what if their interpretation of Jesus' words is in error? Then church history would give witness to the traditional view. Also, some universalists including Hanson (28–30, 32–34) admit that the Jews believed in endless torment.[4] If this is meant to reflect OT teaching, how is it that Christians, according to universalism, departed from the Jewish concept? Finally, in my many years of reading and teaching the earliest Apostolic Fathers I have found not one that supports universalism.

What is interesting to note from this overview of history is the admission that universalism became particularly popular in Germany, where rationalism has virtually destroyed theology, and in the liberal seminaries and churches of America. This admission should say something to evangelicals regarding the dangers inherent in universalism. Moreover, there is an almost entire omission of any discussion of how recent evangelical theology and writers have dealt with universalism. The reality is that these have condemned it as heresy.

---

secondary, unpublished sources.

4. The numbers in parentheses, such as (4), refer to page numbers within Hanson's book.

Chapter 6

Universalism's Distortion of the Witness of the Early Church

UNIVERSALISTS CLAIM THAT UNIVERSALISM was the majority view of the church for the first five hundred years of church history.[1] This claim is without foundation.[2] The claim made by many universalists that universalism was the position of four out of six schools of theology in the early church needs to be clarified as well. In truth this is not the case. Most scholars reject this evaluation.[3]

---

1. Paul Young in his UR paper of 2004, 38–41, cites this claim among the thirty-one points he cites from Hanson, *Universalism*.

2. Buis, "Hell," 116, observes that the early Fathers "gave unanimous testimony in favor of the belief in hell" (116). He cites the Church Fathers Ignatius (died 117), Shepherd of Hermas (c. 115), Barnabas (c. 120), Justin Martyr (d. 165), Irenaeus (d. 200), and Tertullian (d. 220), who was the first to express joy at the spectacle of the lost in hell—an attitude rare in the Bible but common in the Middle Ages. The joy of the saints in heaven relative to the suffering of the unrighteous in hell is discussed by Jonathan Edwards (see Gerstner, *Heaven and Hell*, 33–38). Edwards argues that the rejoicing of the righteous over the suffering of the sinful is not sinful because the glory of God is their concern, and their loving is perfect because God's love is perfect (34–36).
   Also, Kelly, *Doctrines*, 483–4, says that "the general view" of the early church was that the punishment of the wicked would be eternal; and by the fifth century this view was "everywhere paramount." *This is the exact opposite of the claim of universalists.*

3. This claim is made by Knight, *Religious Knowledge*, 12:96. However, what the author says is that the "six schools," as significant cities (there was a strong Christian influence), included four in the eastern part of the Empire (Alexandria, Antioch, Caesarea, Edessa) that were universalist, one (Ephesus) that held to conditional immortality, and one (in the West: Carthage or Rome) that taught endless punishment for the wicked. But Knight's terminology is simply that the Eastern Church was "inclined" to it until AD 500. Indeed, the later editor of this same article says that this is overstated. He says that the majority of present scholars would "disapprove" of ascribing universalism to many of the ancient and subsequent theologians and institutions. All that can

How important is this historical study? Universalists stake much of their entire case for universalism on this study. The view of the first five hundred years should be quite convincing. Hanson writes (4):

> The opinions of Christians in the first few centuries should predispose us to believe in their truthfulness, inasmuch as they were nearest to the divine Fountain of our religion. The doctrine of Universal Salvation was nowhere taught until they inculcated it. Where could they have obtained it but from the source whence they claim to have derived it—the New Testament.[4]

I concur in the importance of early Christian history. However, I assert that universalists are completely wrong in their interpretation of the early church, and that this error is a significant blow to the validity of universalism. If universalism is not the view of the early church then the whole foundation of universalism is seriously shaken. It takes on the vestige of a later creation.

Universalism Makes False Claims Regarding Christian History

Universalism makes several claims regarding universalism in the early centuries to support the larger claim that the early church subscribed to universalism. Hanson claims that the evidence for this view is irrefutable (4), that he cites all the fathers themselves, and that he cites the most distinguished writers of his day in support (4). He claims that the early fathers give incontestable proof that "most and the best successors of the apostles inculcated the doctrine of universal salvation" (6). He affirms that universalism was the prevailing doctrine as long as Greek was the language; the first three centuries were the best; the first advocates of universalism were Greeks; and that the first statement of human destiny by any Christian writer after the time of the Apostles includes universal restoration (37ff.).

---

be "fairly claimed" is that they held to a "larger hope or doubt as to the endlessness of future punishment" (96). This qualification brings the witness of this encyclopedia closer to the actual facts about universalism in the early church, as expressed above. The majority of the church did not espouse it.

One of the fullest treatments, it seems, of the history of universalism is that of R.E., "Universalism," and "Universalists," 657–61. He gives a comprehensive list of advocates of universalism from the second century, beginning with the Gnostic and other sects, to modern times. But the list represents the minority of the church.

4. Hanson, *Universalism*, 4.

In his history of universalism J. M. Austin, another universalist, claims that from the Apostles until the present universal salvation "has been believed and advocated in the Christian Church by the most eminent and learned men in different ages."[5] Whether this claim is true or not depends on who these people are and how many. But it is patently false to give the impression that this is the majority view of the church or the most informed view. On the basis of my study and the teaching of the Apostolic Fathers for forty years, I will show that all of these claims by Hanson, Austin, and contemporary universalists[6] are false.

What we need is proof for such claims. And there is hard evidence that proves that the claims of universalism regarding the first five centuries are patently false.

The Apostolic Fathers are our earliest writings after the NT. These include Clement (identified as 1 Clement), Ignatius, Polycarp, the Didache, and others such as 2 Clement, Barnabas, the Shepherd of Hermas, and The Epistle to Diognetus. The lives of some of the people (Ignatius and the author of the Didache) who authored these works overlapped the life of the Apostle John. These Fathers would presumably know how best to interpret the NT. They could ask the Apostle John! And all of the Apostolic Fathers wrote in Greek. This is significant, since universalists claim that only Greek fathers can be trusted to give the true meaning of the text.

The material that universalism uses to support its claim regarding the first five hundred years by and large skirts over the Apostolic Fathers of the first one hundred years (roughly the date from AD 50–150). Universalists champion Clement of Alexandria (180) and Origen (220) of the next century.

Hanson does cite the Didache (also known as "Teaching of the Twelve Apostles") and the Apostles' Creed. Yet his most persuasive argument for universalism in these sources is that none of them says anything about endless punishment. But this is an argument from silence. He argues that this silence shows that endless suffering was not part of the belief system of the early church, that it was following the teaching of the NT in this regard. However, this view rests on proving what the NT teaches. It is just as plausible that the silence of these sources represents the fact that the church held such a belief in endless suffering. It is also pertinent to note that there are no statements regarding the salvation of those in hell.

Indeed, the statements of the Didache actually support the idea of endless torment (as I show more fully below). Even Hanson quotes statements

5. From Young, UR, 84.
6. Bell, *Love Wins*, 107–9.

(8) that refer to "the terrors and judgments that shall come"; that the "fire of trial" will come on all so that many will "perish"; and that some sins "shall not be forgiven." While he reads these as agreeing with universalism he is reading into the text definitions of these terms that are not there.

Similarly, Hanson (9ff.) deals with the Apostles' Creed (second century). He cites it as giving no word about the duration of suffering. Yet this is another argument from silence. The Creed does mention that Christ will come to "judge the living and the dead." This idea of a future judgment runs counter to the beliefs of universalism. Also, this Creed says nothing about a hope beyond death, about heaven. Hanson (10) admits that Irenaeus (AD 180) cites another form of the Apostles' Creed that includes a reference to the judgment when God will "cast the wicked into eternal fire" but believes that "eternal" does not mean "endless." It is terribly convenient to be able to redefine terms "willy-nilly"!

The apparent silence of both the Didache and the Apostles' Creed concerning eternal punishment may be explained by noting that both documents were written to guide Christian conduct and confession. They were not written to describe the end of the wicked.

There is something else that is significant about the Apostles' Creed. Hanson (9) admits that one phrase of the Apostles' Creed, the one that says that Christ "descended into hell," is a later edition. But (as it will be seen) universalists use this phrase to affirm that it represents earlier Christian sentiment that the wicked are offered a second chance to believe the gospel after death. However, most modern scholarship rejects the historicity of this phrase and its interpretation. It was probably added to explain the preceding phrase, "he was buried" and simply meant "he descended to the grave." Jobes notes that the Creed was never adopted by any church council, and that the Westminster Larger Catechism has always understood the words, "he descended to hell" as an explanation of "he was buried."[7] As will be later shown, to find a biblical basis for the descent of Christ to hell between his death and resurrection lacks adequate support. It is tied to the impact of 1 Enoch 13, 33–34 (to which Hanson also appeals) on the Christian community as the source of belief in endless punishment.

Hanson (11–14) does take up later creeds of the church of the fourth and fifth centuries (those of Nicea, 325; Constantinople, 381; Ephesus; and Chalcedon, 451) and notes that none of them includes any reference to the endless suffering of the wicked, and as well have no condemnation of universalism. Again these are arguments from silence. These creeds were

---

7. See Jobes, *1 Peter*, 236, and her extended discussion of this creed in light of the interpretations of 1 Peter 3:18ff. The *descensus* view is no longer in vogue.

deeply concerned about the nature of Christ, not the destiny of the lost. They deal with Christology not eschatology. Yet they did continue the affirmation that Christ "will return to judge the living and the dead."

Other Arguments about the Supposed Universalism of the Early Church

Hanson (15ff.) and others devote a lot of space in arguing for universalism on the basis of the "cheerful" attitude of the early church. In a world of darkness and despair the gospel came with "sweetness and light," hope, joy, and cheerfulness. Such a new day was informed by an eternal destiny that had no place for eternal suffering. Eternal suffering, it is claimed, was the conviction of the pagans and other ancient religions, but Christianity offered a new, better future.[8] This idyllic description of early Christianity is later contradicted by Hanson's own lament that the early church was corrupted by mixing paganism with Christianity! Further, to conlcude that such a description of the new day being "sweetness and light" means that there is no eternal punishment begs the question.

Interestingly, Hanson (17) also denies that the doctrines of "substitutional atonement, resurrection of the body, native depravity, and endless punishment" were professed by early Christians. Instead, early Christians believed that man "is the image of God, and that the in-dwelling Deity will lead him to holiness."

The informed reader will recognize here the foundation for modern liberalism. It is not surprising that universalism is but a step removed from a complete denial of the core doctrines of evangelical faith: the deity of Christ; the substitutionary atonement of Christ; the resurrection; the fallen nature of humanity. Contrary to the claims of universalists, these doctrines are directly confessed by the Apostolic Fathers. Yet some of these doctrines are implicitly denied in the modern fiction of *The Shack* and other fiction and nonfiction of universalism.[9] Hanson (17) also laments the "discarding of reason" that accompanied, in his view, the rejection of universal salvation. This concern is an implicit confession of the ultimate role that reason

---

8. Interestingly, this argument that the idea of hell came from the pagans, not from the OT nor from the NT, has recently been restated by Brian McLaren in his *The Last Word* (see Part 1 above).

9. Bell, *Love Wins*, 136, 188-9, says that the basic doctrines (atonement, redemption, justification, reconciliation, etc.) are culturally limited and determined and not universal; and the basic meaning of Christ's death is simply an example of death and rebirth (and implies that it is nothing more). This view rejects penal vicarious substitution.

and rationalism will play when universalism in later centuries will virtually destroy the Puritan churches of New England in early America (see the pertinent chapter below).

1 Clement Affirms Eternal Punishment

All of the foregoing claims of universalists about early Christian history is contrary to the evidence provided by the Apostolic Fathers, who cover the first one hundred years after the NT.[10] I simply list here all of the various clauses that touch upon the future destinies of people.

1 Clement reveals the following beliefs, and they are opposed to universalism. The blood of Christ has "won for the whole world the grace of repentance" (7:4); "the Master has given an opportunity for repentance to those who desire to turn to him" (7:5); "Noah preached repentance, and those who obeyed were saved" (7:6); lay aside "the jealousy that leads to death" (9:1); the Master "destines to punishment and torment those who turn aside" (11:1; similar to Matt 25:46); "those who question the power of God fall under judgment and become a warning to all generations" (11:2); "May the Lord utterly destroy all the deceitful lips" (15:5); "the face of the Lord is against those who do evil, to destroy any remembrance of them from the earth" (22:6; quoting Ps 34); "we may be shielded by his mercy from the coming judgments" (28:1); "for those who do these things [e.g., hatred of God, pride, etc.] are hateful to God" (35:6); "Who are the enemies [that are the footstool of Jesus' feet]? Those who are wicked and resist his will" (36:5). Those who act contrary to his will "receive death as the penalty" (41:3); leaders should "walk in fear and love" (51:2); those who rebelled against Moses were condemned; they "went down to Hades alive and 'Death will be their shepherd'" (51:4); God purposed to "destroy [the Israelites] completely" (53:3); "when you call upon me, I will not listen to you" (57:5); "a searching inquiry will destroy the ungodly" (57:7; citing Prov 1:23–33); "You, Lord, are ... righteous in your judgments" (60:1).

There is nothing here that even hints at universal reconciliation. Throughout the sixty chapters there are no other statements that deal with the future of the wicked after death. While a few of the statements above might allow for a deduction that grace extends beyond the grave, the rest of them provide a context that makes impossible the final interpretation of them as supportive of universal reconciliation.

---

10. For the translations cited see Holmes, ed., *Apostolic Fathers*.

2 Clement Affirms That the Destiny of Eternal Punishment Cannot Be Altered

From 2 *Clement* the following statements regarding the future of the wicked occur. It is necessary to "save those who are perishing" (2:5). Regarding those who do not keep the commandments of God, God "will throw them out" (4:5). God has the power "to cast soul and body into the flames of hell" (5:4). "If we disobey his commandments, then nothing will save us from eternal punishment" (6:7; citing Matt 25:46); for the one "who cheats in the heavenly contest . . . he says their fire will not be quenched" (7:6). "After we have departed from the world, we are no longer able there either to confess or to repent anymore" (8:3). The pleasure of the present brings "great torment" (10:4). The kingdom of God is "love and righteousness" (12:1). "Let us, while we still have time, turn again to God who has called us, while we still have one who accepts us" (16:1). "The day of judgment is already coming as a blazing furnace" (16:3). "Prayer . . . delivers one from death" (16:4). "Let us repent . . . lest any of us should perish needlessly" (17:1—twice). Those who deny Jesus are "being punished with dreadful torments in unquenchable fire" (17:7). The "ungodly are judged" (18:1). "I fear the coming judgment" (18:2). "The divine judgment punishes a spirit that is not righteous" (20:4).

In the preceding 2 *Clement* stands out as explicitly denying that there is an opportunity to repent after death (8:3). Note the other statements that counter universalism.

The Epistles of Ignatius Support the Evangelical View

Ignatius (died about 108) wrote seven letters to various churches of Asia, some of them to the same seven churches of Revelation 2–3. He wrote his letters while being escorted by Roman soldiers to his martyrdom in Rome. In five of the seven letters he makes references to the afterlife; in *Romans* and in *Polycarp* he does not. In his letter to the *Ephesians* he refers to the "wrath to come" (1:1), the "powers of Satan" (13:1), the "penalty of unquenchable fire" (16:2), and "living forever" in Jesus Christ (20:2). In his letter to the *Magnesians* he writes: "all things have an end, two things lie before us, death and life, and everyone will go to his own place" (5:1). To the *Trallians* he writes: "by believing in his [Jesus Christ's] death you might escape death" (2:1); and he warns of the "poison of heresy" (6:1–2). To the *Philadelphians* he writes about the "eternal blood of Christ" (Introduction). He warns that "if anyone follows a schismatic, he will not inherit the kingdom of God" (cf.

1 Cor 6:9); if "anyone holds to alien views, he disassociates himself from the Passion" (3:3); and "if anyone fails to speak of Jesus Christ, I look on them as tombstones and graves of the dead" (6:1). To the *Smyrnaeans* he writes: "even heavenly beings and the glory of angels and the rulers, both visible and invisible, are also subject to judgment if they do not believe in the blood of Christ" (6:1). He adds: "faith and love are everything; nothing is preferable to them" (6:1). "It is reasonable for us to come to our senses while we still have time to repent and turn to God" (9:1). This last statement implicitly rejects the idea that people can repent after death.

Other Early Christian Writings Are Clear

In *Polycarp to the Philippians* (dated about 110), Polycarp refers to "Jesus—the Judge of the living and the dead, for whose blood God will hold responsible those who disobey him" (2:1). He adds: "we must all stand before the judgment seat of Christ" (6:2); and the "one who denies judgment is the first born of Satan" (7:1). In the *Martyrdom of Polycarp* (dated 156–171) it is written that martyrs purchased "at the cost of one hour an exemption from eternal punishment" (2:3). It adds: "They set before their eyes the escape from that eternal fire which is never extinguished" (2:3). This work also refers to "the fire of the coming judgment and eternal punishment, which is reserved for the ungodly" (11:2).

The Epistle to Diognetus (dated about 150; some date it about 300) refers to God sending Christ as "Judge" (7:6), and the need to fear "the real death, which is reserved for those who will be condemned to the eternal fire which will punish to the very end those delivered to it" (10:7). What a powerful statement this is!

The *Didache* (dated between 70–130) refers to "forever" (10:3, 5), to "sin not forgiven" (11:7), and that "all humanity will come to the fiery test and many will fall away and perish" (16:5). Finally, the *Epistle to Barnabas* refers to "the pit of death" (11:2) and that "everything will perish together with the evil one" (21:2); and there are more references.

These documents from the Early Church show that the terminology and understanding of the Apostolic Fathers are very close to that of the NT. As noted above they cover the period from about AD 70 to 150. There are no statements that could be construed as agreeing with universal salvation.

Statements from the Next Century (150-250) Support the Evangelical View

In addition, the witness to eternal punishment is common to Justin Martyr, Irenaeus, and Tertullian.[11]

In his *Second Apology*, Justin Martyr writes several times that wicked people (chaps. 1, 2, 8, 9) and the wicked angels and demons with men (chap. 7) shall be "punished" or afflicted with "eternal fire."[12] He writes that "each man by free choice acts rightly or sins," not by fate. "Angels and men will justly suffer in eternal fire the punishment" their sins call for (chap. 7).[13] Moreover, in his *Hortatory Address to the Greeks*, he writes that this torment in hell will be conscious (chaps. 25 and 27); and that Plato's affirmation of the same was learned from the OT prophets (chap. 27).[14] In his *Dialogue with Trypho*, Justin argues against reincarnation and affirms that "the souls of the pious remain in a better place, while those of the unjust and wicked are in a worse, waiting for the time of judgment" (chap. 5).[15] The "word of God foretells that some angels and men shall be certainly punished . . . but not because God had created them so" (chap. 141).[16]

Irenaeus writes that souls "extend their existence into a long series of ages in accordance with the will of God their Creator" (*Against Heresies*, 2, 34, 2), and that "souls henceforth endure [forever]" (2, 34, 4).[17] Christ will "send . . . the wicked and profane among men into everlasting fire" (1, 10, 1; 5, 27, 1).[18] This same idea is repeated in similar terms several times in 1, 32, 1; 2, 34, 1; 3, 4, 2; 4, 26, 2 ["among those in hell"]; "the fire is eternal" (4, 28, 1); "the punishment . . . is not merely temporal but rendered also eternal" (4, 28, 2); ". . . there shall ye be damned forever" (4, 28, 2); "the Lord . . . lets go for eternity those whom he does let go" (4, 28, 3); ". . . inhabiting eternal darkness" (4, 34, 1).[19] Also, in an allusion to the parable of the sheep and the goats, Irenaeus writes that "the same God . . . prepared the eternal fire for the ringleader of the apostasy, the devil, and those who revolted with him, into which [fire] the Lord has declared those men shall be sent who have

11. See Morey, *Death*, 273ff.
12. Roberts and Donaldson, *Ante-Nicene Fathers*, 188, 190, 191. This punishment will be as the "prophets foretold" and as "Jesus teaches" (chap. 8).
13. Ibid., 190.
14. Ibid., 284.
15. Ibid., 197.
16. Ibid., 270.
17. Ibid., 411, 412.
18. Ibid., 331, 558.
19. Ibid., 411, 417, 497, 501, 511.

been set apart by themselves on his left hand . . . preparing . . . eternal fire and outer darkness" (4, 40, 1).[20] Finally, Irenaeus argues against reincarnation; and interprets the parable of the rich man and Lazarus as teaching conscious torment or bliss after death (2, 34, 1).[21]

Another source that agrees with my assessment of the early church fathers is a recent issue of *Christian History* magazine (2011).[22] Edwin W. Tait traced the views of hell as held by fifteen church fathers or documents from the period, AD 30-500 (which extends beyond the earlier fathers dealt with above). Of the earliest fathers, Tait discussed only the Didache, the Epistle of Barnabas, and the Apocalypse of Peter—the latter two holding to eternal punishment. Of the subsequent fathers, Justin Martyr, Irenaeus, Tertullian, Athanasius, John Chrysostom, Jerome, and Augustine held to eternal punishment. Only Clement of Alexandria, Origen, Gregory of Nyssa, and Maximus the Confessor rejected eternal punishment. Gregory Nazianzen did not take a stand, leaving the question to God. This survey shows the inaccuracy of the claims that universalists make for this period.[23]

Summary Observations

The weight of these citations is that the concept of eternal or everlasting punishment was known and frequently written about in the earliest time after the NT. What is more, these church fathers believed that destinies could not be altered after death. These statements parallel the teaching of the NT. There is absolutely nothing in the earliest Apostolic Fathers to suggest an escape from hell by repentance after death. It is ignorance of these earliest church fathers that allows Christians today to be duped and deceived by later teaching.

In addition, universalism claims that it became the minority view in the later centuries because of the rise of powerful Latin fathers. Yet this assumed reversal could also mean that with greater study and knowledge the church came to discern more clearly what was error and what was not. This is what happened regarding the understanding of the nature of Christ. The church had to deal with Arianism, which denied the eternal deity of

---

20. Ibid., 523.

21. Ibid., 411.

22. Armstrong, ed., "History of Hell," 4-8. The entire issue of thirty pages is devoted to this topic.

23. Other writers in this issue traced the idea of hell as found in the Middle Ages (four persons) and from 1500 to the present (twenty-six people). Again the majority of those surveyed held to eternal punishment. The last seven pages surveyed the many books and other sources available on the topic.

Christ. Arianism was predominant in the early part of the 4th century, but the Council of Nicea (AD 325) determined that it was heresy and this eventually became the judgment of the majority in the church. It validated what Christians always believed. It seems that universalism suffered a similar fate of being anathematized, after it developed in the second and third centuries, and justly so.

Hanson's Additional Arguments Claimed in Support of Universalism

In his treatment of the history of universalism in his book, *Aiōn, Aiōnios*, Hanson begins his section on the early church by citing the Peshito's rendering of *aiōn* in the NT as "the world to come" (147), and the Syriac's rendering of *aiōn* as *ōlam* or *eon* ("age") (148). But this argument can be easily reconciled with "everlasting life" since the "the world to come" is the eternal or everlasting state. There is no other period after it.

As shown above, Hanson argues that the idea of "endless torment" is not hinted in the Apostles' Creed, the earliest creed of the church. But neither is there a hint of heaven! This is another argument from silence. It is also curious for a universalist to cite a creed at all since universalists assert that they believe in no creeds and that creeds are wrong. In addition, both this creed and the Nicene Creed (AD 325) speak of Christ's coming again to "judge the living and the dead." These words assume that there are wicked who are accountable and conscious after they die and that their judgment is to be final. As far as arguments from silence are concerned, I can appeal to the silence about a second chance after death to repent and escape from hell, if these creeds represent the majority beliefs of the first centuries!

Hanson cites Beecher as saying that the ideas of eternal life and eternal punishment go unaddressed in the apostolic fathers until the latter part of the second century, by Justin Martyr and Irenaeus. This is patently false. In the previous pages I cited the witness of 1 Clement, 2 Clement, the Didache, Ignatius, Polycarp and others who are in line with the NT as evangelicals have interpreted it, and their witness is the earliest that we have after the NT (from AD 50 to 150). Hanson is incomplete in what he says about Ignatius. While he cites the Sibylline Oracles (dated from 500 BC to AD 150 by Hanson) (148) as speaking of God's delivering the damned from devouring fire and the gnashing of teeth, this work is not counted as among Christian writings, whereas the Apostolic Fathers are clearly Christian.

Hanson misrepresents the statements of Justin Martyr ("others are punished so long as God wills them to exist and be punished") (149), of

Irenaeus and others by reading into their statements about the future punishment of the wicked his predetermined understanding of *aiōn*. While they may have also believed in annihilation, their statements could reflect the Revelation's teaching (20:14) that the wicked die a second death.[24] If it should be, as I've sought to show in the pages above, that Hanson's interpretation of *aiōn* in the NT is false, then the reading of his view into the church fathers is also false.

The Central Role of Origen in Supporting Universalism

For Hanson and universalists in general, Origen (about 185-254) is the champion of limited suffering. Hanson devotes more pages and more praise and adulation to him than to anyone else. There is no doubt that he was the greatest biblical scholar of his day. It is true that he embraced the restoration of all things, as I stated in the Introduction. Yet his defense of the restoration of the devil is not so clear, and I discuss this in the pages that follow. But Hanson may misrepresent Origen. He claims that Origen clarifies the meaning of *aiōn* in the creeds and in the NT by his belief in the restoration of all things. The claim is that if there is a restoration then Origen could not understand *aiōn* punishment (Matt 25:46) to be "eternal" in these texts. Yet on the basis of my understanding of the earliest church fathers Origen could be re-interpreting, not interpreting, the texts as they had been interpreted until then. He would be engaging in novel interpretation.

This suggestion finds support in the observation that it is Origen who brings forward the allegorical interpretation of the Bible. He finds three meanings in Scripture: the literal, the moral and the allegorical. This hermeneutical approach saddled the church with a foreign approach until the time of the Reformation. It is reasonable to think that Origen the allegorist felt freedom to reinterpret the destiny of the wicked in a way that counters the usual interpretation, with the result that none suffer everlasting torment.

Before I evaluate Origen's views it is important to mention the view of Eusebius (4th century), the universalist father of church history. Hanson quotes him (154), that "if the subjection of the son to the father means union with him, then the subjection of all to the son means union with him." But this is logically fallacious. There is no parallel. There are many reasons why the Son is in union with the Father, such as his being of the same essence

---

24. Hanson wants to take the belief in annihilation as proof that the later Apostolic Fathers took *aiōn* as limited in duration, since people would cease to exist. But just as properly annihilation can be viewed as an "eternal" condition since it is unalterable.

or nature as the Father (as Hebrews 1:2–3 affirms). Also, Scripture makes it very clear that the wicked are not in union with Christ but are subject to him as forming his footstool where he stomps on them (so Ps 2:7; 110:1; Matt 22; Heb 1:3, 13; Col 3:1–3; and other texts). Subjection may be voluntary and loving, or it may be an involuntary conquest. The latter is the experience of the wicked (Col 2:15).

The Anathematizing of Origen As a Teacher of Heresy

Hanson states that Origen's doctrine of restoration was for "the first time condemned and anathematized as heretical" in AD 544 at a local, not general, council in Constantinople called by Justinian the Emperor. This action declared him a "heretic of the worst kind," and was followed by a similar action toward the universal restitution beliefs of Theodore of Mopsuestia (died in 427) at a council in 553 (152).[25]

Hanson interprets this anathematizing as curtailing the predominant belief of the early church and led to the reign of the doctrine of "future eternal punishment" during the middle ages until the Reformation (152). In a similar manner the universalist Austin gives his "spin" to these events.[26] He blames this on "ignorance, superstition, and corruption." Instead of seeing this as a "censure" of universalism he takes it as a "compliment" since universalism is "too enlarged, too enlightened, too liberal, to be tolerated in an age of barbarism and darkness." He believes that dishonest and corrupt prelates condemned a doctrine "so grand and heavenly."

Yet by an evangelical interpretation of the NT and the witness of the Apostolic Fathers the acts of these church councils may just as fairly be understood as putting down an increasingly strong deception of the church that begins vigorously with Origen in the third century AD and by Theodore. As time went on Christian people became more and more astute in recognizing deceit and error. This is certainly what happened regarding the

---

25. The decree of 544 stated: "If any one says or holds that the punishment of demons and impious men is temporary, and that it will have an end at some time, that is to say, that there is a restoration of demons or impious men, he is accursed" (160 in Hanson). According to R.E., "Universalists," 658, this was not really an ecumenical or church council (the Latin Church refused to recognize it), but a local council called by the emperor Justinian in Constantinople to declare the Nestorians (who believed in universalism) to be heretical. This council was followed by the similar local council in AD 553 to pronounce Origen's belief in universal salvation to be heretical. Again the main player was the emperor.

26. The following quotes come from Young, UR, 85.

doctrines of the person and the nature of Christ, the Holy Spirit, the canon, and other crucial doctrines.

Hanson appeals to the prevailing mood of six theological schools in these centuries, and yet this witness is misrepresented (as I have shown in the pages above). The proclivity of Hanson to misrepresent the truth and misinterpret the evidence is disturbing, but not unique, as I've discovered in my research.

Hanson claims that the very fact that Justinian used another term ("endless") to clarify *aiōn* in the phrase, "endless punishment," shows that *aiōn* itself was not understood to mean "endless" (157). Yet it could also mean that since there are contexts in the NT where *aiōn* does not mean "endless" (as all acknowledge) he sought to be clear and unambiguous as to what was being anathematized.

Hanson appeals to other universalists within and without the church, orthodox and unorthodox (155–7). He acknowledges that many "doctors" held the view of eternal punishment, but asserts that the "more highly distinguished in Christian antiquity any one was for learning, so much the more did he cherish and defend the hope of future torments some time ending" (160). In this way universalists reject Augustine for helping to quash universalism. Yet he is one of the greatest teachers of the church, one of the "more highly distinguished"!

It is amazing that this same apology is used today. The more learning one has (as defined by liberal theology) the more a person will be inclined to disavow eternal torment. But defining what "learning" is becomes a very subjective matter. Above I dealt with how the Apostle Paul deals with the learning of this world (in 1 Cor 1–2).

Note also that Hanson speaks of the "hope" that future torments would end. This is classic universalist speech, as I pointed out in the introduction to this book. It began with Origen and continues in modern writers such as Talbot, McLaren, Young, and Bell (111).

Another False Claim by Universalists about the Early Church

It is also patently false for Austin to say that before AD 190 there is "a distinct recognition of the salvation of all men" (unless again he refers to only a handful of people).[27] As shown above, the only view of salvation found in the earliest writers, the Apostolic Fathers, and, indeed the general view in

---

27. Ibid., 84.

the first five hundred years, is not universalism but the traditional, evangelical belief of everlasting suffering from which no one can escape.

Austin cites various sects from about AD 120 and the later Sibyline Oracles (AD 150) that followed universalism. Yet these are "sects" and writings falsely claiming to be authoritative (which Austin admits), and thus little credence should be given to them. It could hardly be that they represented the "prevailing doctrine" among Christians. Instead, they represent heresy, just as universalism does. Austin goes on to commend Clement of Alexandria, Origen, and others as noteworthy leaders of the church who espoused universalism.[28]

Re-evaluating Whether Origen Was an Universalist

Closer examination of the evidence for Origen as the chief champion of early universalism, the "darling" of universal reconciliation, reveals that his position is uncertain. More recent scholars argue that Origen's view must be seriously qualified. Henri Crouzel shows (1) that Origen both affirmed and did not affirm universal reconciliation, (2) that he saw that the latter contradicts free will, (3) that wickedness in fallen humanity and fallen angels probably becomes their nature from which free will cannot separate them, and (4) that he could only "hope" for universal reconciliation because of God's goodness.[29] These are four very weighty caveats to what is usually said about Origen. Crouzel shows that Origen contains "numerous qualifications, hesitations, discrepancies" about his view of the restoration of all creatures.[30] Henri De Lubac makes a similar, but briefer assessment of Origen.[31]

Just because their universalism was not opposed by others (if this is true) is an argument from silence, since we don't have the writings of others. For Austin to cite about seven church fathers and "many others" (who are not named) means little in light of the fact that there were hundreds of such leaders who lived and wrote during the first five centuries. Austin is contradicting the truth when he claims that universalism "was the orthodoxy of the early Christian Church." How can this be the orthodoxy when the

28. Ibid. All the references to Austin in this paragraph come from Young at the place cited here.

29. Crouzel, *Origen*, 179ff., 242ff., 262–6. Note that the contemporary, insincere claim of universalists that they only "hope" for the reconciliation of all carries on the dubious claim begun by Origen. It seems loving and generous, yet how can people dare to hope for something that God asserts is, in effect, beyond hope?

30. Ibid., 265.

31. De Lubac, *Origen*, xxxix–li.

traditional view was the belief, the orthodoxy, of the earlier Apostolic Fathers and the majority of the rest? Austin fails to cite some powerful leaders of the fourth and fifth centuries, such as Athanasius and Augustine, among others.[32]

Austin continues his distortion of history to modern times. In route he cites heretical sects (the Nestorians) and a few people who adhered to universalism during the Middle Ages. [33]

McLaren has his own interesting take on the history of heaven and hell during the ages.[34] Christianity became more and more a plan of escape from the physical world. Because of Neoplatonic philosophy, Christianity became more spiritualized, and shifted away from seeking God's will to be done on earth. The plagues of the Middle Ages caused the hope of an afterlife to blossom. The church promised to solve problems and settle issues after death so it didn't need to address problems of this life.

This is a pretty simplistic way to treat the history of belief in heaven and hell. The Crusades themselves witness to the church's interest to expand Christ's dominion on earth. And the rise of Catholic orders, monasticism, and mysticism show the church's concern for the needs of the common people.

---

32. Young, UR, 84. In my book, *Lies*, 205–16, I show that Athanasius was absolutely not a universalist. It was necessary to devote appendices 2–3 to Athanasius because Young and Kruger believe that their beliefs are in line with orthodoxy as found in Athanasius.

33. Ibid., 85–88.

34. McLaren, *Last Word*, 169.

Chapter 7

Universalism's Subversion of the Church Since the Reformation

What about the Protestant Reformation?

I TURN FIRST TO consider one more important period of history. The year 2017 marks the 500th anniversary of the Protestant Reformation. This event had the greatest impact on European understanding of biblical doctrine, church order, Bible translation, state-church relations, and many other matters. Not since the time of Jesus and the Apostles had the Christian church been so awakened to errors in its beliefs and practices.

In its reformation of Christian doctrine the Reformation embarked upon a clarification of the destiny of the unsaved. It rejected Roman Catholic teaching about purgatory and the role of indulgences to secure one's escape from greater judgment after death. The Reformation upheld the biblical teaching about the destiny of the lost—that they will undergo eternal judgment.

When Luther sparked the Reformation with the nailing of his 95 theses to the door of the Wittenberg Church on October 31, 1517, #32 reaffirmed the judgment after death. Luther wrote: "Those who believe that they can be certain of their salvation because they have indulgence letters will be eternally damned, together with their teachers."

As part of his 67 Articles, Zwingli in 1523 wrote (#57): "The true divine Scriptures know naught about purgatory after this life." Calvin similarly upheld the judgment of the wicked in hell.

UR runs counter to Protestant teaching and the Reformation.

In this year 2018 we could do no better than to reaffirm our belief in the biblical teaching about the everlasting judgment of those who are non-Christians, who have not believed in Jesus Christ.

However, with the Reformation and the openness it created universalism "speedily revived" and was embraced by several including the Anabaptists "generally" and many Arminian theologians, Austin claims.[1] Again the significance that Austin gives to this record is not straightforward, for these advocates of universalism were still in the minority. Only "some" Anabaptists and Arminians embraced it.

Universalism's Tie to German Rationalism and Liberalism

It is especially interesting to see how Austin reports the rise of universalism in Germany in his day (the mid-nineteenth century). It was apparently sweeping the country, especially with the rationalists embracing it and influencing others. Yet rationalism in league with higher criticism is the same destructive force that was leading all of Continental Europe away from evangelical faith by its denial of miracle, the deity and resurrection of Christ, the authority and nature of Scripture, and other supernatural matters. It similarly influenced England. With this rise of rationalism universalism found a strong (not strange) bedfellow![2]

If Austin were alive today I'm not sure that he would be pleased to see all of Europe so highly afflicted with this other heresy that the church has virtually died out there! Did universalism contribute to this demise? It seems that it did. The warning for the United States is clear!

Universalism in Early Europe

Austin reports that when the British delegates gathered to form an Evangelical Alliance at a convention in London they refused to be convinced by American delegates to include words in their alliance condemning universalism. The reasons given included the conviction that the belief in endless punishment was not essential to salvation—people can be saved without

---

1. All the quotes and material from Austin in these first several pages come from Young, UR, 85–88.

2. Earlier, at the end of the 18th century, universalists had spoken strongly against rationalism. Jung-Stilling, a universalist, had been an "able defender of Christianity against German rationalism" (so R.E., "Universalists," 659).

believing it. Others doubted the doctrine, and others rejected it. This "infection" of universalism was condemned in the United States.³

Universalism in America

It is interesting to have Austin praise the writings of a Professor Stuart of Andover Theological Seminary, described then as "the great orthodox institution of New England." Stuart praises universalism's pervasiveness in Germany. Then Austin quotes Professor Timothy Dwight as saying that universalists, in comparison to other Christians, have a deeper sense of the "odiousness of sin" and a more "ardent gratitude" toward Christ, and are "brighter examples of piety": in their "charity and love" they should be imitated.

Yet today this same seminary is one of the most liberal institutions in America. Its denial of all aspects of the evangelical faith is well known. Somehow the meaning of sin, love, and piety has become terribly distorted.

Austin cites several Americans, from the time of the Revolution to his day, who believed in universalism. These include Benjamin Rush, a signer of the Declaration of Independence, John Murray, a chaplain of the Rhode Island Brigade, Benjamin Franklin (which is no surprise), a Dr. Redman, and a few others.⁴ Austin concludes his history on an optimistic note, believing that universalism is spreading throughout all the "partialist sects of our country."

To write a brief history of universalism in America is challenging but informative. It is challenging because there are several strains to universalism that have developed in the United States. To trace the developments of its tenets or beliefs is difficult because the group prides itself as not adhering to any necessary tenets.

But it is informative. To decipher its development is instructive for understanding contemporary trends in evangelical and wider circles. There are parallels between the past, when Christians shredded their beliefs in ever bolder ways till there was nothing evangelical left, and the trends today, for example, in the emergent church. Moving from a theology anchored in the person of Jesus Christ as the divine Son of God and the authority of Scripture to one that denies both of these beliefs is a trend toward universalism past and present. Yielding to reason and rationalism, universalism past

---

3. In the excursus at the end of this book Shedd provides more information about European universalism.

4. See further information about universalism in early America in Walker, *History*, 478–9.

and present rejects the institutional evangelical church and its adherence to such doctrines as the deity and resurrection of Jesus Christ.

The Puritans who were among the first to come to the American colonies in the 1630's were anchored to the Reformation. They embraced the Calvinistic teaching regarding the election of some to salvation and the predestination of the rest to eternal suffering. As universalism came to the colonies from England and Europe it gradually made headway in the Puritan churches. While the Puritans first condemned universalism they soon came to embrace it. How did this happen?

How Universalism Took Over Puritan Churches

Historians, such as Sydney Ahlstrom, point to at least three factors that contributed to this subversion of the Puritan churches.[5] The Enlightenment of the 1800's exalted reason over the revelation of the Bible as the final authority. The Bible and its miracles and supernatural claims were forced to pass the test of reason, and, if found lacking, were rejected. Calvinism was biblically based but also carefully reasoned. The writings of the Puritans demonstrate such reasonableness. Universalism exalted reason and what is rational. The Puritan's love of reason and pride of intellect made them susceptible to this appeal.

The congregational form of the government of the Puritan churches was an important factor. This form of church polity meant that there was no central authority to keep the churches in line, to remain orthodox in belief and not to be lured by heresy. Each congregation was an independent entity and could fashion its own beliefs and destiny. In contrast, the early Methodist churches had a monarchial form of church polity that meant that a bishop supervised a group of churches. He could exert tighter control over his circuit riding preachers and the individual churches were much less susceptible to heresy.

The third major influence was the commercial wealth of New England. Commercial shipping on the seas brought prosperity, and with prosperity came a certain aloofness, smugness regarding faith, and indifference toward Puritanical faith. The spirit of luxury meant that the security of what humans could accomplish without God had a special attraction. People did not fear nor need God.

Overlapping these influences were other causes. A more recent writer identifies four sources for American universalism which parallel closely the above three influences. They are liberal humanism, mysticism, reaction

---

5. Ahlstrom, *Theology*, 40.

to Calvinist double predestination, and egalitarian political aims.[6] These causes will find exposure in the following discussion.

In this way universalism found a fertile soil among the churches of New England. Among the first practitioners and preachers were, quite naturally, people from other religious backgrounds. Many universalists came out of a Baptist background because Baptists were characterized by "populist dissent, folk authenticity, and autonomous polity."[7] Universalists had in common their opposition to the doctrine of eternal damnation. From the start evangelicals stood as the major opponent of universalism.

The Significance of the Great Awakening

The Great Awakening of the 1730's–40's came to blunt the tide of irreligion existing throughout the colonies. Under the leading roles of Jonathan Edwards and George Whitefield great numbers came to have a new, fresh relationship with God, often through highly emotional experiences. They embraced a Calvinistic, evangelical form of faith. It is highly reliable to assert that about one out of every six people was converted to Christ during this time. Most historians affirm that this awakening had a powerful impact on improving the morality of the colonies and provided the theological underpinnings for the pursuit of independence from England in 1776. Many people were converted and swelled Baptist churches and other denominations.

It is this resurgence of Calvinism, now accompanied with personal vitality of expression, that turned others against the gospel. Consequently, the appeal that universalists made to reason found fertile soil again. As a whole, universalism opposed the Great Awakening, and many converted to it. Similarly, Unitarians opposed the Awakening.

At the center of the controversy over the Great Awakening was the teaching of conversion or the new birth, as Robinson points out.[8] This teaching was a threat to the strict Calvinist churches who relied heavily on divine election. The preaching of the new birth suggested that salvation was the choice of the individual. What Whitefield and Gilbert Tennent wanted to achieve was to replace a head knowledge of salvation with a heartfelt conversion that would create new people and a new society. Of course, this is what Jesus taught (John 3). While they were Calvinists, the revivalists saw that salvation involved both divine sovereignty and human responsibility.

6. See Ludlow, "Universalism," 204.
7. Robinson, *Unitarians*, 49.
8. Ibid., 10.

Thus when John Murray converted to universalism, coming out of Anglican Calvinism and American Methodist and Baptist influences, he preached a universal election of all to salvation. He allowed for a limited time of suffering in hell that most people would have to experience.

The Early Years of Universalism in America

Several early movements were challenges to universalism. The first was that of Unitarianism which preceded it in the colonies. In the 1700's universalism confronted Deism, in the 1800's it confronted higher criticism and evolution, and in the 1900's it contested with modernism and humanism. In each of these confrontations universalism first contended with the newer teachings, and then surrendered to them, becoming more and more liberal in the process. This process prepared it to unite formally with Unitarianism in 1961.

At the time of the Revolution, Deism, another outgrowth of the Enlightenment, was rampant. This distortion of biblical faith taught that God was impersonal and transcendent only; he was not involved in the daily affairs of people. Being based in reason, Deism rejected anything supernatural, including the deity of Christ and his resurrection. Thomas Jefferson is a prime example of an American deist. He removed from his Bible all the pages that spoke of the deity of Christ and anything that reason or rational thought could not accept. Deism rejected all revelation and opposed all churches. It moved well beyond both universalism and Unitarianism.[9]

The mention of Deism in this history of universalism is important, for Deism played a part in the consciousness of what it meant to be a universalist. For a while many viewed universalism to be a mediation between evangelical belief anchored to Scripture and Deism. At least early universalism allowed one to continue to believe the Bible, in a supernatural God, and the deity of Christ, yet still reject the limited election of some to eternal life as propounded by Calvinism.

The Link of Universalism with Unitarianism

The story of how universalism grew in America is inseparably linked, from beginning to end, with the history of Unitarianism. In recent years these two heresies joined to form one church. But at the beginning the differences were stronger than the similarities. How is it that two different strains of

---

9. Gaustad, *Documentary History*, 293.

distortions of evangelical faith came to join together? The following seeks to explain this from the perspective of both universalism and Unitarianism. We cannot understand one movement apart from the other.

From their beginning in America, both Unitarianism and universalism had Calvinism as their common enemy. The latter seemed to stress divine will over human choice. If Calvinism emphasized the justice of God and the election of some, universalism stressed God's goodness and his love for all, Christ's death for all, and the salvation of all.[10]

Both universalism and Unitarianism are separate streams of religious liberalism in America that only gradually merged. While universalism was chiefly concerned with the nature and goodness of God, Unitarianism concerned itself with the nature and goodness of man.[11] Universalism evolved from the original New England Puritan churches while Unitarianism originated in challenge to these churches.[12]

As universalists opposed the Great Awakening, so did Unitarians. Charles Chauncy's opposition to the Great Awakening was threefold: a commitment to "logic and reason in theology;" a critical and historical biblicism, and a "concern for moral aspiration" in Christian religion.[13] Thus the issues are rationalism, biblicism and moral aspiration. These issues are still vital today.

In the words of Robinson, Chauncy had a strong commitment to biblical authority but to a rational interpretation of it.[14] By applying his rationalism he opposed the "enthusiasm" of the Great Awakening which he believed was against reason. Chauncy also condemned the disorder and disputation and sought a "moral as opposed to a theological standard of judgment."[15] At the beginning Unitarianism viewed itself as a preserver of order, not a challenge of church order. But this soon changed, so that Robinson writes that the history of Unitarianism shows "a gradual reversal of this self-conception."[16]

The seeds for the embrace of liberal theology were sown early in Unitarianism. The intellectual revolution of Newton and natural theology exalted the place of reason. It was believed that science and Scripture were consistent in all their parts and not inconsistent.

10. Ibid., 280.
11. Ibid., 283.
12. Robinson, *Unitarians*, xi.
13. Ibid., 12.
14. Ibid., 13.
15. Ibid.
16. Ibid., 14.

The first Unitarian church was formed in 1785 when members of King's Chapel in Boston voted to exclude all mention of the Trinity from its services.[17] In 1794 a leading English Unitarian, Joseph Priestley, came to America and became a friend of Benjamin Franklin. Robinson asserts that it was he who influenced Thomas Jefferson to personal Unitarianism (although the latter became more radical).[18] Priestley rejected the Trinity and the deity of Christ, and traced the beginning of these beliefs to Justin Martyr. He held to the Socinian view of Christ, not the Arian view. The latter maintains that Christ had a beginning, but was divine; Socinianism rejects Christ's deity altogether, so that everything he did he did as a mere man aided by God. Socinians worship Christ as a mere man who "obtained divinity by his superior life."[19] The modern Unitarian church is a "lineal descendant of the Socinians of Poland, who were first called Unitarians in Transylvania about 1600."[20] Unitarianism came to America via Poland, then Holland, then England.

In Boston, the clergy began doubting Calvinism and emphasized human free will and dignity rather than human depravity. Liberals attacked Calvinism for its original sin and election to salvation as undermining "human moral exertion."[21] People were not depraved sinners but had a strong moral sense and "reliable powers of reason."[22] The emotional excesses of the Great Awakening and the threat that itinerant preachers posed to the established clergy led the Boston ministers to embrace a liberal and rational theology.

Unitarianism grew by its embrace of liberal theology. In 1805 the liberal Henry Ware was elected professor of divinity at Harvard among opposition from evangelicals. In 1819 William Ellery Channing preached his sermon, "Unitarian Christianity," to call liberals together under a new denomination. In 1820 the courts allowed Unitarians in the churches of Massachusetts to control and to keep the original church properties. Many Puritan churches thus became Unitarian. The American Unitarian Association was formed in 1825 to further aid Unitarian identity. These churches held to the doctrines of the goodness of man, salvation by the development of character, the unity of God, the humanity of Christ, and the "immanence

---

17. Cairns, *Christianity*, 457.
18. Robinson, *Unitarians*, 23.
19. Cairns, *Christianity*, 384.
20. Ibid.
21. Robinson, *Unitarians*, 17.
22. Gaustad, *History*, 283.

of God in the human heart."²³ At this point the Unitarians declared that they were not part of the Christian church. The foundation of Unitarianism was thus in place by the 1830's.

Unitarians soon split between Transcendentalists, led by Ralph Waldo Emerson and Theodore Parker, and standard Unitarianism. The former espoused direct intuition of God. It was highly individualized and opposed ecclesiastical organization. It was more reformist in its political outlook.²⁴ It was the precursor of later "free religion" and humanism.

Prior to the Civil War Unitarianism became involved in antislavery and, during the war, pushed medical care for the wounded. In 1865 the National Conference of Unitarian Churches was formed with a desire for a liberal religion with greater universal appeal. This desire found parallel development among universalists at their 100th anniversary in 1870.

While Unitarians sought greater cohesive identification the radical Transcendentalists resisted the formation of a creed by the National Conference of Unitarian Churches or the American Unitarian Association. They formed their own group, the Free Religious Association, to spread "free religion."²⁵

The radical form of Unitarianism spread to the Midwest and the West and insisted on a "creedless religion tied to an ethical basis rather than a theological dogma," in the words of Robinson.²⁶ The radicals and conservatives reached compromise at the National Conference in 1894. The denomination was to be "uncompromisingly non-creedal."²⁷

In the 1920's humanism arose to define liberal theology on a "completely non-theistic" basis.²⁸ Humanism sought to continue the radical theology of Transcendentalism. It so redefined the idea of God and its place in religion that God no longer exists. Somewhat in reaction to humanism James Luther Adams (of the 1930's) called for a revival of liberal religious principles that recognized the "tragedy" of human life and human progress and the need for active "commitment" to remedy such a tragedy.²⁹ After this crisis and after World War 2 Unitarianism and universalism worked

23. Cairns, *Christianity*, 456.
24. Robinson, *Unitarians*, 5.
25. Ibid., 6. The leaders were committed to a "completely noncreedal, and largely post-Christian outlook" (6). They put stock in the "evolving progress of the human race" and argued in a non-supernatural way that God "worked in and through human nature" (6).
26. Ibid., 7.
27. Ibid.
28. Ibid.
29. Ibid., 8.

toward consolidation. While hindered by the social upheavals of the 1960's, including the Vietnam war, civil rights and feminism, there was a growing need for common identity within diversity. Hence the universalists joined with the Unitarians to form the Unitarian-Universalist Association (1961). Robinson reflects that this union will persevere because there is a common identity having a common object of vision, as rebels against established ways of thinking.[30]

The Early Parallel Growth of Universalism in America

As Unitarianism became progressively more liberal and more heretical, universalism had a more checkered beginning. There were several key leaders in the early years.

John Murray, identified as the founder of American universalism, came to America in 1740. He had a Calvinist base and was also influenced by Methodism and Baptist teaching. By 1760 he had embraced universalism in the sense that he believed that all people are elect, not just a smaller number of people. He was influenced by the English universalist James Relly and his work, *Union* (1749). Murray's preaching (begun in 1770) led to the formation of a universalist meeting house in 1780. Murray's story explains how British universalism came to America.[31]

The Baptist minister, Caleb Rich, preached universal salvation after having several visionary experiences that gave him the assurance of salvation. In 1774 his followers formed the first universalist society in America.[32]

Another American patriot and universalist is Jonathan Mayhew (1720–66). He is known for his desire to adapt Christianity to the "world view of the eighteenth-century Enlightenment."[33]

The next significant figure is Elhanan Winchester, a converted Baptist preacher (1781). Robinson holds up his movement through several phases of "Protestant evangelicalism toward Universalism" as "a paradigm for many early converts."[34] In his work, *The Universal Restoration* (1788), he argued that the word *aiōn*, translated often by "eternal," means only a "limited period" of time. Suffering in hell is thus for only a limited time. Winchester appealed to the love of God and the idea that sin and evil had to

---

30. Ibid.
31. Ibid., 49–50.
32. Ibid., 50.
33. Cassara, *Universalism*, 79.
34. Robinson, *Unitarians*, 51.

be conquered.[35] He argued that if the worst of sinners could be saved, then all could be. He also argued against a frequent accusation leveled against universalism, that it led to moral laxity.[36]

In the excursus after chapter 8 I present Isaac Backus' powerful response to the universalism of both James Relly and Elhanan Winchester.

George de Benneville was both a preacher and physician who brought his universalism with him from Germany. He emphasized the pietism of his background.

Benjamin Rush best illustrates, in the words of Robinson, the "convergence of democratic millennial faith and theological universalism."[37] He was well suited to the millennial orientation and political optimism of his day. He affirmed God's ultimate power and will to save, that God has universal love for all, and that there will be final restoration of all to happiness. Rush was rooted in a "Calvinist and Christological sensibility"; yet at the same time he was the forerunner of a more rationalistic universalism.[38]

In 1790 the universalists held a convention in Philadelphia and, in 1792, formed the New England Convention of Universalists.[39] In 1803, at Winchester, N.H., those of New England adopted the Winchester Profession of Faith, which continued in the 19th century to define universalism. I give the content of this Profession, and others, in chapter 6.

The Influence of Hosea Ballou

One of the most important figures in the history of universalism is Hosea Ballou. About a year after the Winchester Profession (1803), Ballou wrote his *A Treatise on Atonement* (1804–05). Robinson calls this the most "significant theological work in the history of American universalism."[40] As the Winchester Profession summarizes the 18th century, Ballou's work captures the essence of universalism in the 19th century. The growth of universalism paralleled the growing influence of Ballou in that century.

While Unitarianism was struggling with the radically more liberal Transcendentalism in the early 19th century, Hosea Ballou led universalists in a different direction than John Murray had led them. Ballou broke with Trinitarianism and the Calvinist-based theologies of Murray, Winchester,

35. Ibid., 52.
36. Ibid., 53.
37. Ibid., 54.
38. Ibid., 55.
39. Ibid., 4.
40. Ibid., 61.

and Rush, and pushed universal theology in the direction of Unitarianism. As early as 1795 Ballou had embraced a Unitarian theology. The old approach was "the old orthodoxy with a heretical outcome"; the new approach of Ballou sought to demolish Calvinism once for all, even though the latter was not his specific opponent.[41]

In his work Ballou rejected the whole idea of the vicarious substitutionary atonement of Christ for the sins of the world so that all might be reconciled to God. Ballou came to reject altogether future punishment after death. All were saved without any suffering. There is no hell. Ballou defended his view that there is no future punishment in his book, *Examination of the Doctrine of Future Retribution*.

The basis of Ballou's theology drew upon strains of Deism, Arminianism, and quasi-pietistic determinism.[42] The most important work that influenced him toward rationalism and the Enlightenment was Ethan Allen's *Reason the Only Oracle of Man*.[43] While he had no formal education he gained a reputation for his preaching ahead of his writing. His writing reflects his many encounters with his opponents. He was heavily influenced by Jeffersonian democracy which put faith in the common man. At that time the "typical Universalist was a Jeffersonian democrat."[44]

In his attack on Calvinism/evangelical faith Ballou argued against the orthodox view that "infinite sin against an infinite God required an infinite sacrifice, the death of Christ, or infinite suffering, everlasting torment in hell."[45] Infinite sin is "impossible in a universe formed by an infinite and benevolent God,"[46] who is "eternal, unchangeable love."[47] Rather sin is finite; it came into being by the will of God in his plan to accomplish a greater good.[48] Thus sin is an ultimate good to form a human being into a better creature in union with God than he would have been without the existence of sin. Sin enables God to exhibit atonement.[49]

---

41. Ibid., 61.

42. Ibid., 62.

43. Cassara, *Universalism*, 18. Ballou felt that evangelical defendants of Christianity damaged the faith more than Deism (19). His work synthesized Deism and his own religious piety.

44. Ibid., 20.

45. Robinson, *Unitarians*, 63.

46. Ibid.

47. Cassara, *Universalism*, 21.

48. Robinson, *Unitarians*, 63.

49. Ibid.

If Ballou's beliefs seem to make God the author of sin, they do, as even he and his reviewers acknowledge.[50] A more orthodox position is that God allowed sin into his universe to accomplish his purposes but he did not will it. Ballou's view means that the end justifies the means. But is making God less than holy a justifiable end, when Scripture considers it unthinkable (Lev 19:1; Rom 3:3–8; 7:12; Jam 1:13–17; 1 John 1:5; Rev 4:8)?

This view is also deterministic: Ballou rejected human free will since it would violate God's omnipotence. Hence humans are limited in their choices by the options that come from God. However, the evangelical response to this is that this conclusion does not arise if God originally created humans with the freedom to choose or reject him.

It is not surprising that Ballou's reviewers acknowledge that the God of Ballou, "like the God of the Deists, emerges as a man-centered God." God "glorifies himself in making man happy."[51]

Ballou's theology also included the following points.[52] (1) Sin is the chief cause of human misery. Indeed, "sin and misery are one."[53] (2) The atonement was done to reconcile man to God, not God to man, since God is not estranged from man. Human love for God is renewed in the atonement, not God's love for man. (3) The sacrifice of Christ demonstrated God's love for man rather than being an act satisfying God's anger toward sin. (4) The atonement of Christ was the effect not the cause of God's love to man (100). (5) "Atonement and reconciliation are the same," a "renewal of love," to cause mankind to "hate sin and love holiness" (119). (6) Christ is a "created, dependent being" (111). Hence there is no Trinity. (7) The atonement was essentially moral: the "literal death of the man, Jesus Christ, is figurative" (122–3). This is close to Unitarians' idea of salvation as character formation. In "following Jesus, the embodiment of God's love, man can be reconciled to God."[54] (8) Hell is not a place of endless punishment; God is not "an enemy to the sinner" (126). (9) Hell is not merely a place of punishment but a state of rebellion against God and unity with him. (10) Hell cannot be endless for then an eternal dualism would deny God's omnipotence. (11) The "consequence of atonement is the universal holiness and happiness of mankind" (138).

---

50. Ibid., 63; Cassara, *Universalism*, 22.

51. Cassara, *Universalism*, 21.

52. I've summarized these points from Robinson, *Unitarians*, 64–66; the numbers in parentheses refer to the pages of Ballou's work.

53. Cassara, *Universalism*, 21.

54. Ibid., 22.

In addition, Ballou doubted the existence of the devil. But if he did exist, then God is a worst being than the devil, for the latter only desires to have people miserable but God intended and purposed many for such a destiny.[55] Ballou also maintained that sin punishes itself.[56]

I will take up all of these assertions in the subsequent chapters on the interpretation of Scripture. Many of these arguments are still being made by universalists today, including Young and McLaren in their fictions and Young and Bell in their nonfiction espousing universalism.

Ballou led his "ultra universalists" (as his followers came to be known) in rejecting all future punishment after death. Sin is punished only in this life. His opponents came to be known as "restorationist universalists": people would be corrected by the fires of hell after death before all would be restored to God. The cryptic phrase to identify Ballou's view was "after death glory." This was the first major schism in universalism. Yet both groups held to universal salvation, biblical authority, the centrality of Jesus (although he is redefined by Ballou) and his atonement.[57] Unitarians, on the other hand, were becoming more liberal and rejecting the Bible and the deity of Christ, and embracing modernism.

Until he died in 1815, John Murray strongly opposed the universalism of Hosea Ballou. He saw Ballou as propagating errors, as one whom he called "a Socinian, Deistical, Sadduccean Universalist."[58] Ballou was installed as minister of the Second Universalist Society on December 25, 1817. In 1819 Ballou began the weekly *Universalist Magazine*. While Ballou had virtually embraced Unitarianism, the Unitarians of Boston, the citadel of Unitarianism, were of a higher social order and Harvard educated; they did not welcome him. They tried to deny that they were universalists.

By the mid 1800's ultra-universalism was on the wane and eventually universalists came to reject Ballou's denial of future punishment and denial of free will. The latter was out of step with American optimism (according to Cassara), so that Arminianism won the day.[59] Those who did not return to classic universalism went over to Unitarianism. By the mid 1900's many had given up the idea of an afterlife altogether.[60]

---

55. Ibid., 104. All universalists, including those singled out in this book, virtually ignore the devil or have him saved out of hell.
56. Ibid., 159. This statement is virtually identical to what Young has "Papa" say in *The Shack* (120).
57. Robinson, *Unitarians*, 5.
58. Cassara, *Universalism*, 23.
59. Ibid., 27.
60. Ibid., 165.

John Murray and Hosea Ballou were the theological leaders of universalism in the 1700's and 1800's respectively. They led churches in their struggle against being taxed to support the established or official churches, as well as their embracing a more liberal theology than Calvinism. Their efforts against taxation paralleled those of the Baptist Isaac Backus in his struggle against the established church in Connecticut and Massachusetts. Yet Backus was a convinced Baptist and evangelical and wrote in opposition to universalism (see the excursus on Backus after chap. 8).

Subsequent History of Universalism

Throughout their history universalist churches were congregational in polity. These joined in loose associations for mutual encouragement but not for any control of the churches. Eventually state conventions, begun in 1785 and 1790, absorbed the associations. Finally, as early as 1834 a national convention was held. By the 1850's the total membership was estimated to be 800,000.[61] These numbers declined substantially by the 1930's due to the fact, according to universalists, that so many in the established denominations had become "closet" universalists and did not need to join with the universalist churches.[62] This is probably still the case.

Over the years universalists have begun their own schools, beginning in 1819. Interestingly, Horace Mann, a Unitarian who believed in universal salvation, made it his goal to remove sectarian religion from the public schools, allowing only the reading of the Bible without comment.[63] Eventually, universalists began colleges including Tufts, Buchtel (now the Uni. of Akron), and Throop (now the California Institute of Technology). Various print media were begun, including magazines and a serious journal, *The Universalist Expositor* (1830).

Prior to the Civil War universalists became increasingly anti-slavery. The Universalist General Reform Association was formed in 1849 as a fruit of this concern.[64] In 1863 universalists ordained the first woman minister in the United States.[65]

---

61. Ibid., 28–29. It was the sixth largest denomination in 1888 (39).

62. Ibid., 39. It had declined to one of the smallest denominations (39). Could not the decline also reflect the influence that the World Wars had on the humanist optimism about the nature of human beings and the gravity of evil in the world?

63. Ibid., 32.

64. Ibid., 190.

65. Ibid., 211.

Anti-Christian Challenges That Conquered Universalism

As traced above in the brief history of Unitarianism, universalism was also challenged by movements that went to the heart of Christian faith. Two of these, higher criticism and evolution, arose in the 19th century and reveal just how far universalism would stray from Christian faith. Because of its "love affair" with reason and rationalism from its very beginning, universalism "came to adapt to new truth," to higher criticism.[66] This movement arose in Germany, and within a short time had influenced the scholars of the Continent and much of England to deny the historical accuracy and the setting of Scripture. In America, universalism came to reject the inspiration of Scripture and its infallibility. Many of the events of the Bible were inauthentic, and the miracles of Jesus were explained as misunderstandings or even myth and legend.[67]

Regarding the challenge from evolution, universalism gradually embraced it more and more and "absorbed it" within its "theistic system." Universalists moved from "one concept of God to another"—from a Creator to one who worked through evolution. This argument led to "wholehearted acceptance of evolution."[68] It is not surprising that the creed of 1899 dropped the reference to "restoring" humanity in the creed of 1803 because the idea was out of line with Darwinism's conviction that "man was evolving to higher and higher forms."[69]

In the 1900's the universalists, while more conservative than Unitarianism, began to become socially defined in response to the challenge of the social gospel. The 1917 Declaration of Social Principles adopted by the Universal General Convention stressed that "evil is the result of 'unjust social and economic conditions.'"[70] Drafted by Clarence Skinner, a "social gospelist," this identified universalism as "economic and social as well as spiritual."[71] The Declaration was viewed as a "program for completing humanity" and called for four new orders: economic, social, moral, and spiritual.[72] Thus universalism defined the gospel as meeting social needs rather than proclaiming the need for personal regeneration.

66. Cassara, *Universalism*, 35.
67. Ibid., 35–36.
68. Ibid., 37.
69. Ibid., 38.
70. Robinson, *Unitarians*, 7.
71. Ibid. See Cassara, *Universalism*, 247ff. He also cites the universalist views of P.T. Barnum (245ff.).
72. Ibid., 140. The words regarding the new social and economic order, it seems to

UNIVERSALISM'S SUBVERSION OF THE CHURCH SINCE THE REFORMATION 139

Facing the challenge of humanism in the 1930's to the 1950's, universalism again succumbed to a wholly man-centered faith. The Humanist Manifesto (1933) declared that man had to have faith in himself, not in a deity, to reorder society and bring world peace and plenty. There is no God, and "the time has passed" for theism, deism, modernism, and other forms of new thinking.[73] Universalists came to embrace the manifesto because they already had become "the most basic of humanists."[74] In their Bond of Faith (1935), while still affirming their belief in "God as Eternal and All-Conquering Love," they looked to "the power of men . . . to overcome all evil and progressively [to] establish the Kingdom of God."[75] As Cassara admits, this accommodation to humanism was a step of universalists that "carried them beyond Christianity."[76] In effect, universalism is no more Christian than is Buddhism, Hinduism, and Taoism. Indeed, universalism adopted the scriptures of these religions as its own along with the Christian Scriptures.[77]

Universalists Reject the Name "Christian"

Since the mid 1900's universalists by their own definition acknowledge that they are not Christians.[78] This should pose a significant barrier to "Christian" universalists who want to keep the name "Christian." The formation of the Christian Universalist Association (2007) is probably a vain attempt to stem this slide toward Unitarianism. In their fiction and non-fiction, Young, McLaren, and Bell are right in line with this assertion of universalists, since they disavow the word "Christian."

This accommodation to humanism indicates just how far their syncretism will go. Universalists are convinced that "man can successfully create a new, world religion that can bridge the cultural differences which perpetuate a superficial division among the nations and tribes of the earth."[79]

---

me, reflect the wording of the *Communist Manifesto*.

73. Cassara, *Universalism*, 259–61. He cites all fifteen theses of this "religious humanism."

74. Ibid., 41.
75. Ibid., 42.
76. Ibid. See also 272.
77. Ibid., 42–43.
78. Ibid., 273.
79. Ibid., 43.

Universalists have been staunch supporters of the League of Nations and the United Nations.[80]

Clearly universalism has placed prior authority in human reason rather than in God who alone is all wise. It has come to reject the great truths that Paul expounds in 1 Corinthians 1-2 regarding the wisdom of God being greater than the wisdom of human beings. It is not surprising that universalism succumbed to the other challenges of the 19th and 20th centuries as well, including the social gospel, humanism, liberalism, socialism, and others. Indeed, universalist authors constantly champion the idea that universalism is liberal and is opposed to evangelical faith.

This overview of universalism's history shows that when challenged by higher criticism, evolution, the social gospel, and humanism, universalism compromised and succumbed to the new ideas. Universalists went so far to syncretize the Christian faith that they professed with other ideas that they ceased being Christian. This was a foregone consequence for a group that early on made rationalism rather than divine revelation their source of authority and belief. And this has had consequences not just for belief but for life and living as well.

Throughout their history universalists have rejected the notion that their theology of no lasting hell leads to immoral living, that with no fear of final judgment people will live as though there is no God. Yet the history of universalism tends to argue the opposite, at least as far as religious fervor is concerned. It is interesting that with universalism's adoption of ever increasingly liberal beliefs in the 20th century, commitment to preaching and missions has waned. Cassara's admissions are telling:[81]

> The distinctive message of universal salvation seemed less important, and the desire to preach and spread it less pressing. Like some other American denominations, the Universalists affirmed their attachment to Jesus in increasingly mawkish terms. He was no longer the great Savior with a transcendent mission but more a friend and companion. Universalists experienced a "rosy glow" when they thought of the friend they had in Jesus.

Both universalism and Unitarianism thus became more and more liberal and socially defined. It is not surprising that they found common ground to form the Unitarian-Universalist Association of 1961. It was preceded by attempts at merger with the Congregationalists, and then the forming of the Free Church Fellowship of the 1930's and the Council of Liberal Churches of 1953.

80. Ibid., 42.
81. Ibid., 39.

Historically, universalism constantly changes and adapts; it has refused to be pinned down about beliefs. One of its adherents wrote around 1920: "Universalists are often asked to tell where they stand. The only true answer to give to this question is that we do not stand at all, we move."[82] The same is true today: universalists disdain doctrinal identification (as related in the previous pages of this book).

Yet universalists have met periodically to put in writing what they believe. In America universalists formulated creeds from the very beginning of Colonial days and continued to do so into the twenty-first Century. The next chapter cites these creeds and brings Part 3, the study of church history, to a close.

---

82. Ibid., 44.

Chapter 8

The Creeds of Universalism

Before closing Part 3 on the history of universalism, I wish to cite the creeds that universalists have articulated over time. Then I interact with a modern contemporary scholar. The creeds of universalism are not many, since universalism eschews any creed at all, in keeping with its universalist identity. Thus none of the creeds was considered "seriously binding" in contrast to the importance attached by orthodox Christians to historic creeds of the early Church.[1] I briefly evaluate each of these that follow.

The Creed of 1790

The first creed was that agreed on by the Philadelphia Convention of 1790 and polished off by Benjamin Rush. Since the Trinity was under debate at the time, reference to such is not explicit.

> Sect. I. Of the Holy Scriptures.
>
> We believe the scriptures of the Old and New Testament to contain a revelation of the perfections and will of God and the rule of faith and practice.
>
> Sect. II. Of the Supreme Being.
>
> We believe in one God, infinite in all his perfections; and that these perfections are all modifications of infinite, adorable, incomprehensible and unchangeable love.
>
> Sect. III. Of the Mediator.

---

1. Cassara, *Universalism*, 31.

We believe that there is one Mediator between God and man, the man, Christ Jesus, in whom dwelleth all the fullness of the Godhead bodily; who, by giving himself a ransom for all, hath redeemed them to God by his blood; and who, by the merit of his death and the efficacy of his spirit, will finally restore the whole human race to happiness.

Sect. IV. Of the Holy Ghost.

We believe in the Holy Ghost, whose office it is to make known to sinners the truth of their salvation, through the medium of the holy scriptures, and to reconcile the hearts of the children of men to God, and thereby to dispose them to genuine holiness.

Sect. V. Of Good Works.

We believe in the obligation of the moral law, as the rule of life; and we hold, that the love of God, manifested to man in a Redeemer, is the best means of producing obedience to that law, and promoting a holy, active and useful life.

There were also recommendations passed by the same convention. They concerned war, going to law, opposition to slavery, oaths and submission to government.²

From an evangelical standpoint the above creed clearly shows the essence of universalism. The Scriptures only "contain a revelation" of God, rather than being such inherently in their entirety. There is an inherent contradiction, even from a logical standpoint, to speak of God as "infinite in all his perfections" and then to say that the perfections are "all modifications" of "infinite love." The statement highlights the belief of universalism that all of God's attributes, including his holiness or justice, are limited by his love. Implicitly, then, God is not perfect in all his attributes, and thus ceases to be God. Section III clearly asserts that all people are already reconciled or redeemed to God and that all will be "finally restored" to God. There is no punishment after death, although this may be assumed, just as the Trinity may be. The work of the Holy Spirit is given as making known to people the "truth of their salvation" that they already have. Clearly this creed may be confessed today by Christian universalists. It is as current as the writings of Young, McLaren, and Bell. A significant omission common to all universalist creeds is the mention of faith and the need for people to believe the gospel and to place faith in Jesus Christ as Savior.

---

2. Ibid., 181–2.

The Winchester Profession of 1803

It is a short declaration and is repeated here in full. It is as revealing for what it does not affirm as for what it does affirm. It was drafted, among some debate with those who opposed any creed at all, by Walter Ferriss.[3] He probably used the Philadelphia articles of faith as a guide.

> Article I. We believe that the Holy Scriptures of the Old and New Testament contain a revelation of the character of God, and of the duty, interest and final destination of mankind.
>
> Article II. We believe that there is one God, whose nature is Love, revealed in one Lord Jesus Christ, by one Holy Spirit of Grace, who will finally restore the whole family of mankind to holiness and happiness.
>
> Article III. We believe that holiness and true happiness are inseparably connected, and that believers ought to be careful to maintain order and practice good works; for these things are good and profitable unto men.

This profession has three simple points that define universalism: the revelation of the Bible, the final restoration of all people, and the need for good works. It is very much like the confession of 1790. While Robinson thinks that the first article places universalism "squarely in the evangelical tradition,"[4] the words, "contain a revelation of God," fall short (as in the creed of 1790) of what evangelicals affirm, that the Bible *is* the revelation of God. The language of the second article is general enough to allow for restoration of all to occur either before hell or after suffering for a limited duration in hell (note these differing views as given above in the discussion of Hosea Ballou). The second article is not evangelical since it identifies God's character/nature as only love, and allows for no permanent suffering in hell. Also, there is no explicit mention of the Trinity. The third article is a polemical defense against the charge that universalism leads to moral laxity. The history of the movement shows that it indeed does lead to both moral and doctrinal decline. It reflects the contemporary debate on whether religion is vital to morality. Christians have always maintained that it is.

---

3. Robinson, *Unitarians*, 58. Cassara, *Universalism*, 110.

4. Robinson, *Unitarians*, 56.

The 1878 Creed of Universalism

The universalists formed early organizations and issued other forms of creeds (that of 1878 and 1899) whose central tenets are similar to those embraced by followers of universal reconciliation today. A study of the statement of the universalist ministers of Boston of 1878 is especially revealing.[5] There are eight paragraphs in the statement. Several are quite mainline theology.

Love Limits Justice

The very heart of universalism, its distinctions, is given in sections four and following. I point out those assertions that are clearly in conflict with evangelical theology. Four is the chief one for it describes "divine justice" as "born of love and limited by love." One must obey love for God and for one's neighbor, and until such obedience is forthcoming, one will be disciplined "for as long a period, as may be necessary to secure that obedience which it ever demands."

The Meaning of Salvation

Statement five affirms that salvation is "from sin rather than from the punishment of sin" and that Christ must "continue his work till he has put all enemies under his feet, that is, brought them in complete subjection to his law."

One's Destiny Can Be Altered After Death

Statement six asserts: "We believe that repentance and salvation are not limited to this life." It concludes: "the obedience of his children is ever welcome to him."

God Is Unjust to Allow Any to Perish in Hell

Section seven asserts that "To limit the saving power of Christ to this present life seems to us like limiting the Holy One of Israel." For God to allow those who have had only a meager opportunity to hear the gospel to suffer means that "their endless damnation would be an act of such manifest

---

5. Paul Young cites the full statement on pages 89–90 of his 2004 document, "Universal Reconciliation" (identified throughout this book as UR).

injustice as to be in the highest degree inconsistent with the benevolent character of God."

Salvation Will Take Place After Death

The eighth statement affirms that salvation may be "affected here or in the future life." The statement concludes with the assertion that in eternity when all are restored, "Justice and mercy will then be seen to be entirely at one, and God be all in all."

Evaluation of the Statement of Universalism: It Is Heresy

In a sense my whole study is an evaluation of these statements at the heart of universalism. What is truly surprising is what the statement omits, what it fails to say. There is not one verse of Scripture cited; not even one reference is given. Perhaps this was strategic. While some points may be backed up with Scripture, most cannot be. So it seems that the choice was made not to have any so as not to draw attention to where Scripture is lacking. It is not surprising that the creeds of universalism affirm belief in Scripture as "containing a revelation" of God, but not *as* the revelation of God.

Another great omission is any mention of faith or belief in Christ as the means of receiving salvation. Indeed, the statement affirms that "salvation, secured in the willing mind by the agencies of the divine truth, light, and love, essentially represented in Christ." The domination of love is recognized, but not faith.

The final great omission is a reference to the Holy Spirit. Yet Scripture speaks of his work in bringing about conviction of the need to repent and exercise faith. Just how are people going to repent, be forgiven and be regenerated if the Spirit in not involved nor his existence affirmed. Indeed, there is no reference to the Trinity as such. This is not surprising in light of the fact that the universalists joined the Unitarians prior to this "statement" (in 1859).

Surely any one can recognize, in light of these assertions and omissions, that universalism is heresy. In 1859 (less than twenty years before the Boston statement) universalism joined Unitarianism which declared in 1825 that it was no longer part of the Christian church. Universalism is distinctively not Christian by its own assertion and by traditional understanding.

The Creed of 1899

By the end of the 19th century, the beliefs of universalists had become so liberal by accommodation to higher criticism, evolution, and the social gospel that a new statement was needed to account for the new views of the Bible which denied its literal interpretation. Thus the "conditions of fellowship" adopted in 1899 in Boston were stated so generally that Cassara calls it "a masterpiece of theological dexterity."[6] The creed of 1899 reaffirmed the Winchester Profession of 1803, done at Winchester, N.H. Then these conditions of fellowship were articulated.[7] They are as follows.

1. The acceptance of the essential principles of the Universalist Faith, to wit: 1. The Universal Fatherhood of God; 2. The spiritual authority and leadership of His Son, Jesus Christ; 3. The trustworthiness of the Bible as containing a revelation from God; 4. The certainty of just retribution for sin; 5. The final harmony of all souls with God.

The Winchester Profession is commended as containing these principles, but neither this nor any other precise form of words is required as a condition of fellowship, provided always that the principles above stated be professed.

2. The acknowledgment of the authority of the General Convention and assent to its laws.

As seen by a comparison with the preceding creeds, this statement of fellowship is itself more general and at the same time renders the authority of the preceding ones less so. It reinforces the view that universalism does not want to be identified with a doctrinal creed.

Knight also identifies the general system of doctrine to which most universalists subscribe as including the following.[8] The Bible contains "a revelation from God" mixed with human and fallible elements. God is "a person of infinite excellence," whose nature "is best expressed in the one word, love, at least the other attributes are entirely consistent with this one." The view of the nature of Jesus Christ is split between those who view him as entirely human and those who view him as a being ranking "half-way between God and man." The Holy Spirit is either "God the Father himself or is impersonal." "Salvation is from sin and its sequences" and "unto

---

6. Ibid., 243.

7. From Knight, "Universalists," 95. See also R.E., "Universalists," 662, who gives the same matter.

8. Ibid.

righteousness, holiness, and a perfected humanity, and is constantly going on." This is "the so-called moral salvation, and contains no element of substitutional satisfaction or transfer of guilt or merit." Punishment is "a sequence of sin, is divinely appointed as a remedy therefore, and is consequently one of the agencies of salvation both in this world and in the next." The clergy "have no apostolic succession." The "Church universal is the great body of all professing Christians, of which body a humble member is the Universalist Church." "Religion is right relations with God, and therefore includes right thoughts . . . right feelings . . . and right acts." Universalists have always "been zealous for doctrine for the honor of God and for social reforms and charities." The two sacraments are observed. Future life is basically "a continuation of the present life" but without the body of flesh. There will be "no resurrection of this body, and no general judgment, no annihilation of the wicked, no endless punishment . . . and no second coming of Christ."

This summary clearly reveals how universalism in general clearly parts company with evangelical faith. Many of these elements are also embraced by contemporary Christian universalism or universal reconciliation as dealt with in the preceding chapters. What is missing are two critical doctrines: the deity of Jesus Christ; and the need for people to believe in him for their salvation. As pointed out above, the words "have faith in" or "believe in Christ" are totally lacking in this summary and in others.[9]

The 1935 Bond of Fellowship

In 1935 universalists adopted the Bond of Fellowship. It reveals how far universalists had embraced the social gospel of the day. There is no explicit statement regarding a distinctive belief in universal salvation.[10] It reads:

> The bond of fellowship in this Convention shall be a common purpose to do the will of God as Jesus revealed it and to co-operate in establishing the Kingdom for which he lived and died.
>
> To that end we avow our faith in God as Eternal and All-Conquering Love, in the spiritual leadership of Jesus, in the supreme worth of every human personality, in the authority of truth known or to be known, and in the power of men of goodwill and sacrificial spirit to overcome all evil and progressively establish the Kingdom of God. Neither this nor any other

---

9. These words are lacking also in R.E.'s larger listing of the beliefs of universalism. See his "Universalists," 662–3.

10. Ibid., 257–8.

statement shall be imposed as a creedal test, provided that the faith thus indicated be professed.

It is obvious that there is no longer any statement regarding Scripture, a personal God, the Trinity, the authority of Jesus, suffering for sin, the need to believe the gospel, and other matters. There is more faith expressed in human beings to overcome evil than there is in God. It is also inherently contradictory to affirm that there is no creedal test and then to affirm that "the faith" must be professed!

Lessons to Learn from This History for the Current Struggle with Universalism

There are several lessons from this history that are instructive for contemporary Christians in America. First, the three factors that made the Puritan churches fertile soil for universalism then exist in America today. There is love for the intellect, for learning and education with the potential that reason will be exalted over revelation. The higher criticism that won over Europe in the 20th century is on constant attack today in higher education including evangelical seminaries. The Evangelical Theological Society is probably the most influential group of evangelical scholars. While they resist the universalism and anti-supernaturalism of others, such as those in the Society of Biblical Literature or, worse yet, the American Academy of Religion (which are now combined), there is the continuing challenge of dealing biblically with innovation and creativity. Recent movements such as neo-orthodoxy, process theology, the new perspectives on Paul, "open theism," and reevaluations of the meaning of the atonement witness to these pressures.

A great number of evangelicals attend independent, congregational churches or loose associations of churches (for example, the Southern Baptists). The recent struggles among the Baptists over the authority of Scripture and inerrancy witness to the temptation for independent churches to explore new directions. The emergent churches are the outworking of these explorations. It is not surprising that many of these are toying with new doctrines, including Brian McLaren and Rob Bell with their denial of hell and the word "Christian."

Finally, the great wealth of American churches makes them susceptible to indifference and compromise. Wealth robs the vitality of faith, deceiving people into trusting money and its illusion of security instead of trusting God. It is notable that churches in the third world, in the 20 x 40 window of the world, are growing faster and experience greater vitality than those in the West. It is a situation that the state of the church in Ephesus (Rev 2:17) fits and which warns us today: it had lost its first love.

Thus the three factors making Puritans susceptible to universalism are prominent today. It is not surprising to find universalism growing today as never before.

There are other lessons to note. The Puritans did not stop in their movement from evangelical faith to universalism. They went on to embrace even more apostate forms of faith as expressed in Unitarianism. The latter denies the deity of Christ and his atonement on the cross, and the Trinity. It is not a Christian form of faith at all. Contemporary leaders in the emergent church are questioning the Trinity as well.

In addition, the Puritans did not move quickly from evangelical faith to universalism to Unitarianism. It took over two hundred years for the Puritans to move from the doctrine of the Reformation of the 1500's to their embrace of universalism in the 1700's; and it took another two hundred years for them to embrace Unitarianism in a formal union in 1961. From a questioning of eternal punishment in hell these former evangelicals came to deny the reality of hell altogether. They have given up resisting higher criticism, evolution, the social gospel, humanism, and modern liberalism, and have heartily embraced them all.

Today, leaders in the emergent church and elsewhere, such as Brian McLaren, openly seek to "deconstruct hell" and redefine the gospel, Christianity, and what a Christian is. Paul Young and Rob Bell do much of the same. The gospel is not so much about personal salvation but the social gospel—compassion for the poor, the diseased, the gay culture, LGBTism, and others seemingly disadvantaged. In his recent nonfiction (*Lies*) Paul Young seeks to "deconstruct" or redefine hell, sin, the cross, the nature of God, the children of God, the plan of God, and the death of Christ, among other beliefs.

It is also interesting that the liberalism of the universalists found connection with the political liberals of their day. Today, this connection continues to find validation.

Finally, it is the evangelical church both as an institution and as affirming a particular set of doctrines that stands as the formidable opponent of universalism. Let evangelicals affirm again their crucial role in the preservation of the truth.

The Testimony of William Barclay, a Universalist

William Barclay is a modern universalist and authored, "I am a Convinced Universalist." Barclay is a well-known scholar who has written studies on biblical words and other books. Because universalists like to cite him I draw attention to the distinctions of his universalism and answer them.[11] He is also an example of the fact that being an expert in Greek does not save one from heresy.

Barclay puts heavy emphasis on the love of God. Yet he affirms that many would have to experience the "severest punishment before they were fit for the presence of God." But what kind of "fitness" is this? The Bible speaks of God making us fit, giving us his righteousness, by means of our placing faith in Christ (Rom. 3:21–26). The Bible never says that punishment makes us fit for God, for this suggests a salvation by works or personal merit.

Barclay puts in opposition to acceptance of "God's offer and invitation willingly" the option of taking the "long and terrible way round through ages of purification" in hell. Note that this implies that salvation after death is unwilling. Again the true nature of universalism is exposed: it is a forced repentance which contradicts love.

Another point that Barclay insists on, as Young does, is that the "purpose of punishment is always remedial." But is it? What about the death penalty where all efforts of remedy have failed? When someone has murdered another person, only the taking of the second human life is adequate to do justice and love for the community. Capital punishment was instituted by God through Noah (Gen 9), recognized by Jesus as something that Caesar might do (Matt 22) and never abrogated by him (see Matt 5), and affirmed strongly by Paul the Apostle (Rom 13:1–7). Similarly the flood wiped out civilization except for the family of Noah. Even the second coming of Christ is not remedial (note Rev 19 especially).

The second half of Barclay's statement appeals to the NT. He claims that the use of "all" justifies his "belief" in universalism (he never speaks about "belief" in Christ). This is woefully inadequate for a scholar such as he. I've addressed this topic above.

He next appeals to the meaning of "eternal torment" (*aiōn kolasis*) in Matthew 25:46. He argues from its Greek background, that the word for "eternal" (*aiōn*) can be used only of God and then he says: "Eternal punishment is then literally that kind of remedial punishment which it befits God to give and which only God can give." Yet the other half of the verse has

---

11. Taken from his work, Barclay, *A Spiritual Autobiography*, 65–67, and quoted by Paul Young in UR, 91–92.

Jesus promising "eternal life" to the sheep, his people. If "eternal" befits God alone, and the adjective is here used to describe both punishment and life, do these not take on the attribute of at least "everlasting"? It hardly seems possible that "life" may take on God's attribute of eternity but not "punishment" when they are used in the same verse, back to back and parallel to each other. Isn't the meaning here that however much of God's "eternity" (or what we might call "everlasting") can be applied to non-human and human beings can be said of both punishment and life? And the text says nothing of punishment being "remedial." I treat this parable in greater length below.

Barclay's third point is that he believes that the grace of God knows no limits in this world or in the next, that it is as "wide as the ocean." In essence the grace of God is limitless, but God does not force it on people. The saints will live for eternity reveling in the grace of God. Those who choose to spurn the grace of God continue to do so in an endless eternity of suffering, and, like their rejection of God's love, God respects their choice. His holiness is also limitless.

Barclay's final point is that he believes "implicitly in the ultimate and complete triumph of God."[12] He asserts that if anyone remains outside of God's love at the end of time then that one "has defeated the love of God—and that is impossible." God is Father "more than anything else." Barclay then proceeds to talk about a father's love for his children, that he wants his offer of love to disobedient children answered "by the return of love. The only possible final triumph is a universe loved by and in love with God."[13]

But is this the case? Let's pursue the analogy a bit further. Am I a loving father if I punish my child for rejecting me, and punish him so much that he is coerced to love me in return? Does not a loving father love his child's freedom not to love in return? The father does all kinds of loving deeds, and seeks his return. But the return is up to the child, up to her/him to love. No wonder that McLaren cites others who think that universalism is coercion!

Think of the parable of the prodigal son. The father did not afflict his wayward son or coerce his return. He did not "teach him a lesson." The son made a free decision to come back and to love the father. Universalists regularly speak of hell's fires being remedial and restorative, and assume

---

12. It is interesting that Barclay says that he can believe in a lot of "things" but never says that he believes in Jesus Christ.

13. Interestingly, this section in Barclay is found almost word for word in a section found in *The Shack*, chap. 11, and reflects a similar passage in Brian McLaren. And Rob Bell reflects Barclay's thinking: the purpose of punishment is correction (86-88); God fails to get what he wants if all are not saved (98); God is not thwarted in his purpose—all will be reconciled (100).

that because God "casts people into the lake of fire" (Rev 20) he causes the suffering for this purpose. They never speak of God *using* the fire of hell to bring repentance. The ministers of Boston, in their second statement, affirm that "God renders to every man according to his works"; and in their third statement, that God does "not afflict willingly nor grieve the children of men; but though he cause grief, yet will he have compassion according to the multitude of his mercies."

All the biblical statements regarding the source of the sufferings are true. What universalists have in error is the purpose of them, to bring repentance after death. The Bible never says this. God is not going to cause any one to suffer to force repentance. Again, God has willed that people have a free choice to respond. If people will not to respond, God respects that will, but the consequences are certain—because of the person's choice, not God's.

Also, note Barclay's words above that if anyone at the end of time remains outside God's love then that person has defeated God's love. Perhaps time is the crucial issue. For in the eternal age to come, which the Bible calls the "new heavens and the new earth," time as we know it will be no more (note Revelation chapters 21–22). Thus those lost everlastingly are "left behind" in the present reality and are not considered as ever in the new realm. In this case there is no one left outside of God's love.

Misrepresentation of Evangelical Belief in the Twentieth Century

Universalism makes another appeal to the impact that church history should have on Christians' views of universalism. Young cites three options that contemporary Christians have: the majority view—eternal torment; the minority view—annihilation, eternal death; and the remnant view—eventual salvation through Jesus Christ.[14]

This is a strange way to list the options, and extremely biased and misrepresentative. For the majority view also affirms "salvation through Jesus Christ." In addition, the first view holds both that there is everlasting salvation and life to those who place faith in Jesus Christ, but everlasting suffering for those who reject the gift of salvation. The third view is given a misnomer, for it suggests that the "remnant" is a godly category derived from Scripture (see Rom 9). The third view should be characterized as follows. It is the view declared as heresy by the other two: universal salvation for all, humans and angels alike, including all those in hell.

14. Paul Young constructs this summary of views near the end of his UR paper, 99-102.

But putting this aside, universalism proceeds to list the Scriptures that each view uses to support its view. It gives eight for the "majority view" (Matt 25:31–46; Mark 9:38–48; Luke 16:19–31; Matt 12:24–36; John 3:35–36; Rev 19:19–21; 20:7–10, 11–15). What is interesting about this list is that hardly any text speaks to the need to have faith to appropriate salvation. Yet this is the core of evangelical faith. Instead, as seen throughout the entire discussion above, universalism lists passages that mainly refer to "eternal" or "forever"—words that don't mean what seems obvious but mean only "age." In addition, there are lists of passages about the lake of fire. This selective listing biases the reader against the majority view and suggests the superiority of the "remnant (universalist) view" with its seventy-three texts listed!

The evangelical view would want to list all those passages dealing with "faith" and "believe" and related terms that are essential to possessing salvation and eternal life. It turns out that there are about 336 passages in the OT and in the NT dealing with "faith" and about 280 dealing with "believe."[15] Universalism's listing of eight passages is misleading and distorts the biblical record.

For the minority view (annihilation) there are twelve texts. By and large these assume that "destruction" is eternal annihilation when the contexts involved usually point to something temporal.

Following this listing of texts for the minority view Young introduces the case for universalism (designated the "remnant view"). Once again he makes the spurious claim that for the first five hundred years the Christian church held to the "remnant view"—universal reconciliation. Augustine is the culprit for aiding its rejection. The dark ages seemingly held the church in captivity to the majority view.

Yet if this is so, why haven't the centuries since the end of the dark ages seen the resurgence and triumph of the minority view? Finally, universalism faults evangelists of the majority view for using Scripture "to scare people into their church or into the kingdom." I have dealt with this *ad hominem* argument above.

---

15. *Strong's Concordance* was the basis of this calculation.

Excursus

Isaac Backus: An Early American Refutes Universalism

THE NAME, ISAAC BACKUS, is hardly a house-hold name recognized in contemporary America. But this man was a giant in Colonial America. Not only did he more than any other to influence the dis-establishment of colonial or state churches in early America but he helped to expose the heresy of universal reconciliation in his time. He is a champion of both political and spiritual freedom.

Universal reconciliation (UR) is not new for our day. It has a long history of entangling itself among Christians and subtly trying to destroy evangelical churches. It goes back as far as some early church fathers (so-called): Clement of Alexandria, Origen, and Cyprian. Origen is the most prominent of these and the one to whom modern universalists appeal for finding some historical basis for their belief. But I've shown in chapter 6 of this book that a complete understanding of early church history reveals that the vast majority of Christians and their leaders believed that the Bible shows that UR is wrong, that it is a heresy worthy of being condemned at early church councils.

As I've related in the preceding chapters, UR came to America in the 1740's in the person of John Murray. From the mid 1700's this teaching grew in popularity for over a hundred years. But God raised up leading Christians of the day to expose UR. They helped to bring about its gradual decline for the next century or so. Chief among these is Isaac Backus.

Isaac Backus was born in 1724 into a Puritan family. But he wasn't a Christian until he was saved (in 1741) during the Great Awakening of the 1740's. Almost at once he realized that the Congregational church that he was attending was not faithful to the truth of the Bible (it baptized infants and unbelievers), so he and some others formed a Separate or New Light Church (1746). He soon received his call to the ministry and then started a Separate church in Massachusetts (1748). A few years later Backus became convinced that the Bible did not support infant baptism so he began the first Baptist church in Mass., at Middleborough (1756).

The revolutionary events of the times found Isaac Backus leading a church movement of the Baptists to resist the paying of taxes to the established Colonial church. He wrote several pamphlets and a book to justify such civil disobedience: *An Appeal to the Public for Religious Liberty Against the Oppression of the Present Day* (1773). This book carefully unfolded why the comingling of state and church was wrong; why Baptists should not have to pay taxes to support the Colonial church; and concluded with five reasons to justify civil disobedience—just as the Colonies were beginning to use civil disobedience against England (the Boston Tea Party erupted in 1773).

Backus' influence initially failed to lead to a united civil disobedience. But as the years unfolded after the Revolutionary War, Backus, representing Massachusetts, supported ratification of the new Constitution of the U.S. (1788). He had particular interest in the First Amendment protecting freedom of religion. He believed that the American Revolution was as much spiritual as it was political. In contrast to Jefferson and Madison who believed that America would become a secular state by 1830, he believed that one day Christians would be in the majority in America. He died in 1806, having pastored the same church for 58 years and having preached over 9,800 sermons. His work led to the disestablishment of the last state churches in Connecticut in 1818 and in Massachusetts in 1833.

Isaac Backus exerted a strong influence in early America, not only for freedom of religion but also for biblical truth. He wrote thirty-seven books and pamphlets, and many articles, on many topics of interest to Christians. His three-volume history (1796) of the Baptists in America is still considered essential reading for understanding early America.

Among his many religious books was one on universalism titled, *The Doctrine of Universal Salvation Examined and Refuted, containing A concise and distinct Answer to the Writings of Mr. Relly, and Mr. Winchester, upon the Subject* (Providence: 1782). This forty-page book is still available today. What he wrote then still has merit for us today—to see the errors in universalism and how to refute them—and why it is urgent to do so. In the following words I review his arguments that provide for us today a heritage of biblical truth.

The catalyst for Backus' writing was the alarming increase in popularity of universal reconciliation due to the preaching and writing of John Murray, James Relly, Elhanan Winchester, and others. The last was once a

Baptist minister. By their preaching and writing these all became leaders of the universalist movement.

Backus first takes up the arguments in a pamphlet by James Relly. Relly asserted that all people find salvation in Christ because they are united in him. He rejected the substitutionary atonement of Christ—that Christ chose to die in the place of sinners and for them. This must be, he claimed, since each person must die an eternal death for his own sin. He rejected the idea of sin as separating people from God. Instead he insisted that people out of necessity were united in Christ before the world began, and chosen without sin in him (so Eph 1). None had a choice in this matter. Also, all people by nature are united in Adam. Thus Jesus did not choose to provide atonement; it was by nature his necessary lot as embodying everyone in the church. Relly argued that all people as part of the body of Christ are born without sin because they were by union with Jesus who as head of the body was so born. Faith is unnecessary since people are already united to Christ; they had no choice in the matter. Relly appealed to the nature of the universe as demonstrating this union (4–5; 17). In this manner Relly was rejecting penal substitution.[1]

Backus observes that this denial of personal sin runs counter to the biblical view, that the "evil of sin appears greater in his sufferings, than it could have done in the eternal damnation of all the human race" (5). He points out that the power of thinking and choosing are essential to the nature of all immortal spirits. He notes that Relly is deceived: faith is necessary for salvation. Otherwise, why did the disobedient Israelites have to first believe and then look at the brass serpent in order to be healed. By Relly's argument they were already healed before they looked (8)!

Relly next argues that his view about union is persuasive because Scripture says that as in Adam all die, even so all shall be made alive in Christ (Rom 5:12–21; 1 Cor 15:22). [I note that this is a standard argument of universalists]. Yet Backus points out that the life found in Christ must be received (Rom 5:17). "All the blessings of salvation were provided by covenant in Christ, before the world began; but the only way for any to enjoy them, is by receiving them freely by faith" (10). In contrast, our identification with the sin of Adam is the lot of all who are naturally born.

Relly criticizes those who proclaim the gospel as promoting fear, but the obedience of faith is without fear. Since Jesus Christ has once been judged for sins, and all are united to Christ, there is no longer any future judgment for anyone (11). Backus replies that Relly worships a god but not

---

1. It is surprising how most of these statements find contemporary expression in Young's *Lies*, chapters 2, 3, 7, 13, 17, 19, 24, and others. See my book, *Lies Paul Young Believes about God*.

the God of the Bible. He goes on to show in parallel columns over several pages (12–14) what the Truth of the Bible says in comparison to what Relly says. Highlights of Relly's claims are that "by Jesus we inherit, by him we have atoned"; and "your unbelief cannot make his grace of none effect" (13). Relly appeals to the inward desires for good that mark one as having Christ, to allow one to reckon oneself as dead unto sin.

Yet Backus quotes several Scriptures that affirm the need to be in Christ, that to deny sin is self-deceit, that faith is necessary, that loving God means keeping his commandments, and that one must beware of the errors of the wicked. Backus describes Relly's system as "a filthy dream" (15). He points out the fallacies of setting reason over revelation, of taking pride in discovering a new system which claims certainty. Relly's attempt to deny any place for future judgment by the sword (after Christ's death) promotes anarchy toward government. Backus points to Felix's refusal to believe (Acts 24:24–27) as a "soul-damning crime" (16).

Backus points to the contradiction when Relly claims that imperfect men of old (Noah, Lot, Abraham, David, and others) were types of Christ, yet at the same time they were really perfect in union with Christ (17). Backus points to the need to discern the truth. What Relly does is to take texts of the Bible that pertain to the saints only and applies them to the whole human race. He wants to find the whole human race already reconciled to God (18). Relly is a "liar" for asserting that eternal life is "as fully given to the unbeliever, as to the believer" (19). While people may consider Relly to be evangelical, his contradiction to biblical truth is "for dreamers; . . . it is harder to be received than the belief of transubstantiation" (19). By these words Backus is referring to the view of the eucharist (communion) as taught by Roman Catholicism. Later, in the 19th Century, Nathan Hale Smith (a later convert from universalism to evangelical faith) will write his autobiography and make this same comparison of universalism and Catholicism (see the Conclusion of this book).

Backus concludes his review of Relly by noting that the latter's arguments are similar to those of the serpent in the Garden of Eden who called in question the truth of what God said.

Let me give a few comments regarding this section of Backus' book. It is clear that universalists were using many of the same arguments then as they do now. Further, it is clear that evangelicals found that the witness of Scripture when properly interpreted was an adequate refutation of universalism. Finally, Backus clearly saw how evil and idolatrous, how blasphemous, the universalist position is. He does not mince words in describing the universal salvation of his day.

In part two of his book, Backus takes up the writing of another, leading universalist of his day, Elhanan Winchester. He makes comparisons of the two, basically noting that while Relly built his whole argument for universalism on "an imaginary union with Jesus," Winchester built his on the "benevolent nature of the Deity" (20). Relly asserted that salvation was already complete in Christ, that all men are in Christ, so as to exempt men from all future punishment. Winchester denied the need for Christ's blood to appease any wrath in God but that it is necessary to purge away disorders in nature which are so great as to require the sufferings of many ages until they are removed (20). Another major difference is that the latter asserted salvation for devils but Relly did not speak of such.

Backus points to Winchester's appeal to the second and third centuries, and to Origen in particular, for support for his views. He takes up Winchester's use of Scripture and his departure from the "literal apparent meaning" which makes it difficult to dispute with him (21–22).

At this point Backus sets up two columns, as he did with Relly, to show side-by-side what the truth of the Bible says compared to what Winchester says (22–24). Near the end of this (points 10–12) Winchester labels the curse pronounced on Adam as a "trial" and remarks: "Punishment is never an *arbitrary* infliction upon the sinner" (italics his). He concludes: "Fury, wrath, or anger can never dwell in the fountain of love, but are *only* to be found in fallen nature, separated from the life of God" (24). To oppose this last claim Backus cites Romans 1:18, that the "wrath of God is being revealed from heaven" (24). Backus appeals to God's questions in response to Job: "Who is this that darkens counsel by words without knowledge?" (Job 38:1–38).

Backus remarks that some think that Winchester is so absurd that he doesn't need to be answered. But Backus thinks that the case is otherwise, that "the turning points in both of these pamphlets have caused the greatest controversies that the world or the church have ever been perplexed with" (24). With these words Backus senses just how important the conflict over the error of universalism really is.

Backus next proceeds to raise the questions that moderns, including the contemporary universalists who are the focus of this book, often raise. They go to the heart of the nature of God. (1) "How can a Being of infinite goodness and love make any creature, who shall be miserable without end?" (2) "How can any, who receive great favors from the mediation and merits of Christ, be eternally lost?" (3) "How can it be just with God to damn men forever for not believing his gospel?" (25).

Backus begins to answer these questions by appealing to what the Bible teaches about God and the justification of his anger. If people can be both loving and angry, certainly God can. He argues: Is it possible for a man to love his wife and children and friends "without hating the wretch that would murder them?" Is it possible "to love truth and goodness without hating deceit and cruelty?" Thus Backus argues from the lesser to the greater, not from the lesser "against" the greater (27).

Backus makes other points that center on the account of the fall of Adam and Eve where God expresses his intention to put enmity between himself and Adam and his seed. He takes up Winchester's claim that the atonement of Christ was never intended to quench wrath in the Deity but only "to break the power of death in us, and to overcome the wrath of fallen nature." Winchester went on to assert that the kingdom of God is within all mankind, that Christ is able to raise up "the divine life" in all humanity. God seeks the "recovery and complete restoration" of all. Without this the "good news which Christ commanded to be preached to every creature is mockery, insult, and insincerity" (26).

Backus points out that this "mystic philosophy" and "mystic divinity" has two points, that it is calculated to prevent anyone from thinking that either God or man act with "bad designs" towards each other; and that it raises a "hope that they will all be reconciled" (26). Backus notes that such sentiments oppose one great fact, that God said (in Genesis 3) that he would put enmity between the two seeds, and this enmity remains after thousands of years. This action by God shows his freedom to do as he pleases, and none can "fault" him, in the words of Paul (in Rom 9:13–23).

To answer the three questions above Backus argues about the nature of God and his freedom to do as he pleases or wills. He points out that the role of faith is to carry us off from self to the truth, from trusting in the flesh to trusting in the Lord (28). He faults those who would interpret Genesis 3 figuratively to remove the obvious reference to God's anger. He notes that those who resort to such interpretation are of the devil and worship idols—their own gods. He affirms that we need to have "the infinite excellency of all God's perfections displayed before us in the clearest light" (31). The more strongly we are persuaded that God cannot err, and we obey the revelation of God, the more strongly will be the desire to know and do his will, and have the confidence that brings mutual esteem, happiness, and peace (31). The specter of endless torment teaches everyone not to break God's laws or to neglect his grace.

Regarding question (2) above, Backus argues that nothing is more contrary to the love of God than a disbelief in his word. God has left his witness in every nation which people are responsible to receive. Jesus validated who he was by several witnesses: himself, his works, and the Holy Spirit doing the works. Thus the rejection of the witness of the Spirit, Jesus said, is so serious that it could never be forgiven (Matt 12:24–32), contrary to universal reconciliation (32). So the conflict of the ages is over the point, "whether all that God says is *true*? Or, if true, how it can be *equal*" (italics his)? Those who reject the witnesses about Christ "will justly be damned" (33).

In regards to the (3) question above, Backus points out that Scripture may affirm that Christ has purchased all (2 Pet 2:1) and make other broad statements about the deliverance of all. Universalists thus assert that all have been reconciled. But in these texts the word "all" is limited or defined by the context to mean only some (33). He points to other texts (1 Tim 4:7–10; 1 Cor 10:4, 5). Backus also appeals to God's permission that allows some to reject the grace of God (33–34) and to divine sovereignty (35–36).

Backus answers the charges that God lacks the power, the wisdom, and the goodness to make every creature happy. First, Backus notes that all the creation belongs to God and, following clear property rights, Jesus can bestow the fruits of his death on whomever he wishes. It is "the height of madness" to deny him that right to property (36). Second, Backus asserts: "No pardon was ever promised to men who *presumptuously* and *deceitfully* acted against the light" (italics his) (37). Here Backus seems to be saying that there is no forgiveness for those who reject forgiveness, that God honors the choice of people to disbelieve. He cites the example of Israel in the wilderness who were judged when they refused to believe, to obey God (see Hebrews 3–4). It is not a matter of impotence or lack of wisdom in God but a matter of human obstinacy.

Backus next brings forward Winchester's (and UR's) argument: the words "everlasting," "forever," and such are used in a limited sense. The suffering in hell is not without end. Backus cites several texts where "everlasting" must be without end—especially the verse at the end of the Parable of the Sheep and Goats (Matt 25:46). Backus cites the example of Judas to show that at least he will be finally lost—and if this one person is eternally lost then UR is false. According to Winchester, Jesus meant that if Judas had died in the womb it would have been good for him because then he would be at rest, where the wicked "cease from troubling." But Backus argues that Judas was not an object of God's love (in light of what Rom 8:28 means: that all things work together for the good of all who are the objects of God's love). This principle could never be applied to Judas.

Backus completes his refutation of Winchester by giving several principles that should guide local churches. Basically he exhorts that churches with Christ as their head should only admit Christians, teachers should use sound and clear speech, men should lead but women be heard, love should prevail, to be on guard against teachers who stir up passions, and to avoid slothfulness but be fervent in spirit. Regarding the last encouragement

Backus warns against the two extremes of being overbearing with authority and on the other hand allowing licentiousness with freedom (39).

Finally, Backus writes about three matters that attend his refutation of UR (40). (1) Everyone needs to be on guard against pride and must not regard self above God. (2) UR is characterized by self-condemnation and conscience-blinding, as well as deception. There will be degrees of punishment in hell for devils and for people. (3) Everyone should seek to live in conformity to the will of God since this affects one's present and eternal welfare.

Backus' very last words appeal to the logic of the greater loss that attends UR. He writes: "Could it therefore be possible, that the torments of the damned would have an end, yet we are certainly as safe as our opponents; but, on the other hand, what a risk do they run in their way! If reason can be heard, it will make everyone in earnest to know and live to God" (40).

In this brief excursus on Isaac Backus' refutation of the claims of UR in early America one thing stands out. The contemporary arguments of universalists differ hardly an iota from arguments used in Colonial America, and even earlier. "There is nothing new under the sun," said the Preacher (Eccl 1:9). Today we can take encouragement from those who have striven to defend the truth.

Part 4

The Appeal to Texts of Scripture

Chapter 9

The Appeal to Texts with "All" and "Whole"

THE FOURTH MAJOR DEFENSE that universalism makes is its appeal to Scripture. It argues from many texts that the view of universalism is the correct interpretation of the Bible. Universalists cite many of these texts because they use words such as "all" or "world" or "whole world," seemingly to support universalism (John 1:29; 3:16–17; 4:42/1 John 4:14; John 12:32, 47; Acts 3:19–21; Rom 5:10, 12–21; 6:1–11; 1 Cor 15:20–26; 2 Cor 5:14, 18–20; Eph 1:10; Phil 2:9–11; Col 1:16–23; 1 Tim 1:15–16; 2:4; 4:10; Tit 2:11; Heb 2:9; 9:26; 2 Pet 3:9; 1 John 2:2). McLaren (103) asserts that these texts show that universalism is not "as bankrupt of biblical support as some suggest."

In this and the next several chapters I present the best texts that universalism uses to try to prove its case. I interact with these texts to refute universalism. Then in the following major section of this book I present what I believe are the most important biblical texts that universalism does not answer or cannot answer.

Putting Paul in Opposition to Jesus

Yet before dealing with the texts of Scripture which universalism cites for its position it is important to set the larger context of this discussion. There is a sub-stream of assumptions going on in McLaren's concept of a "new kind of Christianity" (chap. 25) that pits the teaching of Paul and John against the picture of Jesus as derived from the synoptic Gospels (Matthew, Mark, Luke). The three Gospels emphasize social justice and define the gospel. The former, especially Romans, do not give the gospel but give the means whereby Jews and Gentiles are put on common ground in the gospel of the kingdom (149). McLaren claims that Christians use Paul and John to interpret the synoptic Gospels and to define the kingdom; and this creates an "unjust and ineffective religious system" (152). McLaren seeks to rectify this use of Paul and John. Similarly Young (*The Shack*, 152) refers to the institutional church as a demonic system.

This way of dealing with the witness of the NT reflects the old liberal attack on the NT whereby in the mind of Baur and others the thesis of Petrine gospel was opposed by the antithesis of Pauline theology, and this clash produced the synthesis of catholic Christianity. This old Hegelian approach (thesis—antithesis—synthesis) to understanding the development of the church has been effectively refuted by evangelical writers over the last two hundred years, but apparently McLaren's seminary training did not inform him of this.[1] His "new kind of Christianity" is remarkably like the old kind of Baur and his liberal critics. Thus "eternal life" apparently has nothing to do with time but means a new relationship with God. Bell (58-61, 150-151) writes similarly. To know God is to have an "interactive relationship" with him, and McLaren defines this as the "kingdom of God." In addition, Young writes about a "circle of relationship" that includes the Godhead and all people (*The Shack*, 122-4; see also *Lies*, chaps. 27-28). There is no subordination and no authority. While there is an intimate relationship with God that should be pursued, it does not go far enough. McLaren apparently conceives of this "kingdom of God" as "realized eschatology" (there is no future realm to be entered), instead of "inaugurated eschatology" (the kingdom has begun but there is much more to come at the end of the era). Such realized eschatology runs counter to the better view—that both Jesus and all the Apostles affirm inaugurated eschatology across the NT. Jesus Christ is coming again to complete fully the reality of his kingdom, when eschatology is truly realized.

The Meaning of "All"

But the texts of reconciliation may be, must be, interpreted otherwise, as meaning that Christ's death is sufficient for all but effective only for those who exercise faith (see my extended discussion of this below). Otherwise, why does faith have to be exercised? Not surprisingly, believing in Christ and trusting Christ go virtually unmentioned in universalism, yet faith

---

1. Hegelian philosophy is the basis for Marx's communism. Also the preference for Jesus over Paul and the Apostles represents the view of Islam in its understanding of the NT. Islam believes that Paul the Apostle distorts the message of Jesus. Islam accepts Jesus as a prophet but rejects Paul.

is the heart of the gospel and the *only means* of receiving salvation (Rom 1:16–17; Eph 2:8–9; John 3:16–18; and many more).

All People Are "Forcibly Dragged" to Jesus

There is an inherent contradiction in the interpretation of many of the texts. For example, Young (UR, 42–44; see also *Lies*, chap. 13) interprets John 12:31–32 to mean that Jesus will "forcibly draw" or "drag" all people to himself. It is an "act of force that is absolutely unconcerned about the willingness of the person drawn." It is not "wooing or pleading, or some sort of invitation." It "speaks of violence and force, not gentle persuasion." Jesus "will forcibly and irresistibly 'drag' all men into himself."

But is this not contradicted by the claims of universalism that the fires of hell are corrective and therapeutic, not punitive? The standard Greek lexicon, BDAG, defines *helkō* ("draw") in John 12 to be figurative, of the pull on a person's inner life, to "attract" (251). This is far from "forcibly drag."

People Are "Not Forced" to Come to Jesus

Yet universalists just as quickly cite passages (Isa 45:22–23; Phil 2:10–11) from which they conclude that those who bow before the Lord "are not conquered subjects compelled and coerced into bowing and confessing allegiance to a hated but almighty God"; it is not a "forced confession." As with the Apostle Paul (Eph 3:14), it is not "compulsory adulation here, but love and worship and adoration"; it is "worship and adoration freely and spontaneously flowing from every part of his being" under the influence of the Holy Spirit. It becomes "a willing acknowledgment and acclamation." It is the "same worshipful humility that characterized Paul himself, and every tongue is to thank or praise or acclaim Christ as Lord in the glad spirit that characterized our Lord Himself." This loving attitude of the whole universe is to be complete and perfect. Such is the reasoning of universalism expressed by Young (UR, 44–46).

Universalism is in great contradiction here. Either those in hell are "violently forced" to come to Christ or they lovingly come to him and are "not forced." Universalists can't have it both ways. In fact, the contradiction occurs in back to back statements interpreting the same text (Isa 45:22–23)! First, it is "an imperative and carries all the weight of a command . . . that all are to be saved and then [God] proceeds to swear by Himself that He will do it." Yet "this is not a forced confession" but "under the influence of the Holy Spirit . . . a willing acknowledgment" (Young, UR, 44–46).

The hermeneutics of universalism is greatly skewed. The resolution is that the texts mean just the opposite of what universalism says they mean. The John text refers to the irresistible invitation of Christ to humans while they live, but it cannot mean to "forcibly drag" (this would violate the nature of Christ himself). The other texts about all confessing Christ refer to the conquest of all the forces opposed to Christ who before or after death confess him under constraint, not willingly or lovingly or in a saving manner (as discussed above).

Universalists also give faulty or incomplete, and therefore, distorted interpretation. For example, in discussing two texts (1 Cor 15:21–22; Rom 5:12–21), they fail to discuss Romans 5:17 (Young, UR, 48–49). This is the most important verse in the passage, since it affirms that identity in Christ the second Adam comes only to those who "*receive* the abundance of grace and of the gift of righteousness." It is they, not "all," who shall reign in life. This clause places chapter 5 within the context of the rest of Romans where believing in Christ is absolutely necessary to receive God's righteousness and forgiveness (1:16–17; 3:21–31; chap. 4). Thus the identity in Adam is not totally equal, of the same extent, to the identity in Christ. People have to believe in order to be in Christ; they do not have to believe in order to be in Adam. To be in Christ they have to be "born again" (John 3:8, 16). To be in Adam they merely have to be born.

Enemies Are the Footstool of Jesus' Feet

In the other, related text (1 Cor 15:21–22) the "all" ("in Christ *all* will be made alive") must refer only to those who have believed in Christ (as Rom 5:17, discussed just above, shows). In addition, the following verses make it clear that the *final* state of all things (including the state of heaven and hell) reveals that all are not alive—enjoying spiritual reality in heaven in the pleasure of Christ. There are those who will be the enemies of Christ that form his footstool, that is, they are in subjection under his feet (vv. 23–28; as 1 Clement above also asserted). This is not loving adoration (see the similar truth taught by Col 2:13–15 and Phil 2:9–11). Again universalism snatches a verse or thought out of one verse and causes a terrible dissonance and contradiction with the immediate context.

Are All Reconciled to God?

Much of this assessment also applies to the discussion of reconciliation texts, which are central to universalism. Universalists use the text (2 Cor

5:14–20) to claim that since Christ died for all people then all are saved (Young, UR, 49). Universalism points to verses 18–19 as affirming that the world has been reconciled to God. Yet the problem is that Paul the Apostle immediately says in the next verse that his is a ministry of reconciliation by which he pleads: "Be reconciled to God" (vv. 19–20). Being a new creation is conditioned by the words, "if anyone is in Christ" (v. 18). Clearly, then, his other words cannot be taken as realized or accomplished. If reconciliation for all is already accomplished in the death of Christ at the cross, why would he have to exhort people to become reconciled? The indicative statement of what Christ accomplished on the cross for people is followed by the imperative for people to actualize the truth. The gospel is not simply a declaration that one is already reconciled to God. The gospel is a declaration that salvation/reconciliation has been provided in the death of Christ on the cross. But its realization by anyone only comes when one responds in faith to the exhortation, "be reconciled to God." There is the absolute necessity to exercise faith in Christ. In Lies, chapter 13 (118) Young denies that faith is necessary.

In the context of 2 Corinthians Paul clearly distinguishes between the lost and the saved, the reconciled. He writes in 2:15–16: "For we are to God the fragrance of Christ among those who are being saved and among those who are perishing. To the one we are the aroma of death leading to death, and to the other the aroma of life leading to life." In addition, he writes (4:3–4): "But even if our gospel is veiled, it is veiled to those who are perishing, whose minds the god of this age has blinded, who do not believe, lest the light of the gospel of the glory of Christ, who is the image of God, should shine on them." Thus the context reveals that some are perishing, on the way to eternal death, and that believing is the difference between the two groups. It is with this knowledge that we should read 5:14–21. My remarks about this text (2 Cor 5) apply equally to Romans 6:5–8 where identity in Christ and his resurrection is actualized only for those who by their exercising faith in Christ are in him.

By its interpretation, universalism proves too much. If God is reconciled to all already, why even talk about some going to hell where the "corrective" force of the fire brings repentance? Universalism's interpretation of these texts places it only a step away from fully liberal theology, which affirms that all are saved whether or not they believe. The history of universalism given in Part 3 demonstrates how universalism came to embrace the basic beliefs of liberal theology.

This interpretation of reconciliation (in 2 Cor 5) is very similar to the text of Colossians 1:19–23, with faith mentioned in verse 23 ("if you believe"). Faith is necessary to apply Christ's work to each person. Until a person believes there is no reconciliation but enmity (as vv. 21–22 assert) between God and a person—the opposite of reconciliation. Yet Young (in *The Shack*) asserts that God is already fully reconciled to the world including unbelievers (192). Bell (134, 155–7) similarly asserts that all are saved; all are reconciled to God. I discuss in detail these reconciliation texts in Section 2 in the pages below and in my book, *Burning Down the Shack* (chaps. 11-12).

All of these texts have in common the clear instruction of Scripture that there are two "times" of conversion for every Christian. The first aspect of conversion is at the cross. When Jesus Christ died the potential was for the whole world to be reconciled to God. Jesus' death removed the barrier, the condemnation justly deserved by everyone because of sin (note Col 2:15). When Jesus died every believer was dying in Christ so that it can be said by the Apostle Paul that believers have died in Christ, were buried in Christ, and were raised in Christ in his resurrection (which is the whole message of Rom 6:1–11; Col 2:11–15; and elsewhere).

But all of this identification with Christ in his death and resurrection, which is the first "time" of one's conversion, must involve also a second "time" or point or event of one's personal conversion—when one believes all of this. Paul makes it very clear that when one is "baptized into Christ" only then is one "baptized into his death" (Rom 6:3–4; Col 2:11–12). Baptism is the outward sign that one has believed the gospel. It is only with this event that all the work of Christ at the cross and the resurrection comes to be applied to the one who believes. It is only then, at that moment, when a person is forgiven from sin (Col 2:13). So Christ's death is sufficient for all, but it is only actualized by faith.

Christ's death and one's believing—these are the events of every believer's salvation. Without the second event Christ's work remains unappropriated and a person remains alienated from God, not reconciled, and under condemnation (judgment). "Therefore, there is now no condemnation for those who are in Christ Jesus, because through Christ Jesus the law of the Spirit of life set me free from the law of sin and death" (Rom 8:1–2; cf. 6:23).

Chapter 10

The Appeal to Texts Dealing with Choice and Freedom

ANOTHER MAJOR APPEAL THAT universalism makes concerns the purpose of God, that it must be accomplished (Isa 14:24–27; 46:9–11; Eph 1:9–12; 3:8–11) (see Young, UR, 42). Since God is almighty and all powerful, anything that he purposes must come to pass. This seems so obvious.

Yet these texts do not concern the salvation of every individual, whether before or after death. They affirm simply that God has a plan that he will without fail accomplish, and within that plan there is the salvation of some and not the salvation of others. God's plan is never said to be the salvation of all (see the next discussion on 1 Tim 2:3–6), but it does include the acknowledgment or confession by all (by unbelievers under constraint) that God alone is God.[1]

Universalism challenges the traditional interpretation of 1 Timothy 2:3–6, that commands believers to pray for all, for their salvation, when by this traditional view only a few, a mere handful, would ever be affected by that prayer. Such a view represents either foolishness or impotence on God's part, universalism believes (Young, UR, 46). But universalism has missed the point here, the purpose of prayer. After citing verse 1 universalists conveniently jump over verse 2 which gives the purpose of our praying (Young, UR, 46). We pray, not because our prayers effect anyone's salvation, but that God through government might bring about a society free from war abroad and a quiet, dignified, and God-fearing society within.

Universalism also appeals to 1 Timothy 4:9–11. The last part of the passage refers to "the living God, who is the Savior *of* all people, especially

---

1. Interestingly Young denies that God has a plan that includes everything and everyone (*Lies*, chaps. 3-4).

of believers." Universalists argue that the word "of" means that all people will actually be saved, in contrast to the translation "for" which means that Christ is only a potential Savior of all (Young, UR, 46–47). The problem with this is that the Greek text employs the genitive case, which can justly be translated here by either "of" or "for." Obviously, an argument based on the English translation has no bearing unless it corresponds to the Greek. The real point of the Greek grammar is that the genitive here is probably an objective genitive: it simply means that Jesus saves all.

Yet this does not mean that all will actually be saved, for the second clause posits the means for salvation (one must believe), just as in the parallel text (2:4) coming to the knowledge of the truth is the means of being saved. In addition, the word for "especially" may be better rendered "namely, I mean"; and this meaning fits all its other occurrences in the Pastoral Epistles (1 Tim 5:8, 17; 2 Tim 4:13; Tit 1:10). Hence the verse would read: "the Savior of all people, namely of those who believe." In any case, it is by the conditions (knowledge and belief) in the second clauses that God's universal will to save comes to realization.[2] Without proper knowledge and faith people are not saved.

Can God's Will Be Thwarted? An Aside on Hermeneutics

Having discussed universalism's citation of several texts dealing with "all" or the will of God, let me here address some serious shortcomings in the hermeneutics, the principles of interpretation, of universalism. There are some basic principles of biblical interpretation that universalism fails to practice.

Universalism often makes statements to the effect that God's will and purpose will be done; it cannot be thwarted. Hence if God wills all to be saved (1 Tim 2:4) they will be saved (again, Young, UR, 46). I've tried to show that such Scriptural terminology may not be conclusive in light of other statements of Scripture that appear to contradict it or complete it. This allows for the most basic principle of interpretation, namely that context—the whole context of an author, not just the immediate verse or paragraph determines meaning. For the Bible, this also means that ultimately the entire context of the biblical canon must be searched and brought to bear on a particular verse so that its meaning can be discerned. Christians identify this principle of interpretation as the analogy of faith.

---

2. See Towner, *Letters*, 311–2.

The reason that this principle of interpretation must prevail is that this is the only way that we can read any author and understand him/her. If one contradicts oneself, how will we know what to believe about what the author says or means? Even Young and McLaren and other universalists would want this principle to prevail in the understanding of what each of them has written. This is not to deny that Scripture may contain enigma or difficulty or apparent contradiction. But the key word here is "apparent" for in the end God is a God of truth and cannot contradict his promise with a denial of it. As 1 John 2:27 says, the anointing (the Holy Spirit) "teaches you just as he taught you"—that is, the new teaching will not be opposite to or truly contrary to what the Spirit has already taught. It can only be in addition to it and consonant and consistent with what the Spirit has already taught.

Another thought should be stated. I promised above to discuss further the "all" claims of universalism, including the statement that God has reconciled all to himself (Col 1:19–20). Young repeatedly overlooks the possibility that when the text says that God has provided something for all (whether reconciliation for all, or redemption, forgiveness, or atonement; cf. Col 1:19–20; 1 John 2:1–2; John 3:16; etc.), these texts are only saying that something is potential or possible or provisional for all but not actual or realized for all. A condition may be implied or taught elsewhere. To receive the benefits of Christ's death requires something to take place (such as believing) for them to be effective or real (as the *contexts* of Rom 5:1–11; Col 1:19–23 make clear).[3] Other texts in the broader context assert the need to express faith as the means of appropriating these benefits. Virtually all universalists give very little place to the role of faith. This is the principle dealt with above, that the context of the rest of Scripture has to be taken into account to avoid colossal contradiction.

The Issues of God's Will and Human Responsibility

In addition, universalism erroneously asserts that God's will cannot be thwarted (Young, UR, 46–47). Yet, without saying it, the text often assumes that God's will or plan is limited or conditioned by something else he has willed. For example, God may will the salvation of all, but he also wills that people exercise faith for this salvation to be actualized. If people don't exercise their will positively he cannot exercise his will positively. So there is often an unstated conflict between the will of God and the will of humans to choose—what we can call human responsibility. But since his will includes

---

3. R.E., "Universalism," 657, similarly argues.

human freedom to exercise one's will, God's will is done after all. God's will actually is not thwarted.[4]

Here are some examples to illustrate the foregoing. When Jesus lamented Jerusalem's refusal to accept him as the Messiah, he said: "How often I wanted to gather your children as a hen gathers her chicks, but you were unwilling" (Matt 23:37). Jesus wanted repentance but he could not and would not enforce it. In a sense, his will was thwarted by their will (but not truly). Consequently the civil war and destruction of Jerusalem by the Romans in AD 70, leading to the death of thousands of Jews, followed. This calamity could have been avoided by the people but they chose not to receive God's offer of a deliverer. Indeed, Jesus could have forewarned them of the consequences for not accepting him, but he chose not to do so on this occasion (but he does on the occasion recorded in Luke 21). Jesus did not intervene in the potential for judgment and evil. He respected their choice. Yet all of this—his purpose and their response, and the consequences—was included in God's greater plan to accomplish greater purposes that God had planned for or willed. God works through, or in spite of, human, evil intention to accomplish his good.

Joseph the patriarch affirmed this duality of intentions long ago (Gen 50:20). He said to his brothers who had betrayed him and sold him into slavery: "You intended to harm me, but God intended it for good to accomplish what is now being done, the saving of many lives." God incorporates the wills or choices of humans, even their evil choices, to accomplish his will. Universalists ultimately deny such a contrary will to God's will, and thereby universalism is coercive and deterministic. This conclusion is one of the most serious obstacles for universalism.

The Example of Judas

We can learn much from the example of Judas. His betrayal of Jesus Christ is reckoned in light of both divine sovereignty and planning, and also human accountability (Mark 14:21). Jesus himself said: "The Son of Man goes as it is written of him (=divine initiative); but woe to that man by whom the Son of Man is betrayed! It would have been better for him if he had never been born" (=human responsibility).

---

4. Throughout this whole discussion of human freedom to choose, here and elsewhere, I'm not dealing with the heavier matters of how fallen people have the ability to choose. I'm persuaded that faith and repentance are themselves gifts from God. When left to themselves to choose, all people will not choose God or the good. Nevertheless God holds all people responsible for the choices they make, including the choice we all made in Adam to rebel.

Yet universalism disagrees with Jesus' assessment. It asserts that Judas will be in heaven after some "corrective suffering" in hell. But Jesus said that, in light of his future, he should never have been born.

God could have interrupted Judas' evil plan but he allowed Judas to exercise his will and did not stop it. *If God respected or allowed Judas' choice then to do such evil, why should we think that God will not respect the results of that choice*? If God respected or allowed Judas in his life time to exercise his will with evil purposes in mind, and this exercise of choice took Judas to hell, *why should not God continue to respect or allow his will in hell*? If God did not intervene to override Judas's will 2000 years ago, why should we think he will do so sometime in the future?

Is it not the concept of a lesser God that would have him allow Judas' choice but then seek to contravene the consequences of it? Isn't this a love truly balanced by holiness and justice—that he respected (loved) Judas so much that he allowed his will to be exercised, and then respected his choice and its consequences? Yet God still accomplished goals of which Judas was not aware.

Judas' evil choice was included in God's plan. Yet universalists would rewrite God's plan.[5] Judas' judgment is not everlasting. It was okay after all that he was born. Jesus was ultimately wrong in his assessment of Judas—so universalists assert. But if Judas is one person who will be in hell forever, then the whole structure of universalism falls—since it claims that all in hell must come out of it because of God's love. In a distortion of biblical truth Bell says (98) that God fails to get what he wants if all are not saved.

Everlasting Effects of Both God's Choice and Peoples' Choice

If God's sovereignty has everlasting effect or force (as universalism even admits), then why doesn't human freedom and responsibility have everlasting force (especially since God created man this way, in his image and likeness)? So it truly is the case that it is universal reconciliation that destroys human responsibility for people to choose as they wish.

Even for *professing* Christians, who have the highest level of knowledge, there are some things that God cannot do. Scripture says that it is *impossible* to renew again to repentance those who fall away from the truth, because they crucify Christ again and openly disgrace him (Heb 6:6). This places the preeminent value on the meaning of the cross; it is central in

---

5. Young explicitly denies God's plan, claiming that God does not control all and that the cross was man's idea, not God's (*Lies*, chaps. 3, 17).

God's dealing with people. *But universalists assert that what is impossible for God to do they are able to do by their revisionist theology! They do not believe the statement that something is impossible for God. They disbelieve God. In effect, universalists create another, novel theology that allows people to get to heaven without the cross, since according to the text these are crucifying Christ again to disgrace him!* The verbs in the Greek are in the present tense: they "are crucifying Christ again."

Behavior and Its Consequence

McLaren (115-20) gives extended discussion to a wide range of additional Scripture to support universalism of some sort. He seeks to find the "rhetorical purpose" of the passages in the Gospels that deal with judgment. He builds an elaborate chart to show what behavior is expected, the consequences for the behavior, and then the point of the text. It is an interesting approach to interpreting Scripture that McLaren has used elsewhere (as pointed out above regarding the language of hell). In this way he alleviates the impact of the texts on hell since the "rhetorical purpose" of each text is the goal of the study, not the affirmation of the validity or the reality of hell.

Yet McLaren's method is open to criticism. As seen elsewhere in his novel, he is reluctant to give the idea of faith its premier place. McLaren cites a few places, such as John 6, where he acknowledges "faith in Jesus"; but in this one chapter alone (John 6) "faith" occurs almost a dozen times, not just the one time cited by McLaren (120). In addition, the consequence that Jesus frequently gives as a result of faith is to "live forever" (6:27, 35, 40, 47, 51, 54, 57, 58, 63, 68) or "to be raised in the last day" (6:39, 40, 43, 54). Jesus and his Apostles placed a priority on faith in him as the way to escape eternal death (John 11:25-26; 3:16). As I noted above, "faith" and "believe" occur over 600 times in the Bible. Finally, McLaren (121) sums up his charted findings by asserting that Jesus does not teach the idea, "hold the right beliefs, affirm the right doctrines, or anything like that." Rather, McLaren claims, Jesus emphasizes living out or doing the right things.

Yet this conclusion bifurcates believing and doing, when the NT and Jesus himself say that the two conditions must go together. In the Sermon on the Mount Jesus says that it is the one who both "hears and does" (7:21-24) that is blessed. The one who fails both to hear and to do comes under judgement. Hebrews 3:18-19 even uses the two words "believe" and "obey" interchangeably. Throughout the teaching of Jesus it is the holding of the right beliefs that is assumed as the basis of right doing. The wedding of these two ideas is clarified by Jesus himself. "The work of God," Jesus affirms, is to believe in him

(John 6:29). This is the will of the Father (v. 40). Finally, in summing up his entire First Epistle, the Apostle John writes that the command that Christians should obey has two aspects (1 John 3:23): "And this is his command (note the singular): to believe in the name of his Son, Jesus Christ, and to love one another as he commanded us." This is one of the clearest expressions of how faith and action relate. Paul writes similarly (Gal 5:6).

Universalists also use these texts to assert that Jesus "doesn't condemn; he judges, that is, tells the truth about our actions." They also assert that the texts do not say that God will send someone to hell but only that he can do so (McLaren, 119). Young writes similarly (*The Shack*, 192). Yet Scripture frequently assumes or asserts that judgment belongs to Jesus or is associated with him (Matt 13:24; John 3:16–18; Acts 17:31).

Chapter 11

The Appeal to Other Texts That Supposedly Support Universalism

Universalists like to show that there are scores of texts that early Christians supposedly used to support their view that all mankind will be saved. I've already addressed many of these. I draw attention to a few significant texts that I have not addressed before.

Universalism appeals to Hebrews 7:25 ("he is able to save to the uttermost"), to show that there is no end to God's saving design. Yet the words actually mean that Jesus is able to save to the end, completely, finally, or at all times, and the end of the verse tells us who he thus saves: "those who come to God through him." The verse applies only to believers. Any attempt to find universalism here fails because several other texts teach that believing in Christ is the privilege of people not angels, and those who fail to respond have only the prospect of eternal separation from God. I discuss several other texts from Hebrews in Section 2 below. These are among the most convincing proofs to show why universalism is false doctrine.

Universalism appeals to 1 Corinthians 4:5 ("all will have praise from God"), but the words actually are that "each one will have praise from God;" and the verse refers to believers who will be judged by Jesus Christ at his return. Universalism cites James 5:11 as saying "you have seen the end of the Lord that he is full of mercy." Yet the KJV here needs to be corrected as follows: "You have heard of Job's perseverance and have seen what the Lord finally brought about. The Lord is full of compassion and mercy." This hardly needs to point to universal reconciliation. It didn't in Job's time, nor in James' time; and it doesn't in ours. In the immediate context the words apply to Job, then to all who trust in God (as in Job's day and in James' day).

With the deliverance of just one person the words are appropriately spoken of God.

A few other texts must be considered. The list includes 1 Corinthians 3:15, that "all are saved, so as by fire." Yet this is falsely quoted. The verse reads: "If it (a believer's work) is burned up, he will suffer loss; he himself will be saved, but only as one escaping through fire." The text refers to those believers who are judged after death. It doesn't say that they actually go through fire, but it is "as though" they go through fire. The fire is to purify the kind of works that a believer does. Paul is addressing Christians in 1 Corinthians. Purification is not to bring people to faith. It is not a fire to purify the wicked. There is nothing about unbelievers changing their destiny because of the "purifying, corrective fires of hell." The text does not help universalism, for universalism teaches that there is no judgment after the cross.

Brief comments about a few other texts are in order. Romans 11:15 referring to the "reconciliation of the world" must be interpreted, as the other passages discussed above, as referring only to the provision of reconciliation for all, not its implementation for all. In John 17:2, Jesus says that he "will give eternal life to all whom you [the Father] have given to him." This verse is obviously limited to the number of the people that the Father chooses to give to Christ. Daniel 4:35, which refers to the fact that God's will is done in heaven and on earth, is absolutely true.

The great plan of God will be done, and includes the rebellion of the wicked who choose to reject his offer of salvation. God will accomplish his goal in spite of the opposition of the wicked. Neither the schemes of the wicked while alive nor the presence of the wicked in hell comprise a threat to God's accomplishing his plan for his creation and creatures. Nor can it be said that God's "love for the world" has failed because some reject his love. John, who wrote these words about God's love (John 3:16), went on to say that it is only those who "believe" on Christ who receive eternal life. Then in the very next verse he wrote about the judgment facing those who do not respond in faith. Not for a moment was John bothered by the thought that somehow God's love had failed. Implicitly he is acknowledging that God respects people's choice not to believe; God does not force his love on any.

Lamentations 3:31–32 claims that God will not cast off forever, that "he will show compassion, so great is his unfailing love." This is a great text. The immediate context refers to confession of sin to have God's forgiveness (vv. 39–42). It is those who confess that will experience God's compassion and love. There is not a hint that somehow this forgiveness and subsequent love can be experienced after death by those who reject it while living. Indeed, the position of universalism (such as McLaren's) is that the OT had only a minimum belief in an afterlife (but I've shown above that there is much evidence for the reality of life after death in the OT). Thus, from this standpoint, any idea based on the OT that one has a chance to alter one's destiny after death lacks credibility. In its use of the OT to prove salvation after death universalism by its own admission is appealing to a minimal amount of support.

The Failure to Mention Faith in Christ

Universalists appeal to scores and scores of texts (so Young, UR, 92–102; with a whole catena of texts in *Lies*, 241–8, and elsewhere), yet there is hardly a single one that says anything about placing faith in Jesus Christ or believing in him in order to receive salvation. Even the verse so widely loved by Christians, John 3:16, goes unmentioned—not only here but in much of the writing of universalists. In other words, in making their lists of texts, universalists today commit the same error that the universalist ministers of Boston did in 1878. Like them universalists today say virtually nothing about how people escape the terrors of hell, whether before they die *or* after they die! This omission suggests that universalists are possessed of such a strong desire (an obsession?) to prove the conversion of *all* after death that they fail to tell us by what means they are converted. *Nor are they able to tell us*. In their being consumed by a twisted conception of the love of God their vision of God, and of the truth, is blurred. It is not surprising that universalists admit that their zeal for missions and evangelism has waned.

Universalists, including Young, McLaren, and Bell, are not in love with God as revealed in Scripture—our only reliable source of our knowledge of God. *Rather they are in love with their conception of God.*

At the end of his long lists of texts, Young (UR, 102) asks the obvious question drawn from the statement of Psalm 135:6 ("God does what pleases him"), namely "What pleases God?" As a universalist he answers with the citation of four texts: 1 Timothy 2:3–6 ("God desires all to be saved"); 1 John 4:14 ("the Father sent the Son as Savior of the world"); John 3:35 ("the Father loves the Son and has given all things into his hands"); and John 6:39 ("This is the will of the Father . . . that of all he has given me, I should lose nothing, but raise it up at the last day"). Universalists believe that since these texts contain the word "all" they must point to universal reconciliation. Above, in the preceding pages, I have dealt with this argument and these texts.

Universalists complain that the history of exegesis shows the persistent ignoring of many New Testament passages. I don't believe that this is the case. Rather I think that universalists do not like the way that Christian theology for 2000 years has interpreted them because this interpretation does not countenance universalism. Can this complaint really be true, that 2000 years of study have failed to deal with all the texts (indeed a whole host of them)? Isn't the hope that further study will convince the majority of people of the correctness of universalism an empty hope? If universalism is true, would not the church have returned to its moorings by now?[1]

Isn't it more likely that the vast majority of the church finds the interpretation belonging to universalism to be forced, distorted, and based more on emotive concerns and wishful thinking than on solid exegesis of the text which demonstrates the need for saving faith in Jesus Christ? Does not the history of universalism demonstrate this deviation? Its own historians note that universalism has moved further and further to the left, to liberal theology, and away from evangelicalism, so that it finally came to embrace Unitarianism and reject its "Christian" identity.

Seeking and Finding the Lost?

A final appeal for universalism in this section is to the parables that assert that Jesus came "to seek and to save what was lost." The idea is that the Seeker continues to seek until he finds. Again this idea goes beyond the parable which only expresses the Lord's intent or purpose. There is nothing said about his "finding" all humanity in the sense that none perishes in hell. Jesus cannot "find" those who wish to hide from him, the Seeker, and who don't want to be found.

Why Universalists Believe That People Reject Universalism

Universalism believes that people resist the idea of universal reconciliation for several reasons (from Young, UR, 53). (1) People simply have never really considered it as a new paradigm; (2) they have been well trained; (3) it destroys the us/them dichotomy (a common idea to Young, McLaren, and Bell); (4) it calls into question our motivations; (5) the implications are too staggering. It is interesting that universalists do not say that people resist

---

1. I'm rereading this manuscript on October 31, 2017—the 500th anniversary of the beginning of the Reformation. One of the great battle cries of the Reformation was *sola scriptura* ("Scripture alone"). It was a return to the study of the Bible. What Luther said a few years later, at the Diet of Worms, in 1521, was: "My conscience is captive to the Word of God." Christians renewed their commitment to Scripture. Would that universalists today would take a similar stand.

it because they believe that it is unscriptural. This is the main objection of evangelical Christians.

None of the reasons is the basis of my resistance, nor probably is any of them the basis of the resistance of most evangelicals. Evangelicals are convinced of its error because a close examination of Scripture shows that it is a false paradigm, a false teaching that the church has already condemned through the centuries. We believe it is unscriptural. Strangely universalism does not cite this as a possible reason!

Here are the scriptural reasons that evangelicals have. (1) There is no Scripture that asserts that there is a chance for those in hell to repent and get out of their suffering and go to heaven. There is no way to alter one's destiny after death. (2) There is no Scripture that says that God's love overwhelms or trumps his justice or holiness, that "justice is limited by love" (as virtually all universalists assert and their creeds, as noted above, echo). (3) There is no Scripture that says that the sufferings of hell are temporary and corrective, redeeming, restorative, etc. They are a just, deserved penalty—an expression of God's justice (and love).

Universalism claims that love will conquer, that death will hold no more power over anyone anywhere in all God's vast universe, that death shall be destroyed. Sin and rebellion shall raise their ugly heads no more, for God will be all in all. One need only ask: What does love conquer? Elsewhere universalism makes it clear that it is the free will or choice of people to reject God that is conquered by "corrective suffering." Somehow it does not occur to universalists that this is no longer love, but rather determinism and coercion. Somehow it doesn't occur to them that this is inherently contradictory to reason and to revelation.

Universalism Unmasked: No Need for the Death of Christ

Universalism (Young, UR, 53; *Lies*, 113) also appeals to the year of Jubilee which it believes is yet coming as a parallel to universal reconciliation. This is an allusion to the OT cycle of forty-nine years plus one year when slaves were freed and land went back to its original owner (Lev 25). Universalism claims that a future Jubilee is coming when all will be restored to their inheritance. If people do not experience redemption now they must endure the pain and travail of poverty and slavery until the Year of Jubilee arrives.

Yet aside from the fact that the NT and OT never associate the future destinies of people to the Year of Jubilee, there is no call here made for repentance from sin on which elsewhere universalism insists. In the OT the people who were set free in the fiftieth year did nothing by way of repenting from sin to earn or change their destinies. Their suffering was not viewed as therapeutic or corrective. They had done no sin or moral wrong. The event simply occurred according to the natural course of the calendar.

Is this the bare face of universalism unmasked? In the end it doesn't matter after all, according to universalism, whether people who have died even repent from any sin or wrong doing. They don't even have to suffer since they lack "ultimate knowledge," and (as claimed above) God doesn't punish those lacking it. *They all escape hell in mass anyway for some reason at some time somehow. For them there was no need for Jesus to die, nor for him even to become incarnate.*

And so, in this way, universalists "throw Jesus Christ under the bus" driven by their own idea of God.

Finally, More Scripture in Summary

In the rest of this chapter I deal with some final arguments that Young (UR, 54–95) makes in his commitment to universalism. He appeals to many more texts of Scripture to defend his case. He divides them into several categories. There are those that deal with the word "ages"; with free-will and divine sovereignty; with "hell," *sheōl*, and hades; with immortality; with "judgment"; and with "things hard to understand." Then there follows a list of as many as twenty-nine texts that supposedly argue that "all creation shall be redeemed" (these texts use such words as "all," "every," "world," etc.). A second list gives seventy-four texts used to support universal salvation because of the use of "all" or "every" or related terminology. Some of these repeat the verses cited in the previous list.

The Meaning of Texts Having "Age" and "Ages"

While I've addressed many of these texts above, and how they are used supposedly to support universalism, a few remarks are in order. The list of verses that have "ages," "age," or "aeons" in them (Young, UR, 54–67, 93) makes no point other than that there is a variety of translations used to render the Greek terms involved. The claim in the similar section near the beginning of this study, that the Greek *aiōn* should always be rendered "age" instead of "eternal" or "forever," was refuted there. I refer the reader to the rebuttal I gave above. No serious Bible student, and *no* commentator, lexicon or dictionary makes or would make such a claim. By asserting such universalists are violating basic linguistics and Greek.

The Meaning of Texts Referring to God's Sovereignty

In the second section (Young, UR, 93–95) the list of twenty-one texts is meant to show that the texts referring to God's sovereignty outnumber those that refer to free will. Many texts from Isaiah (four texts), John (two texts), and from Romans (eight) are cited. Universalists cite these texts to assert that God's purpose to save is not going to be thwarted by man's free will (as asserted above). God's will cannot be thwarted.

Interestingly, this argument is a double-edged sword. For within the scope of the references from Romans universalism includes without discussion verses that affirm that God has "mercy on whom he wants to have mercy, and he hardens whom he wants to harden" (9:18); and that God "bore with great patience the objects of his wrath—prepared for destruction" (v. 22) and prepared in advance "objects of his mercy" (v. 23). These texts reveal that God is sovereign in creating objects of both mercy and wrath. This evidence seems to contradict the claim of universalism that no one is destined to eternal wrath. Universalism may respond: "But God's love will cause those destined to hell to later repent in the fires of hell and he will deliver them from hell." Yet if this takes place then the whole argument that pleads that God is totally sovereign fails, for those willed for damnation are able to exercise their free will and believe and escape hell. The only argument that sustains God's sovereignty is to say that he determines that some will go to hell and this decree can't be thwarted. This argument finds its balance with the elect—that they are destined to heaven and must end up there; otherwise, if free will can be exercised, then some may get out of heaven. Thus universalism again proves itself to be contradictory and inconsistent. The most challenging text to evangelical belief is that of Romans 11:32, and I dealt with this text above and return to it below.[2]

The Meaning of Texts Affirming Immortality and the End of Death

In another list (Young, UR, 95–96) universalism cites several texts that affirm immortality and the destruction of death. Apparently the intention is that these texts point to immortality for all including those in hell. Yet none of the texts affirms that people in hell have life of the quality that the saints

---

2. Interestingly, and surprisingly, in *Lies*, chapters 3–4, Young argues that God does not have a complete plan, that he is not in control of all, and that God submits often to the plans of people, and these plans include the work of the cross (chap. 17).

have, or that they get out of hell to live forever. Just as well the verses may mean that the wicked in hell stay there "alive" forever.

The Meaning of Texts Referring to Judgment

Universalism (Young, UR, 96) goes on to claim that there are 285 references to judgment in the OT and forty-seven in the NT, and 397 references to "to do right." Some texts (Jer 30:12—31:14) refer to God's dealings with Israel. In addition, universalists remark that, contrary to claims, there is "no damnation" in three texts (Matt 23:33: "You snakes! You brood of vipers! How will you escape being condemned to hell?" Mark 3:29: "Whoever blasphemes against the Holy Spirit does not have forgiveness for ever, but he is guilty of an eternal sin." John 5:29: "Those who have done evil will rise to be condemned"). The obvious meaning of the first two texts leads to just the opposite conclusion—an evil person's destiny is fixed. The second text is especially clear. How can universalism (Young, UR, 96) contradict Jesus' own declaration that the sin against the Holy Spirit will never be forgiven? It can only do so by making its fatuous claim that "forever" and "eternal" (both derived from *aiōn*) must always and only mean "an age." Above I've shown why such an idea is linguistically inept and uninformed.

The Meaning of Texts That Are "Hard to Understand"

Universalism discusses eleven texts (for example, Young, UR, 96–97) that are challenging alike to universalists and evangelicals and all interpreters. But newer translations improve on what the KJV says. For example, in two of these a better translation reads that God "creates calamity" (instead of "evil"; Isa 45:7), and that God "created the destroyer to ruin" (instead of "to work havoc"; Isa 54:16). The third text (Matt 12:32) is the parallel to Mark 3:29, dealt with just above. It reads that the sin against the Holy Spirit will not be forgiven "either in this age, or in the age to come." The answer I gave to Mark 3:29 applies equally here. The fourth text is clear enough. It says that every careless word will be accounted for in the day of judgment (Matt 12:36), so that one's words either justify one or acquit one (v. 37).

The fifth text (Luke 12:46–48) teaches that in the judgment to come suffering will be proportioned according to the amount of knowledge that one has of God's will. This text reinforces the justice of God to do all things right (cf. Gen 18:25). The sixth text (John 6:37, 39, 44, 65) says that "all that the Father gives me will come to me." This text simply assures us that the number of the saved is common to the Father and the Son. None are lost between the two. The seventh text (John 9:1–5) simply declares that God achieved his purposes in the man born blind.

The passages in Romans are similarly answered. The eighth text (Rom 2:14–16) refers to the conscience that will accuse some and defend some, according to their works, on the day of judgment. The ninth text recognizes that God was sovereign over Pharaoh's decisions, to display his power (Rom 9:16–23). The tenth and eleventh texts (1 Pet 3:18–20; 4:6) are used by universalism to teach that Jesus went to hell to proclaim salvation to those in hell, so that the wicked could change their destiny. I dealt with this interpretation above under the section, "multiple visits to hell." It is a better interpretation that no such visits to hell took place.

The Meaning of Texts Affirming That "All Shall Be Redeemed"

In this seventh section, universalism cites twenty-nine passages (Young, UR, 97–99) that presumably affirm that all people will be redeemed because "all" occurs or some similar term ("world," "everyone," etc.). Most of these texts are dealt with above. In some of these texts the context makes it clear that the words are limited in their scope: "all" really means "many" or "all who believe." Also, in light of larger contexts (including the whole Bible), it is clear that God's redemptive or salvific work must be limited to those who receive Christ. The larger context of the Bible speaks of a judgment leading to a destiny of eternal suffering for others and this destiny cannot be changed—an interpretation I defended above. Universal reconciliation is also limited by the teaching about human responsibility which I dealt with above: God's will is "thwarted" by his including in his will the exercise of the will of humans to choose to reject his offers of love. This is an appeal to the very nature of God and the nature of people made in God's image.

Even Scripture acknowledges explicitly that "all" has exceptions. When Paul the Apostle writes that "all will be subjected to God" (1 Cor 15:27), he goes on to immediately add: "But when he says, 'All things are put in subjection,' it is evident that he is excepted who put all things in subjection to him." In other words, when Scripture says that all things are subjected to Christ, God who subjects the "all things" to Christ is an exception to these words.

Another example occurs in this context. The Apostle says that "as in Adam all die, so also in Christ all shall be made alive" (15:22—a verse famous with universalism as this study shows). Yet the very next words clarify Paul's words: "But each in his own order: Christ the first fruits, after that those who are Christ's at his coming, then comes the end . . ." (vv. 23–24a). It is clear that the second "all" in verse 22 does not have the same scope as the first "all," since the second is clarified by the words, "those who are Christ's at his coming, then comes the end." The Apostle doesn't contemplate any others being able to come to Christ later (such as those in hell), to be added to the "all" at the coming of Christ.[3]

Many of the rest of the texts seemingly speak of universal atonement (1 Tim 4:10; Heb 2:9), but they do not necessarily argue for universal salvation (note how 1 Timothy distinguishes "those who believe" from the rest of humanity). In other words, the atonement of Christ was made on behalf of all, but it becomes effective or applied only at the exercise of faith (as Col 1:19–23 makes clear). Christ's atonement is sufficient for all but it is not applied to those who reject it.

Hebrews 2:9 is a major obstacle to universalism. The text says that Christ "tasted death for the sake of all." What universalism fails to realize from this context is that Christ did atone for peoples' sin but could not and did not atone for angels' (including the devil's) sin, for he became human not angelic (2:14–15). He gives help only to humans not angels (2:16). In the pages above I have dealt with all of these arguments given here, and I refer the reader to that material.

Summary of Universalism's Chief Arguments

Young (UR, 103) uses five summary paragraphs to bring his sustained defense for universalism to a close. He probably intends that these are his chief arguments. The first summarizes the view that aeons or ages are undefined periods of time and are not "eternal." Thus the unbeliever does not suffer "eternal damnation," but rather judgment and "aeonian" or age-abiding chastisement. I have dealt with this distorted use of word studies above.

The second paragraph deals with free will and divine sovereignty under the picture of the potter (an apparent allusion to Rom 9). Universalism rejects the notion that mankind and Satan have a free will, but only freedom of choice, with God able to direct and influence people's choosing. Thus God moves all things according to the council of his will. People are not puppets but they are clay in the hands of the great Potter, who fashions all

---

3. Actually, universalists use this text (vv. 20–28) in four different ways to find universalism here. But all of the arguments run counter to the context wherein Paul is dealing with the fact that believers will be made alive and that the rest of humanity will be brought into subjection to Christ, not to salvation. The defeat of death (v. 26) does not mean that resurrection is involved; and this truth does not negate the judgment of all. See Wilson, "Strongest Argument," 805-12. He shows that universalism is not found here.

according to his design and purpose. Yet the obvious element missing from universalism's appeal to God as the Potter is the Apostle Paul's statement that God as Potter fashions some "vessels of wrath prepared for destruction" as well as "vessels of mercy" (Rom 9:22–23). Calvinist and Arminian theologians argue over the meaning of these terms but no one suggests that somehow God remakes the former vessels so that in the end all are of only one kind, so that all are vessels of mercy. Again, universalism indulges in half-truths and wishful thinking, and in the end is more deterministic than the two great schools of theology.

In his third paragraph Young asserts that God's judgment is not vindictive punishment. It is certainly not the "angry outburst of a frustrated, impotent God against an unruly creation" that has broken free from the will of its weaker Creator. Judgment is the ultimate tool in the hand of the great Potter to restore his "cracked and broken creation back to beauty and usefulness." It is the Good Shepherd finding and restoring the "black sheep" back to the fold. It is the loving and ever-patient Father, bringing the "prodigal once more into the family, fully restored."

Yet Romans 9:22 says nothing about reworking the "vessels prepared for destruction" into something that is good or profitable (as the "vessels of mercy" in v. 24). The Greek word for "prepared" is in a tense (perfect) that emphasizes the ongoing results of the preparing, the final form of the vessel. The text virtually excludes changing this state. The prodigal son comes back to the father not under duress but willingly. The father did not beat the son into submission (which is what the "corrective fires of hell" are believed to do, according to universalism).

The fourth statement (again Young, UR, 103) asserts that hell and the lake of fire are not final but places of cleansing from which all the wicked, including Satan and his angels, will be restored to God. Judgment is not "vindictive torment." At the "great white throne judgment" the sins of unbelievers will be judged and this will "effect" their final salvation. Some will be cast into the lake of fire which is the ultimate "process of cleansing," awaiting the final consummation at "the end of the aeons." "Some evidence" shows that the lake of fire will ultimately even cleanse Satan and his angels.

Yet everyone who reads these words asks: Where is the support for such statements? Note the use of the words that unbelievers will be dealt with in such a way as to "effect" their final restoration. What does "effect" here mean if not to "coerce" people to repent under duress? Again, note that there is no mention of those in hell placing faith in Jesus Christ and not a hint that restoration will ever take place.

The fifth and final summary statement concludes that all will be saved by the true and final sacrifice of Jesus Christ. Believers are saved during this "aeon" of grace *by faith* in Christ. Their sins are purged by the "fire of the Holy Spirit" working in them now. Unbelievers will be saved *by sight* at the judgment. Their sins will be purged by the fires of judgment. At the end of the "aeons" the great consummation will take place when sin, death, suffering, and pain shall be no more. All shall be made alive and restored to fellowship with their Father and Creator, and God shall fulfill his Word. Finally, he shall be all in all. This is universalism's vision of the final state of all things.

These five paragraphs make bare the basic elements belonging to the appeal of universalism. Clearly universalism wishes to view all judgment as restorative. Interestingly, universalism asserts that the unbelievers are saved by sight and by judgment, and that their sins are purged by fire in hell. This belief is in direct contrast to believers being saved during this era by faith in Christ. There is no basis anywhere in Scripture for saying such a thing about unbelievers, and it results in two ways to be saved. This belief is abhorrent to the teaching of the Apostles. In Galatians (1:6-9) the Apostle Paul identifies such people who teach this as deserving hell! Also there is nothing in Scripture about our sins being purged by the fire of the Holy Spirit. Rather our sins are purged by the death of Christ; there is no "fire" of the Holy Spirit.

The Total Failure to Make the Case for Universalism

So what shall we conclude about universalism's appeal to Scripture, its use of word studies, its appeal to history, and its appeal to emotive and rational matters? It is my judgment that there is total failure to present a credible case for universalism. There is misuse of the biblical text since universalism often cites only portions of verses, takes verses out of context, or ignores contrary texts. There is misrepresentation of its opponents' views. There is failure to validate its views by citing scholarly resources. It totally fails to interact with traditional evangelical commentaries and theologies. Universalism cites sources who claim to present truthful claims about the history of the church, but these are patently false (especially the claim about the first five hundred years). From this tabulation of failures it is clear that universalism is not biblical, nor scholarly, nor historical, nor theologically sound.

What should we make of this total failure? First, it means that the verdict of the church *throughout* its history is correct. In light of Scripture, universalism is serious error; it is heresy. Second, the proponents of universalism are to be pitied. Is this a case where theological bias coupled with personality change, and bias against evangelical institutions including seminaries and Bible schools, and the institutional church, have rendered universalists blind to the truth that evangelicals can see by God's grace?

Yes, universalists are to be pitied, for their blindness has led them into heresy where the prosperity of their souls is in jeopardy. Yet, even more, they are to be feared. For the souls of others that they influence are in spiritual jeopardy.

In summary, universal reconciliation is theological rape of the gospel. It destroys the only message which is able to save the souls of people and everlastingly suit them for the pleasure of God's presence. *UR is culpable in leading many into the everlasting suffering of hell.*

For universalists to assert that people after death will have a second chance to repent and to turn to God is a terrible charade. There is actually a better chance for my dog to go to heaven than for people to have a chance to repent after death. This is so because the Bible is silent regarding the destiny of dogs but it is quite vocal in rejecting the idea of people having a second chance after death to change their destiny!

Section 2

Correctly Interpreting the Bible
The Case for Everlasting Hell and Evangelical Belief

IN SECTION 1 I have interacted in detail with the position of universalism as propounded by many writers past and present, including the fiction writers, McLaren and Young, and the nonfiction of Young and Rob Bell. I now present several texts of Scripture that argue against universalism. While these are major texts they comprise only a partial list. They are often cited by universalists as obstacles to the traditional view of hell. Other texts have been overlooked or ignored by universalism; others have been inadequately treated.

In addition to dealing with the witness of Scripture, I will also incorporate significant chapters dealing with theological questions regarding the afterlife—about hell— that are difficult for universalism to answer. I will also assert significant, dangerous distortions that a universal position brings, both for belief and for Christian living. Finally, I will deal with implications for the church today and for ministers in particular.

I begin with the most authoritative source by which to deal with universalism, namely the Holy Scriptures. It is the Bible when properly interpreted that stands as the most significant obstacle to universalism, and shows it to be the heresy the church has always understood it to be.

Chapter 12

The Parables of Jesus and His Additional Teaching about Hell

IN THE FOLLOWING PAGES I take up the most significant witness to the destiny of the wicked that can be found in the Bible. It is the witness of Jesus Christ. I concentrate here on the parables that Jesus taught, and then give an overview of his comprehensive teaching about the destiny of the wicked.

The Parable of the Rich Man and Lazarus

In Luke 16 Jesus gives the account of the "rich man and Lazarus." It is usually designated the "parable of the rich man and Lazarus," but it is probably not a parable in the technical sense.[1] It is not labeled such by Luke and its characters have names unlike other parables. It is probably better to understand it as an "example story" similar to the parable of the good Samaritan and the prodigal son. It depicts not a single event of a real individual but a representative one. The conversations need not be real but are literary devices to show the reality of what lies ahead in the afterlife. The words are graphic to emphasize the great separation between the character in paradise and the one in hell, and the unchangeableness of destinies after death. Lazarus is one of the most common names in Judaism and is not to be taken to refer to the brother of Mary and Martha who was raised from the dead (John 11).

The story is a warning to the wealthy, that what one has in this life does not mean that one will have it in the next. In this regard the story is one of reversal. The poor in this life may enjoy great wealth in the next world; the wealthy now may experience tremendous loss and suffering in the next. The

---

1. See Bock, *Luke*, 1362–3. Much of my observation about this story derives from this excellent commentary. See also Marshall, *Luke*, 632ff.

idea of reversal in the afterlife occurs in Egyptian stories and even in non-biblical Judaism.² The story is Luke's second major teaching on wealth (cf. 16:1–13).

The story breaks down into three simple sections.³ In the first section Jesus describes the situation of the rich man and Lazarus in this life (vv. 19–21). In the next section he describes their situation in the next life (vv. 22–23). In the final section Jesus describes the pleas that the rich man makes to Abraham (vv. 24–31). The main proposition is that for the callous rich Jesus affirms the reality and permanence of hell and the separation of the righteous from the rest.

In the first section, in the starkest terms of contrast, Jesus presents the condition of the rich man and Lazarus in this life. The rich man, whose name is unknown, finds his identity in his wealth. Purple clothing is a mark of luxury, as is even the wearing of fine linen undergarments. The Greek text describes his daily life with a term ("making merry") that suggests that he faired sumptuously every day at banquets.

Ignored but not unknown to the rich man is the beggar Lazarus who experiences just the opposite of the rich man. He is so poor and crippled or ill that he lies at the ornate gate of the rich man, and cannot escape the dogs who by licking his sores render him further unclean by Jewish law. The scraps of food that the rich man threw out to the dogs became the only sustenance of the beggar. By all appearances and by the standards of the Jewish law, the rich man was blessed by God but not the poor man.

Lazarus' name is a short form of Eleazar, "God helps." Jesus gives him an appropriate name for while he suffers the extremity of deprivation and suffering, he is known to God and cared for. The next section of the story (vv. 22–23) show that the destiny of each is a reversal of what he experienced while alive.

It is at this very point that the case against universalism begins. For with the passing of time each one dies, but this is not the end of the story. Lazarus is carried by angels to a place of celebration, to Abraham's side or bosom. The latter is the place of blessing and intimate fellowship. It represents the reception of the faithful into heaven itself. It is probably parallel to the OT concept of "being carried to the fathers" spoken of the patriarchs (Gen 15:15; 47:30; Deut 31:16; Jud 2:10; 1Kgs 1:21; 4 Macc 13:17).⁴

---

2. Ibid., 1364, where various examples are cited (ns. #4–5). See also Marshall, *Luke*, 632–3.

3. Ibid., 1363–4.

4. Ibid., 1368. Marshall, *Luke*, 636, rather, suggests that it points to Lazarus' enjoying fellowship with Abraham at the messianic banquet (cf. "bosom" in 13:29; John 1:18; 13:23; 2 Clem 4:5).

In bold contrast, Jesus describes the destiny of the rich man as hell or Hades. He is not carried by angels to his place; he may have been carried there by Satan. Furthermore, he is described as in torment or torture. In both Jewish and Christian (2 Clement 10:4; 17:7) texts the word *basinos* is often used of a slave being punished in order to elicit confession. Finally, Jesus relates how each one is conscious in his place, that each is conscious of the place of the other. Whether Lazarus is in a compartment of hell or Hades is unclear.[5] The place is that of heat—suffering (v. 25; cf. Matt 24:41, 46). The point to note, however, is that the rich man is suffering and Lazarus is comforted. It is a complete reversal of what was known in their lives before death.

In the third part of the story (vv. 24-31) Jesus relates the whole point of the account, devoting more space to describing the three pleas of the formerly rich man than to the other earlier sections. The first plea of the rich man is for a drop of water to relieve his pain and thirst in the midst of the heat and suffering (v. 24). Thirst reflects the image of enduring judgment (Isa 5:13; 50:2; 65:13; Hos 2:3; 2 Esd 8:59; 1 Enoch 22:9).[6] In making his plea the rich man assumes that pre-death conditions still prevail. He asks "father Abraham," terminology which reflects his reliance on his Jewish heritage. He also asks that Lazarus be commanded to bring him water. He presumes that the same pre-death conditions exist. But he is sadly mistaken.

Abraham gives a tender but firm denial for relief. Abraham affirms that the rich man is (note the present tense) in continual anguish (perhaps mostly mental) while Lazarus is comforted.[7] Thus what Lazarus once was the rich man has become. What he failed to provide for Lazarus Lazarus cannot now provide him. It is clear that some "sons of Abraham" will not be in heaven.

Furthermore, Abraham adds that a great gulf "has been fixed" (probably stated in the passive voice to indicate that God himself has set the chasm) so that no one can pass over from one place to the other.[8] Thus

---

5. Ibid., 1369-70. In the OT Hades is the place of both the righteous and the unrighteous—the place of the dead. But in the NT the wicked go to Gehenna and the righteous never do. Marshall, *Luke*, 637, suggests that the intermediate state of the dead before the final judgment is meant, but that torment is a feature of both Hades and the final state of the wicked (see 1 Enoch 22; cf. Wis 3:1; 4 Macc 13:15; 2 Clem 17:7; 10:4). See the discussion in chapter 2. On the reality of the intermediate state, see Cooper, "Bible and Dualism," 459-69.

6. Ibid., 1371.

7. Marshall, *Luke*, 638, cites F. Hauck (*TDNT*, 5:115), that here the reference is to the "spiritual torture of remorse."

8. The form of the verb ("has been fixed"; perfect passive) emphasizes the unchangeableness of the gulf.

the rich man's request for personal relief cannot be granted. "Retributive justice" prevents any help.[9]

In the second stage (vv. 27–29) the rich man pleas for Lazarus to be sent to his family. There is acknowledgement here by the rich man that he has made a fatal, eternal mistake. There is partial compassion, a conversion of perspective. Yet his "conversion" doesn't change his fate as determined by his living before death. Still thinking as he did before, he asks Abraham to command Lazarus to bring a solemn warning to his brothers so that they would not come to "this place of torment."

Again, Abraham rejects the plea. He notes that the living have the instruction of Moses and the Prophets (a reference to the entire OT) which if they are heeded is sufficient to avoid the place of torment. The point is that there is sufficient revelation to deliver any and all from hell or Hades. Revelation found in various texts (Deut, Isa, Jer, Ezek, Amos, Mic, Zech 7:9–10; Mal 3:5) gives sufficient warning about wealth to avoid a destiny of suffering.[10]

In the final stage (vv. 30–31), the rich man, revealing his truly unconverted convictions, makes a third plea that in effect rejects the statement of Abraham. He says "no" to Abraham, that revelation from God in the OT is not sufficient. He didn't respond to divine revelation and he knows from personal experience that his brothers won't respond either. Thus he insists that if Lazarus makes a visit back to the living, perhaps in a dream or vision, it would be a sign convincing enough to bring repentance.

Abraham makes a final refusal. He notes that if (since) the living refuse the revelation of Scripture (a first class condition assumed true) they will not repent on the basis of the sign of one who even may rise from the dead (expressed as a future possibility). The latter idea is more significant than a momentary visit from one who will return to death. The brothers will not change or repent.

The words "to hear Moses and the Prophets" mean to believe them. Thus the issue is faith. Failure to believe OT revelation shows where the heart is, and a person will not be persuaded even if someone rises from the dead. This is an obvious allusion by Jesus to his own forthcoming resurrection. It is not a lack of evidence, or proof, that keeps one from believing, but one's will does (cf. Acts 17:31: some of those who heard Paul "believed"; the majority of those in Athens rejected the gospel). Only faith yields understanding (Heb 11:1).

---

9. Marshall, *Luke*, 638.
10. Bock, *Luke*, 1375.

This story teaches several important points that reinforce the fallacy of universalism. (1) There are only two destinies for all people. One is that of comfort and the other of "terrible pain" (vv. 23–25). (2) A great chasm "has been fixed" (note the perfect tense pointing to ongoing results; it cannot be altered) so that people cannot cross over from the place of bliss to the place of torment, and neither can people cross over from the place of torment to the place of bliss (v. 26).[11] Destiny cannot be altered after death. And this gulf "has been fixed" by God. It has not been "fixed" by man. (3) People must respond to the written Scripture before they die; otherwise there is no "second chance"; they will not repent. There is no indication that the rich man repented, that he came to faith. (4) Even if people are given special revelation by one rising from the dead, from the grave, to tell people to respond, they will not "hear" or obey, since they have rejected Scripture. In other words, if people do not respond to the authoritative Scripture they will not repent before or after death no matter what message is brought to them (including, apparently, the report of how painful separation from God really is). This suggests that even the resurrection of Jesus from the dead will not convince any to repent and believe the gospel. They view the promise of heaven to be a sham. The events following the resurrection prove Jesus' words to be true, for his own people did not receive him even though his resurrection was widely witnessed. Revelation is one whole—Scripture and Jesus himself. (5) The principle is this: how one responds to earlier revelation determines how one will respond to later revelation.[12] Those who reject the OT would not respond by new revelation coming from hell. Consequently those who reject the gospel while they live will not believe the gospel after death. (6) Contrary to a major teaching of universalism, suffering does not lead people in hell to repent. (7) The resurrection does not cause faith; it only bolsters it.[13] Thus after his resurrection Jesus appears only to disciples. The call is to believe God's promise regarding the death of Christ; the resurrection is only a fulfillment of Scripture. People do not reject Christ for lack of a sign but because of a lack of a will to accept him. Signs are of no value if the heart is not right. Miracles will not "convince those whose hearts are morally blind and unrepentant."[14] (8) The parable is a call to people to believe also Abraham and the patriarchs, for they believed God. Therefore, for

---

11. Powell, "Hell," 953–4, points out that there is probably not support here for two compartments of hell. This is more of a Greek idea than a biblical one. Here there are two "altogether different locales and conditions separated by an impassible and fixed gulf."

12. Bock, *Luke*, 1376–7.

13. Ibid., 1377.

14. Marshall, *Luke*, 639.

universalism to reject Jesus and disagree with him is to reject the testimony of God's servants all the way back to Abraham.

Keller notes a couple other points about this parable. The rich man is so self-absorbed that he thinks of Lazarus as he did while living—as his servant. He never asks to be taken out of hell. He assumes that it is a place he deserved to go.[15] He does not complain that his destiny is unfair (as universalists believe!).

For universalism to reject this account as something that Jesus did not really believe is without merit. While there are antecedents to this story, Jesus adds crucial elements, thereby validating the seriousness of it. His teaching in it accords with everything else he taught about the afterlife.

The Parable of the Sheep and the Goats

In Matthew 25:31–46 Jesus deals with the destiny of the nations at the final judgment. The parable of the sheep and the goats poses one of the most significant challenges to universalism. I introduced this parable over several pages in chapter 1.

As far as an overview is concerned this parable is the fourth and last of Jesus' last series of parables prior to his death. The three parables before this one in the Olivet Discourse (Matt chaps. 24–25) warn about wrong attitudes resulting from the delay in Jesus' return. But this final parable is different; it serves to encourage Jesus' followers that their work for him is special and bears eternal consequences. He has special reward for them among the nations and for all eternity to be announced at the judgment at the end of the age.

This parable is a parable in the loosest sense of the term, since it is also apocalyptic prophecy and deals with the subject of the judgment. In this way it is similar to the doubt about the parable of the rich man and Lazarus—whether it should be called a parable. Jesus presents himself in this parable as the one who fulfills OT prophecies of the future, coming King (Zech 14), Shepherd (Ezek 34), and Son of Man (cf. Dan 7:13). We also learn about the coming role of angels attendant to Jesus at the judgment when he will judge the nations. The nations are divided into the sheep and the goats, and there is a third group known as the "least of these my brothers."

---

15. Keller, *Reason*, 77–78. He notes that in hell people are not screaming, "I repent. Get me out of here." People do not seek to get out; they are blind to what has happened; they are filled with blaming others and self-denial; they have based their identity on something other than God (in this case his riches, hence his title, the "rich man"). In *The Last Battle* of the *Chronicles of Narnia*, C. S. Lewis pictures those outside of blessing as ignorant and dismissive of the light all around them.

THE PARABLES OF JESUS AND HIS ADDITIONAL TEACHING ABOUT HELL 199

Jesus makes a distinction between the nations. On the basis of how they responded to him and his people, some are favored (designated sheep) and some are not favored (designated goats). The nations are favored by treating Jesus' people favorably (caring for their physical, social, and emotional needs), as though they were actually treating Jesus Christ that way. The "least of the brothers" (v. 40) must refer, not to the Jewish people nor to all the oppressed people of the world (the liberal interpretation of the parable leading to salvation by works), but to those who are Christians who believe in him, his disciples (cf. 12:46–50).[16] On the basis of how others, the nations, treat Christians in the course of the coming ages they will be rewarded. But these nations are not unbelieving people, but believers. They take compassion on Jesus' people because they believe the witness of Christians concerning Jesus Christ. Their good deeds show where they "stand in relation to the kingdom and to Jesus himself."[17] The "least of these" (v. 45) may be a slightly different group—those who treat not just believers with compassion but all who are needy. The goats are nations that fail to do acts of compassion with a "righteousness of the whole person," from the heart.[18] But in both cases those who are praised in the parable are Christians among the nations. These, the sheep, are called "righteous"—they have embraced the gospel of Christ. They are not pagan peoples who do good toward Christians as though they could earn salvation. The sheep treat Christians well because they have accepted the message embodied by Christians, the "righteous." The goats are those who both reject the message of believers regarding Christ, and persecute Christians.

The central truth, then, of the parable is that at the judgment at the end of the age[19] Christ will divide all humanity into two groups on the basis of acts of charity done for him on his true followers: some (the goats) will go to eternal punishment, and some (the sheep) will go to eternal life (v.

---

16. Carson, *Matthew*, 520. It is unlikely that a smaller group, the apostles, is meant. Turner, *Matthew*, 605, agrees with this interpretation and notes that this view is the "one most widely held throughout the church's history."

17. Ibid., 520. Carson takes up the objection to this identification of the sheep, namely that there is not an adequate distinction between the sheep and the "least of these my brothers." Both groups are believers. He answers that there is "similar ambiguity in Matthew 18," that this interpretation "emphasizes the kind of loving relationships" that must characterize Christians, and that this view "prepares the way for the surprise shown by both sheep and goats"—surprise not at their destiny but at the reason given for their destiny (see 520, 522).

18. Ibid., 522.

19. It is not clear from the parable which judgment this is, that at the end of this era, prior to the Millennium, or after the Millennium, the Great White Throne Judgment (Rev 20). The surety of the judgment, not its timing, is Jesus' emphasis.

46). It is this clear, distinguished destiny that is the difficult obstacle for universalism.

Jesus concludes with the words: "and these (the goats on the left) shall go out to eternal torment, but the righteous (the sheep on the right) [shall go out] to eternal life." The parallelism of the clauses makes it clear that the length of the destiny of each is equal: it is "eternal" or "everlasting." Since everyone believes that the righteous have a destiny of life without end, it is inescapable that the unrighteous have a destiny of torment without end. If there is not an "eternity" of torment for the wicked, there can be no heaven that has "eternal" life. If there is no such heaven, if heaven is temporally limited, then the whole point of redeeming the wicked out of hell offers only a little respite. What follows then for those in heaven? There is an obvious conclusion. *There can only be an eternal heaven of bliss if there is an eternal hell of punishment.* The one gives meaning to and validates the other.[20] This text is one of the five or six that comprise the most difficult texts for universalism to overcome.

As noted in chapter 1 above, Jesus' use here of the term "torment" (*kolasis*) points to divine retribution. Further, it is used of hell by the Jews, Josephus, and Philo. It is used by the church fathers: the Martyrdom of Polycarp 2:3 ("exemption from eternal punishment"); 11:2 ("eternal punishment reserved for the ungodly"); Ignatius in his work at Romans 5:3 ("cruel tortures of the Devil"); and 2 Clement 6:7 ("save us from eternal punishment"). It occurs only twice in the NT (Matt 25:46; 1 John 4:18). It is among the strongest terms used to refer to the future destiny of the wicked, and it comes from Jesus Christ. In 1 John 4 the word occurs in the context of not having fear but confidence in the day of judgment.

The parable presents the surprise of both the sheep and the goats at their reward. Neither realized the eternal significance of their works while they did them. What the "sheep" did for fellow believers was being done to Jesus himself! The judgment pronounced on the nations who are the goats would vindicate the witness and sacrifice of Jesus' people.

The parable is significant for showing that all humanity falls into only two categories. It reveals Jesus Christ as the Judge (as well as the King, the Shepherd, and the Son of Man). It is a reminder that when Christians serve others they are serving Christ himself. This is a tremendous encouragement to a genuine expression of social concerns. The use of this parable by the social gospel comes wide of the true meaning of the parable.

Yet something more significant needs to be said about two verses of this parable. It is not just the last verse that is difficult for universalists, but

---

20. I dealt with this logic and reasoning in the excursus above, after chapter 5.

so are verses 34 and 41. In verse 34 the sheep are pronounced as "blessed by my Father." This represents a perfect tense in the Greek text, and connotes a lasting state that is ongoing. The sheep exist in an ongoing state of blessedness. In addition, they are promised the kingdom "prepared from the foundation of the world" (another perfect tense). The implications are that their being blessed to inherit the kingdom began before the making of the world. It reinforces the doctrine of election.

In contrast, verse 41 uses different verbs in the perfect tense for the wicked, the goats. These are pronounced by Christ as "cursed" (indicating an ongoing state and its results) and their destiny is "everlasting fire prepared for the devil and his angels" (another perfect tense). The implications are that the wicked cannot change their destiny which is something prepared for the devil and demons. The wicked join the forces of the devil and participate in the judgment he deserves. The destiny of the goats is not fatalistic.

These verses (vv. 34 and 41) form an obstacle to universalism as weighty as verse 46, but these verses are rarely addressed. The parallel clauses make the ideas of both annihilation (conditional immortality) and universalism wishful thinking. The "eternally excruciating experience of hell is unspeakably worse than these two metaphors [fire and deep darkness found elsewhere in Matthew] portraying it."[21]

Some protest that these verses tend to turn people into infidels. But, as Carson observes, human response "is a secondary consideration and may reveal as much about us as about the doctrine being rejected." The question is not how people respond to a doctrine but "what Jesus and the NT writers actually teach about it."[22] Universalism has greater concern to satisfy a natural sense of love and justice than to adhere to the teaching of Scripture.

Other Parables

The parable of the sheep and the goats presents teaching that finds reinforcement in Jesus' teaching in the parables of the sower and the weeds (or, tares). In the former the evil one snatches away what is sown in the heart (Matt 13:19, 40–44). If the devil is able to do this during the present era, to those who are hardened and do not understand the truth, what is to prevent him

---

21. Turner, *Matthew*, 610.

22. Carson, *Matthew*, 523. Carson goes on to remind of two things (which are pertinent to universalism): (1) there are degrees of punishment in hell just as there are degrees of reward in heaven (Matt 11:22; Luke 12:47–48); and (2) there is no "shred of evidence" that hell ever brings about repentance. "Sin continues as part of the punishment and the ground of it" (523).

from doing so in the state after death? Every attempt by people to come to truth in hell (so universalism teaches) will be blocked by Satan. In regard to the parable of the weeds, Jesus taught that the devil sows evil people among the righteous. At the end of the age angels will gather everything that causes sin and all lawbreakers and throw them into a fiery furnace where there will be weeping and gnashing of teeth (13:40–43). The righteous will shine like the sun in the kingdom (v. 44). Jesus presents this as the final disposition of people; he does not hold out a future hope for a time when all will be righteous and when there will be no "evil one" (the devil).

The three other parables that precede the parable of the sheep and the goats are instructive concerning future destinies. These are the faithful and wise servants (Matt 24:45–51), the parable of the ten virgins (Matt 25:1-13), and the parable of the talents (25:14–30). All these parables exhort the disciples to abide faithful while the Lord delays his return. The parable of the ten virgins portrays Christ as the bridegroom. At the wedding it is he who enters the house with his bride and five of the virgins. When the other five who have gone away to buy oil come and try to enter, they find that the door is shut. When the five cry out to be admitted the bridegroom declares that he never knew them. He refuses access. This text is very similar to that in the Sermon on the Mount that pictures Jesus as the Lord who doesn't know those who have failed to do the will of the Father (Matt 7:21–23). He is also the way of access by the narrow gate to the way that leads to life as opposed to the way that leads to destruction (7:13–14).

In all these parables the message is the same. When Jesus Christ returns, it is he who opens the way to life and blessing, and closes entrance to those who do not obey him. It is he who is in charge of the punishment of those who disobey him. Jesus said: "I am the way, the truth, and the life; no one comes to the Father except by me" (John 14:6).

The Broader Teaching from Jesus on the Destiny of the Wicked

In addition to his parables, Jesus had much more to say about hell. Indeed, he teaches more about hell than anyone else in the entire Bible. We learn more about hell from Jesus Christ than from anyone else. He affirmed the reality of hell in clearer and stronger terms than anyone else.

There are some other broad statements that need affirming. Jesus Christ is the key to this teaching as he is for all other doctrines of the Bible that Christians confess. In a sense there is nothing new in the rest of the NT; the Apostles merely add to or clarify what Jesus taught. We are Christians;

we are not Paulites, Johnites, Peterites, or other -ites (even though the Corinthians were close to becoming such; 1 Cor 1:12).

Universalists Discount Hell

As shown in the pages above, universalism seeks to discount the significance of Jesus' teaching about hell in several ways. They claim that Jesus did not really believe in hell (so Brian McLaren in his *The Last Word and the Word After That*). Instead the Pharisees borrowed the belief from pagan sources (Egyptians, Babylonians, Persians [Zoroastrians], and Greeks) and used it as "power language" to scare scapegoats (the poor people) into submission to them and their beliefs. They sought to place blame and shame on the poor people. Jesus came along and used the Pharisees' language to turn the tables on the Pharisees, but he didn't personally believe in such a place of judgment. This is one approach that universalists embrace.

Attendant to this approach is to assert that the beliefs about hell do not come from the OT, that it is virtually silent about punishment after death and the afterlife. Thus again the beliefs about hell are not authoritative, for they have no OT precedent. Finally, as also seen in the pages above, universalism rejects the evangelical interpretation of the Bible about hell and seeks to impose some liberal view on the text that often has no other basis but wishful thinking. In one way or another, universalists trivialize or minimize Jesus' teaching about hell.

Nagging Questions about Hell That Universalism Can't Answer

Yet such approaches have serious shortcomings. There are nagging questions that cannot be answered by the universalists' views. Here are some of them. (1) Where did the ancient peoples get their view of the afterlife? If they could create such a belief, why could not the Jews? (2) If the Apostles follow Jesus' teaching regarding hell and continue it, does this not validate it for all Christians as true and to be believed? (3) Is not Jesus our source for all doctrine and its authority, wherever it came from? (4) Is not Jesus and the Holy Spirit our guides into all truth (John 14:26; 1 John 5:18–20)? (5) Is not Jesus the only one in all of history to visit the afterlife following death and to return, never to die again? Does this not qualify Jesus' views on this issue more than anyone else's? Should not his words about the afterlife have greater weight than anyone else's? (6) If Jesus experienced eternal separation from God for the moments he was dying for sin on the cross, does not this and his entire afterlife experience affirm that eternal judgment after death has always existed, at least since the rebellion of Satan against God? If an afterlife exists in the experience of Jesus, it has always existed. It could not have begun in the experience of Jesus. (7) Even a more basic question is this. Is not Jesus our leader and pioneer and perfecter of our faith, as Hebrew 12:2 asserts? We do not qualify what our leader says; we do not question it; we do not dispute it. Rather we obey him and believe what he says about any matter. He claimed that all authority belonged to him, hence he commanded his followers to obey him (as in the great commission: Matt 28:19–20).

Ultimately it is not a question of where Jesus got any of this teaching, as we properly seek to interpret him. Perhaps he borrowed much as, for example, in the Sermon on the Mount. The issue is whether he believed what he taught and meant for his followers to believe it. It is a question of the authority he invested in the beliefs he held. We are commanded to believe God and him (John 14:1: "You believe in God; believe also in me").

Actually universalists reject, distort, or reinterpret Jesus' teaching about hell because of another, prior reason. It is a philosophical, not a biblical, view. It is because universalists believe that God's love is so great and overwhelming that he cannot allow finally anyone in the end who has rejected his love. Contingent with this line is the belief regarding God's justice. A loving God cannot "send" people to a place of eternal suffering for failure to believe on him during a relatively short human lifetime. His love has failed if there remains anyone not overwhelmed by it, if evil continues in hell.

The most obvious objections to this view are the following. God could justly consign people to an eternal hell if they continue to reject him in hell, thus validating the decision they made during life. Also, the eternal judgment is no more inequitable than the outcome for those who believe in Christ for a brief lifetime. Believers spend an eternity in heaven for trusting Christ during a mere lifetime or less. Finally, *the view of universalism on hell is more scary and threatening than the evangelical view.* I demonstrate that this is so in my excursus on the permanency of hell in the pages above (after chap. 5). *One result of universalist thinking is the destruction of heaven*!

Jesus' Pervasive Teaching about Hell

As we review Jesus' teaching regarding hell there are some general observations. Matthew presents more about Jesus' teaching about hell than any other gospel. John the Baptist introduces the suffering of hell (Matt 3:7–12).

Then the Sermon on the Mount mentions hell several times (5:20–30, esp. vv. 22, 29–30; 7:13–27, esp. vv. 13, 14, 19, 21–23, 24–27—where Jesus is the keeper of the way to life and the way to judgment). In the narrative of 8:10–12 there is outside weeping and gnashing of teeth. It is in the commissioning of the disciples (10:28), and occurs in the parables of chapter 13: the weeds (13:36–43, 49–50) and the net. In the narrative of 18:6–9 Jesus mentions eternal fire, citing the last verses of Isaiah (66:24) dealing with the new heavens and the new earth: "where the worm dies not and the fire is unquenchable." It is an ongoing horror, as expressed also in other non-biblical Jewish literature (in Judith, 1 Enoch, the *Sibylline Oracles*) when they comment on this text in Isaiah during second temple Judaism.[23] *And the everlasting fire is not quenchable by universalism or by annihilationism.*

Jesus continues to instruct about hell in his opposition to the Pharisees (23:33) where he refers to "inescapable punishment." The "son of hell" is one who belongs to hell this side of hell as well as in his destination.[24]

As shown in the parables above, Matthew 24–25 perhaps presents Jesus' most significant teaching about hell. All four parables teach future punishment with the fourth emphasizing this in the strongest terms. In addition we have the parable of the rich man and Lazarus from Luke 16.

In light of this instruction it is quite clear that hell was a matter of very serious concern to Jesus. Why is this? Probably it is because its reality was so certain, sober, and real to him and he wanted as many as possible to escape it. Out of love Jesus sought to warn all humanity.

As interpreters have considered the scope of Jesus' teaching about hell they find three characteristics of what he teaches about hell. They find that he emphasizes three things that help to answer the question: What is hell? Hell involves punishment, destruction, and banishment (a stronger idea than mere separation). Many, including C.S. Lewis and Christopher Morgan, have discovered these ideas.[25] These three ideas represent "an inaugurated eschatology"—that the end has already begun but the full realization of these three ideas takes place at the very end.[26] It is like the judgment on the sin of Sodom and Gomorrah that represents "hell before its time," as Chrysostom the church father of the fifth century observes in his comments on Romans 1.[27]

23. See Morgan and Peterson, *Hell*, 82.
24. Ibid., 73.
25. Ibid., 135ff.; n. 5, 142; n. 11, 145.
26. While Christians often speak of the kingdom under the idea of inaugurated eschatology we should reflect on hell as inaugurated eschatology. Every so-called "natural disaster" is a warning of the judgment to come—as Jesus taught (Luke 13).
27. Chrysostom, "Homily IV: Romans 1:26, 27," in De Young, *Homosexuality,*

These three ideas go together and all three occur in several texts together (Matt 24:45—25:46—the parables dealt with in the above pages; cf. Paul in 2 Thess 1:5–10, esp. v. 9; and Rev 20:1—22:15). The three terms may also be understood more broadly: punishment may also be described as rejection and deprivation; and banishment may also be described as separation, retribution, and disintegration.[28] The idea of destruction does not mean that one ceases to exist, as in annihilationism, but that one ceases to experience real life as it normally is before death.

Hell Is Punishment

How does Jesus' teaching give expression to these three ideas? The following texts show how far reaching Jesus' instruction is. First, Jesus portrays hell as punishment. It is worse than death and earthly suffering. He says that it is better to enter life maimed than to enter whole into the eternal fire of hell (Mark 9:42–48). It is punishment for sin (as the Apostle Paul also writes in Rom 1:24, 26, 28). Punishment is based in the proclamation of Isaiah 66:24, cited above regarding the undying worm and the unquenchable fire. This reality of hell exists side-by-side with the reality of the new heavens and new earth. In the text of Mark 9, God is the agent who effects the punishment/judgment (vv. 47–48). This is a far cry from universalism's arrogant claim that God could not send anyone to eternal punishment. This text is parallel to Matthew 18:6–9 where "eternal fire" (v. 8) and the "fire of hell" (v. 9) also occur.

Hell Is Destruction

Jesus portrays hell as destruction in several texts. In Matthew 7:13–14 he describes the broad way as leading to destruction; and in 7:24–27 he asserts that the house built on sand will collapse. In the parable of the servants (Matt 24:51) people are cut to pieces and there is weeping and gnashing of teeth. In Luke 13:3–5 Jesus cites the examples of those who are destroyed when Pilate murdered them and those on whom the tower of Siloam fell. In both cases he asks whether the people who died were worse sinners than the survivors. The answer is "no," but unless the survivors repent they shall likewise perish. Jesus does not ask nor deal with the obvious question as to why the innocent seemingly suffer unjustly. Jesus' point is that it is a marvel

---

268–72.

28. Morgan and Peterson, *Hell*, n. 5, 143.

that God's grace prevails most of the time when all people deserve his justice and wrath for rejecting him.

Other texts emphasizing hell as destruction include one of Christians' most endearing texts, John 3:16. Whoever believes in Christ "will not perish." Other texts found in the Apostles include this same idea (2 Thess 1:5–10; Rev 20:14; 21:8).

Hell Is Banishment

The third idea characterizing hell is separation, even banishment. Jesus portrays those who reject him as banished from the kingdom (Mark 9:42–48; Matt 3:1–12; 7:21–23), to be "away from me" and the kingdom. The kingdom is "at hand" (Matt 3:6) and there is "coming wrath" (3:7). This idea is reflected especially in the last scene of the Bible, where the wicked are outside the New Jerusalem (Rev 22:14–15). In other texts the wicked are "thrown outside [by God] with weeping and gnashing of teeth" (Matt 8:12); the wicked are thrown into a "fiery furnace, with weeping and gnashing of teeth" (13:41–42); the wicked are separated from the righteous and thrown into fire (Matt 13:49–50); the unprepared five virgins are excluded from the marriage feast by Christ (Matt 25:10–12); the unfaithful servant is thrown outside "into darkness, with weeping and gnashing of teeth" (25:30); the goats, the nations who reject the gospel, are commanded by Jesus to "depart into eternal fire prepared for the devil and his angels" (25:41); Jesus says that the rich man is separated forever from the righteous (Luke 16:19–31); and finally, the branches who do not bear fruit are removed and burned in the fire (John 15:1–7).

Some final observations about Jesus' warning about hell are pertinent. Jesus believed in hell and we are compelled as his followers to believe in it as well. The reality of hell becomes part of his teaching that he gave to his apostles to teach others, and we are heirs of this instruction (in the great commission; Matt 28:18–20). We are called to follow Jesus Christ, not Plato and the Greeks, and certainly not the emergent church and universalists, who have betrayed the teaching of Jesus Christ. We are not more holy and more loving than Jesus and his Apostles regarding the belief in hell as though they never thought about the serious consequences of hell or did not have concerns about eternal suffering. Yet they chose to be faithful to God's word, to submit to the truth of Scripture and to God who is both loving and holy. How arrogant of anyone to think otherwise!

Chapter 13

The Apostles on Judgment and Hell
Paul, Peter, Hebrews, John in The Revelation

THE WITNESS OF THE Apostle Paul to the reality of unchanging destinies is especially crucial. There is no one, after Jesus Christ himself, who has contributed more to the doctrine of the Christian church than the Apostle Paul. His teaching concerning the suffering of the lost in hell is especially helpful in understanding the meaning of reconciliation and the universal aspects of Christ's death. Universalists cite several core texts from Paul to show that all have been reconciled to God by Christ's death on the cross (e.g., Rom 5:18; 1 Cor 15:22; 2 Cor 5:16–21; Col 1:18–23; Phil 2:9–11). It is such texts as these that give universal reconciliation its name. Yet a contextual interpretation of Paul's epistles shows that universal reconciliation is neither universal nor is it reconciliation.

In the pages that follow we will discover that Paul reinforces Jesus' instruction about hell, and carries Jesus' instruction to further refinement. From his perspective after the cross, Paul under inspiration interpreted in particular detail the meaning and implications of the cross.

In this section I present the material from the Apostle Paul in the following format. I present first the claims of universalism concerning several of Paul's texts. I find six major claims. Then I respond with the evangelical interpretation of these texts that Christians have held since the time of the New Testament and early church.

The First Major Claim of Universalism: God Has Reconciled All Already

The first of the six major claims, and perhaps the most significant claim that universalism makes, is that God has reconciled all people to himself already. Reconciliation means that people have come to peace. Universalism claims that God does not need to be reconciled to anyone but people need to be reconciled to God. All were reconciled to God by the cross.

Universalism cites various texts to support their claim; but instead these texts show that God is not reconciled to those who do not believe, and those who do not believe are not reconciled to God. Everything about reconciliation hinges on the act of faith. Our Lord's atoning work on the cross makes reconciliation available for all but it is not applied until an individual believes and accepts that Christ's work was done for him/her. There is universal provision for reconciliation but not universal realization or application. Contrary to what universalism claims about several texts, these texts show that one is not reconciled until one believes.

Colossians 1:20

One of the key texts is Colossians 1:19–23. Universalists cite verses 19–20: "For he [God] was pleased to have all his fullness [of deity] dwell in him [Christ], (20) and through him [Christ] to reconcile all things to himself, having made peace through the blood of his cross—[through him],[1] whether things on the earth or things in the heavens." On the basis of the words that begin verse 20 universalists claim that by means of the death of Christ on the cross God has reconciled (meaning "brought into peace") all people to himself and he has made peace with all. Thus there are none who remain not reconciled to God.

Yet this claim claims too much, and cannot be sustained as the meaning in light of the very next verses. Verses 21–23 record:

> And you who once were alienated and enemies in your minds as expressed by your evil works, (22) he has now reconciled [you] by his physical body by means of death to present you holy and without blemish and blameless before him, (23) if indeed you remain in the faith having been established and being firm and not being moved from the hope of the gospel which you have

---

1. This second use of the phrase, "through him," is a textual variant found in some manuscripts and may simply duplicate the first use. It does not materially affect the meaning of the verse, whether genuine or not.

heard and which was preached in all creation which is under the heaven, of which I Paul became a servant.

These verses clarify that the Colossians were not reconciled to God when Jesus died on the cross, for Paul describes them as not reconciled at the time they heard the gospel. These verses make clear that the exercise of faith was necessary to change the readers from alienated, hostile enemies characterized by evil deeds (thus not reconciled) to reconciled people. Earlier in the book Paul writes that he thanks God for the readers and prays for them "because he had heard of their faith in Christ Jesus" (1:4) and their love and hope "which they heard beforehand in the word of truth, the gospel" (1:5).

The only way to reconcile Paul's statement in 1:20, that God was pleased to reconcile all things to himself by the blood of Christ's cross, and the statement in 1:21, that the readers were once not reconciled but now are, is to posit the essential role that faith has in applying or actualizing the reconciliation available because of the cross. Reconciliation is potential and available for all, as it appears from a human perspective, but all do not appropriate this reconciliation by the cross. By believing the gospel the transition from enemies to reconciled people is made. *If universalists are right in their interpretation, Paul would have said simply that the Colossians were reconciled by Christ's death approximately thirty years earlier.* He would not have dealt with the difference that faith made. Indeed, there would be no need to exercise faith if reconciliation is simply accomplished by Christ's death.[2] The words of 1:23 make it clear that there is *a condition* to their reconciliation. If faith is renounced, if they stop believing, then they would not be reconciled to God.

In chapter two Paul reinforces this essential role of faith. In 2:6–7 he exhorts the readers to walk, to live, in what they have been instructed, (7) having been rooted and being built up in Christ and "being made firm in the faith just as you were taught . . ." In a following verse (v. 12) Paul speaks of the readers as having been raised spiritually in Christ "by means of faith in the working of God who raised him [Christ] from the dead."

Another meaning for Paul's words is also plausible. In 1:20 Paul includes in his words of "universal reconciliation" not only those who believe the gospel (such as the Colossians, explained in vv. 21–23) but also those who are reconciled by conquest and become the footstool of Jesus Christ's future reign. They are conquered opponents who have refused to exercise faith. This idea appears in 2:15 where Paul says that by means of the cross

---

2. This is exactly what Young, *Lies*, 118, asserts: all people are reconciled whether they believe or not. So Bell (188–9) also asserts.

(note v. 14) God has "disarmed the rulers and authorities (mentioned as unseen forces created by Christ in 1:16) and made a public disgrace of them, having triumphed over them by him [or, it—the cross]." This is a triumph that has been won. It is *de jure* (accomplished in God's plan) but it is not yet *de facto*—actualized in history.

In either case, the universalist interpretation of 1:20 will not hold up in light of the meaning derived from the larger context. Clearly not all are yet reconciled to God so as to be saved. Clearly, in order for the Colossians to be reconciled faith made all the difference.

2 Corinthians 5:16-21

Another text very similar to the Colossians 1 text is that of 2 Corinthians 5. Here again reconciliation is the theme. Universalists appeal to several verses. Verse 15 says that Christ "died for all"; and verses 18-19 read:

> And all these things are from God who reconciled us to himself through Christ, and who has given us the ministry of reconciliation. (19) In other words, in Christ God was reconciling the world to himself, not counting people's trespasses against them, and he has given us the message of reconciliation.

As they do on the basis of the texts from Colossians, universalists claim that these verses also speak of universal reconciliation. They cite the words, "in Christ God was reconciling the world to himself." What could be clearer? The whole world was reconciled when Christ died.

Yet the immediately following words show that the verses cannot mean this. Verse 20 reads:

"Therefore we are ambassadors for Christ, as though God were making his plea through us. We plead with you on Christ's behalf, 'Be reconciled to God!'" It is clear that everyone could not be reconciled to God if it is central to Paul's ministry to exhort people to be reconciled to God. The preceding chapter describes those who have not believed (4:3-4): "But even if your gospel is veiled, it is veiled only to those who are perishing, (4) among whom the god of this age has blinded the minds of those who do not believe so they would not see the light of the glorious gospel of Christ, who is the image of God." A few verses later (v. 13), Paul emphasizes the role of faith: "But since we have the same spirit of faith as that shown in what has been written, 'I believed; therefore I spoke,' we also believe, therefore we also speak."

From these verses it is clear that there are those who are perishing—who are not reconciled to God—who do not believe the gospel. These are not reconciled until they believe.

Some may want to make a difference regarding those needing reconciliation. They cite 5:19 as saying that God is reconciled to people on the basis of the cross, but people are not reconciled to God. Reconciliation is a two-way street, as it were, and God has done his part. He has accomplished peace for all, but all are not at peace with him, Young claims.[3]

Yet this cannot be. *If God is truly at peace with all people regardless of their response, even with a response of rejection, then he could not show wrath toward them.* Yet Romans 1:18–32 and 2:1–16, and other passages (Eph 2; John 3:36), show that God does have anger toward those who reject him. Also our text above includes Paul's statement that "because he knows the fear of the Lord" he seeks to persuade people (5:11). This verse indicates that God is a source of fear for those who do not believe the gospel. This hardly supports the idea that God is reconciled to all including those who do not believe. Further consideration of Paul's teaching in the following pages support this observation.

Other Texts Dealing with All Being Saved

There are several other texts used by universalists to point to universal salvation. Two are especially significant and similar. Romans 5:18 asserts: "Consequently, just as condemnation for all people came through one transgression, so too through the one righteous act came righteousness leading to life for all people." Similarly, 1 Corinthians 15:22 reads: "For just as in Adam all die, so also in Christ all will be made alive." Universalists claim

---

3. This is the claim of Young in *The Shack*, 192. Papa speaks: "so now listen to me carefully: through his (Jesus') death and resurrection, I am now fully reconciled to the world." Mack replies: "The whole world? You mean those who believe in you, right?" And Papa replies: "The whole world, Mack. All I am telling you is that reconciliation is a two way street, and I have done my part, totally, completely, finally. It is not the nature of love to force a relationship but it is the nature of love to open the way." Yet, as I've shown above, there is no Scriptural support to say that "God is fully reconciled to the world." Young is inherently contradictory here, for if reconciliation is a "two-way street," then the assumption would be that there is not any reconciliation if one of the ways is not actual or real. Yet he insists that God is "fully, totally, completely, finally" reconciled to the world. There is no condition of a believing response. This is without Scriptural support. In his more recent work, *Lies We Believe about God*, Young continues without reservation to assert universal salvation (chap. 13), even apart from faith. No one needs to "get saved" because everyone is already saved. Bell (155), too, says that Jesus saves everyone.

that the numbers identified in Adam—all—and the numbers identified in Christ—all—are the same. In the end, everyone will enter heaven since the promise is that "all" will be identified in Christ just as all are identified in Adam. It is surprising how often one hears this remark.

Yet universalism again overlooks the immediate context where it is clear that "all in Christ" is not the same number as the "all" in Adam. Those in Christ are a smaller number and come to be in him by way of exercising faith. Romans 5:17 reads: "For if, by the transgression of the one man, death reigned through the one, how much more will those who receive the abundance of grace and of the gift of righteousness reign in life through the one, Jesus Christ."

This verse is the only one in the passage (vv. 15–21) that distinguishes the number of those in Adam from the number of those in Christ. Verse 17 makes clear that life comes only to those who "receive" the grace and gift of righteousness available in Christ. Clearly, some will not receive such a gift. Even the word, "gift," suggests that there is something given to be received. In the case of humanity's identification in Adam there is no "gift" to be "received." All one needs to do is to be born, and the way one lives validates the judgment of Scripture that one is in Adam and lost. But if one will receive the gift, Christ and the forgiveness offered in him (Col 2:13), one becomes identified in Christ and will have eternal life. *One needs merely to be born to be in Adam and under judgment; but one needs to be born again to be in the kingdom of Christ (John 3:5–8).*

Similarly, the context of 1 Corinthians 15:22 ("For just as in Adam all die, so also in Christ all will be made alive") shows that believing is necessary to be alive in Christ and no longer dead in Adam. Receiving the gospel (15:1-2) was that by "which you [the Corinthians] are being saved, if you hold firmly to the message I preached to you—unless you believed in vain." Verse 11 reads: "Whether then it was I or they, this is the way we preach and this is the way you believed." Verse 14 has: "And if Christ has not been raised, then our preaching is futile and your faith is empty." Verse 17 has: "And if Christ has not been raised, your faith is useless; you are still in your sins." So within the context of verse 22 there are four references to the Corinthians' faith. It was faith that distinguished them from all the rest who remained in Adam. It is those who exercise faith in Christ that become the "all" who are made alive in Christ. In contrast to this, Young asserts (*Lies*, chap. 25) that all people were created in God and all were included in the death, burial, and resurrection of Christ.

A Second Claim of Universalism: God's Will That All Be Saved Will Succeed

Another major claim of universalism is that God's will that all be saved and none perish will be realized without exception. In the end none will be able to refuse the love of God. There can be no lasting hell where evil still exists forever in God's universe. The text of 1 Timothy 2:4 holds major sway here. Verses 3–6 read:

> Such prayer for all is good and acceptable before God our Savior, (4) since he wants all people to be saved and to come to the knowledge of the truth. (5) For there is one God and one intermediary between God and humanity, Christ Jesus, himself human, (6) who gave himself as a ransom for all, revealing God's purpose at his appointed time.

There are two places in these verses where universal reconciliation seems to appear. The text says that God "wants all to be saved and to come to the knowledge of the truth" and that Christ gave himself a ransom, a payment, "for all people." Similar, but a bit different, is 4:10: ". . . we have set our hope on the living God, who is the Savior of all people, especially of believers."

Yet these verses should be understood as those discussed in the pages above where "all" also occurs (Col 1:20; 2 Cor 5; Rom 5:18; 1 Cor 15:22). It is clear from the context that not "all" are saved or ransomed until faith is exercised.

The Clarity of the Pastoral Epistles Regarding the Need to Believe in Order to Be Saved

Faith is assumed throughout 1 Timothy, in every chapter, as the basis for the readers' place and standing before God. In fact there is a *two-fold emphasis on faith* in 1 Timothy. *One emphasis commends and exhorts faith; the other warns of those who have abandoned the faith or stopped believing and are in peril.* The only way that the latter warning makes any sense is that faith is absolutely required in order that God may become one's Savior, for Christ's death to be appropriated as a ransom (payment). *The first emphasis* occurs in several places. In 1:5–6 Paul informs his readers that God's plan "operates by faith" (so the NET), and that love "comes from . . . a sincere faith." Consequently God's plan not only includes his will that all be saved but also the role of faith to make his plan operative. Without the exercise of human faith, God's plan does not enter reality.

Other texts along this same line abound in 1 Timothy. Paul is in the ministry (1:12–16) because God considered him "faithful" (1:12). His personal testimony witnesses to the centrality of faith for his conversion:

> I was treated with mercy because I acted ignorantly in unbelief, (14) and our Lord's grace was abundant, bringing faith and love in Christ Jesus ... (16) But here is why I was treated with mercy: so that in me as the worst, Christ Jesus could demonstrate his utmost patience, as an example for those who are going to believe in him for eternal life.

How much clearer could it be? Paul does not say that he experiences salvation because of God's universal desire or want or will but because of God's particular will regarding him, showing him mercy, and because he believed. Both divine working and human response came together. How God worked in Paul is to serve as an example for others who are going to believe. And there is not a word that unbelievers can exercise faith, that it can be operative or functional, after death.

In chapter two, Paul adds to his personal calling. Immediately after the text loved by universalists (2:4, 6), Paul adds: "For this I was appointed a preacher and apostle—I am telling the truth; I am not lying—and a teacher of the Gentiles in faith and truth." *If Gentiles are already saved and ransomed, why does Paul have to instruct them to believe the truth?*

The other universalist text is 4:10: "we have set our hope on the living God, who is the Savior of all people, especially of believers." In light of the context, where believing is so prominent, it is better to translate this verse: " ... the Savior of all people, particularly, believers." This meaning ("particularly") suits the Greek term involved (*malista*) everywhere else it occurs in the NT (Acts 20:38; 1 Tim 4:10; 5:17; 2 Tim 4:13; Tit 1:10).[4] Regardless of how this word is translated, in light of the context, the verse cannot be affirming salvation for believers and unbelievers. Alternatively, the word "Savior" may refer, not to personal salvation in a redemptive sense, but to Jesus Christ as the Lord of all, by forceful confession, parallel to Philippians 2:10–11.

Paul also exhorts Christian slaves not to treat "believing masters" with less respect because they are brothers, but instead to serve them all the more because they are "believers and dearly loved" (6:2). Near the end of the Epistle, Paul exhorts Timothy to pursue, among other virtues, "faithfulness"

---

4. See *BDAG*, 489.

and to "compete well for the faith and lay hold of that eternal life" for which he was called (6:11–12).

As part of *the second emphasis* regarding faith (warning about abandoning faith) consider the following verses (1:18–19). Paul encourages Timothy to "fight the good fight. (19) To do this you must hold firmly to faith and a good conscience, which some have rejected and so have suffered shipwreck in regard to the faith." It seems that universalists such as Young have "suffered shipwreck." In 2:15 Paul warns women that they must "continue in faith and love and holiness with self-control." In 3:7 he says that among the qualifications that an elder must meet he must "be well thought of by those outside the faith, so that he may not fall into disgrace and be caught by the devil's trap." How can there be those who are outside the faith if Christ is the Savior of all? Universalists reply that they are "outside" only this side of death, and that they move to the "inside" in hell. *But if even believers may be caught in the devil's trap now, will not unbelievers be especially "trapped" by him after death?*[5]

Similarly, deacons are to meet the qualification of "being faithful in every respect" (3:11). Those who serve well as deacons have a "good standing . . . and great boldness in the faith that is in Christ Jesus" (3:13). Paul goes on and identifies the church as the "support and bulwark of the truth" (3:15). Then he gives a wonderful summation of the revelation about Christ that Christianity contains. Of the six elements cited, the fifth is that Christ "was believed on in the world" (3:16). In 4:12 Paul exhorts Timothy himself to be an example "for the believers" in speech, conduct, love, "faithfulness, and purity."

Additional warnings about losing faith occur. He says that the Spirit warns that "in the later times some will desert the faith and occupy themselves with deceiving spirits and demonic teachings" (4:1). *Are we to believe, with universalism, that these will somehow convert after death when demonic spirits will be even more active? If people occupy themselves with such now, will they not pursue them even more after death? Will the "corrective fires of hell" be really that persuasive?* Paul distinguishes these apostates from "those who believe and know the truth"—probably meaning that one group is in view (one Greek article precedes both "believe" and "know the truth") (4:3).

Paul warns Timothy that someone who fails to provide for the needs of his own "has denied the faith and is worse than an unbeliever" (5:8). Later he warns that some "have already wandered away to follow Satan. If a believing woman has widows in her family, let her help them" (5:15–16). As evidence of how heavily faithfulness weighed on Paul's mind, the very last

---

5. See my discussion of the devil's work in hell in the excursus after chapter 5.

words of the Epistle warn Timothy to avoid the contradictions of "falsely named knowledge" which some professing "have strayed from the faith" (6:20–21).

Can God's Wish Be Thwarted? Yes

The special issue raised by 1 Timothy 2:4 is Paul's use of "want" or "wishes": "God wants all to be saved and to come to the knowledge of the truth." Universalists argue that God must bring about his every want or wish (the Greek is *thelei*); otherwise he is impotent and not omnipotent. God's will cannot be thwarted, universalists argue.[6]

I agree that God's attributes of omnipotence and love must go together; but to these must be joined his attributes of holiness and justice. Moreover, he created human beings in his "image and likeness" (Gen. 1:26–27), and such an image includes the will, the capacity to choose wrongly or sinfully, against God's preferred will. Adam and Eve witness to this choice. God wished that they would not rebel against him. Therefore, included within God's will or wants or desires is his will that humans have the capacity to choose, to will, even contrary to God's will. *God has willed that people have the capacity to will contrary to God's will.*

Universalism More Deterministic and Coercive Than Calvinism

Universalism is more deterministic and coercive than any expression of evangelical belief, including Calvinism with its emphasis on divine election and predestination. Universalism decrees (a strange thing to say, since universalists pride themselves in not having a creed) that all must repent and come to faith, either before dying or after dying. God's love triumphs over his justice; his love demands this (which is also strange, for how can love be demanding?) Clearly, universalism finds itself at odds with both biblical revelation and reason.

Clearly the emphasis of 1 Timothy is on the need to exercise faith to realize and experience salvation. And there is no hint that anyone can exercise faith after death.

---

6. Bell, *Love Wins*, 100, says that God is not thwarted in his purpose; all will be reconciled.

The Witness of Peter against Universalism

The preceding discussion also applies to 2 Peter 3:9: "The Lord is not slow concerning his promise, as some regard slowness, but is being patient toward you, because he does not wish for any to perish but for all to come to repentance." This verse is related to 3:15: "And regard the patience of our Lord as salvation, just as also our dear brother Paul wrote to you, according to the wisdom given to him." The verses imply that people need to embrace the gospel before judgment comes (vv. 10–14), that the delay of judgment associated with the return of Christ is to give additional opportunity for people to respond before "the day of judgment and destruction of the ungodly" (3:7). The text of 2 Peter affirms a coming judgment for some that for all intents and purposes is final and unchangeable. *If universalism is correct, why would God have to be patient if he will bring all to repentance after death after all?*

Texts Showing That Faith Cannot Be Coerced

Universalism's claim that God's will cannot be thwarted contradicts the obvious meaning of texts that make faith the condition of salvation, and pose no opportunity to change after death. John 3:16–18, 36 is classic here:

> For this is the way God loved the world: He gave his one and only Son, so that everyone who believes in him will not perish but have eternal life. (17) For God did not send his Son into the world to condemn the world, but that the world should be saved through him. (18) The one who believes in him is not condemned. The one who does not believe has been condemned already, because he has not believed in the name of the one and only Son of God. (36) The one who believes in the Son has eternal life. The one who rejects the Son will not see life, but God's wrath remains on him.

These verses emphasize the role of faith to enter into salvation, to have eternal life, and to escape perishing, condemnation, and the wrath of God. *If God's wrath is already operative (note the present tense of "remains"), when does it cease so that those who die under it and go under it to hell can repent and go to heaven?*

It is not surprising to find that universalism hardly ever mentions the need of faith as expressed in this perhaps the most endearing promise (John 3:16) that Christians claim. In believing, people are exercising their will to believe the gospel. Paul concurs with this will to believe: "For the Scripture says, 'Everyone who believes in him will not be put to shame' . . . will be saved" (Rom 10:11, 14). Note how 10:9–10 make it clear that believing is essential for salvation, and that salvation is the result of a process that involves the sending of a preacher, the preaching, the hearing, and the believing (10:14–7). Without this process faith does not occur (so v. 17). *Who then will be the preacher of good news in hell? How will this process ever get underway there/then?*

Inherent in this entire discussion is the obvious truth that faith must not be coerced but be freely expressed. Universalists' insistence that the "corrective fires of hell" will bring all the wicked in hell to repentance and to faith is a crucial and convincing error in its whole approach. *There is no Scripture that asserts that this is the role of suffering in anyone's life after death.*

Divine Sovereignty and Human Responsibility

The preceding texts make it very clear that there is always a twofold explanation of anyone's conversion. Divine sovereignty—God's choice and role in salvation—is always balanced by the person's exercise of faith. Any attempt to explain anyone's salvation apart from both of these aspects will fail. As shown in the pages below, Romans 9 emphasizes God's sovereignty and election; Romans 10 emphasizes personal faith.

A Third Major Claim from Universalism: All Humanity Will Embrace Jesus

A third major claim of universal reconciliation is that one day all humanity will lovingly confess Jesus Christ as Savior and Lord. Even *The Shack* (248) makes such an assertion. Universalism appeals to several texts to support this view. The implication is that there is no coercion to believe this side of death or after death.

Philippians 2:9–11 is one such text. "As a result God exalted him and gave him the name that is above every name, (10) so that at the name of Jesus every knee will bow—in heaven and on earth and under the earth—(11) and every tongue confess that Jesus Christ is Lord to the glory of God the Father." This passage reflects the prophecy of Isaiah 45:23. It is similar to Romans 14:11–12 (which quotes Isa 45:23 and 49:18): "For it is written, 'As I live, says the Lord, every knee will bow to me, and every tongue will give praise to God.' (12) Therefore, each of us will give an account of himself to God."

Jesus Rules As Conqueror of Some, Not As Savior: Psalm 110:1

Yet the wider context of apostolic teaching reveals that all do not lovingly submit to Jesus Christ or to God. They are forced to submit to a conquering sovereign. Such is not saving faith.

Various metaphors are used to show this. The most frequently cited OT text is Psalm 110:1: "The LORD said unto my Lord, 'Sit at my right hand until I make your enemies the footstool of your feet.'" The text is first employed by Jesus to confound the Pharisees in their understanding of Messiah, who must be both David's son and also David's Lord (Matt 22:44). Following his lead, virtually all of the writing Apostles cite the same text. Here is that of Paul (1 Cor 15:24–25): "Then comes the end, when he hands over the kingdom to God the Father, when he has brought to an end all rule and all authority and power. (25) For he must reign until he has put all his enemies under his feet" (and then Paul cites Ps 110:1). In the following verses Paul does not allow for any "enemy" to become Christ's "friend" in subsequent time. The verses say that when all things are subjected to Christ he will himself be subjected to the Father who caused all to be subjected to Christ "so that God may be all in all" (vv. 26–28). *These final words depict the final state; no other condition is foreseen.* It means, therefore, that some are in everlasting subjection and conquest. This can hardly be a "loving embrace of Jesus Christ." Paul alludes to the same OT text in several other places (Col 3:1; etc.).

In the book of Hebrews this text is cited or alluded to five times (1:3, 13; 8:1; 10:12–13; and 12:2). These several texts emphasize that Christ "is now waiting until his enemies are made a footstool for his feet." Clearly, it is the position of the enthroned great high priest-king (1:1–4).

Finally, 1 Peter describes Christ as the one "who went into heaven and is at the right hand of God with angels and authorities and powers subject to him" (3:22). From this text we learn that not only human beings but also unseen opposing forces are subject to Christ.

In addition to these texts which cite Psalm 110:1, there is the text that pictures Jesus' triumph on the cross as that of a Roman conquering hero who rides triumphantly at the head of the captured forces opposed to him (Col 2:15). This depicts conquest, not a loving relationship. Further, Psalm

2:9 is cited in the NT as describing Jesus as ruling over his enemies not with a rod of gold or jewels but with a rod of iron (Rev 19:15).

Jesus As Judge of All

Then there are many texts that describe Jesus as the judge of those who will be judged before him. People will render account to the one ready to judge the living and the dead (1 Pet 4:5). Judgment will come to those who disobey the gospel (1 Pet 4:17). "Swift destruction" awaits those who teach destructive heresies (2 Pet 2:2–3). God reserves the unrighteous for punishment at the day of judgment, just as he judged the angels who sinned, the world of Noah, and Sodom and Gomorrah (2:4–9). The wicked will be "destroyed in their destruction" and "paid the wages of their harmful ways" (2:12–13). For the wicked the "utter depths of darkness have been reserved" (2:17). There is coming "a day of judgment and destruction of the ungodly" (3:7).

The text of 2 Peter 2:20–21 is especially instructive. It records that the "last state" of those who have forsaken the gospel is "worse than the first" and "it would have been better never to have known the way of righteousness than knowing it and to depart from it." *According to universalism this is not the last state. Yet how can there be a reversal of a "last state"? Universalism makes these statements meaningless. Departing from something once known is not worse after all, for somehow this "last state" is going to be reversed and the last state is better, not worse.* Universalism cannot escape the clear meaning of this text: for some the last state has to be worse (a greater degree of punishment in hell), not better (to go to heaven).

A Fourth Major Claim of Universalism: Jesus Went to Hell to Bring Salvation There

A fourth major claim of universalism seemingly based in the NT is that Jesus Christ went to hell between his death and resurrection, and could return there a thousand times, to proclaim the availability of salvation for those who are there (so Young in UR, 35–37).[7] There are two potential texts to support this: 1 Peter 3:18—4:6; and Ephesians 4:7–9. This descent to hell, universalism claims, is part of the early Apostles' Creed.

Yet these texts more likely have another meaning. Ephesians 4 rather affirms that at his incarnation Christ only descended to the "lower parts,"

---

7. Young favorably quotes a universalist who identifies the evangelical teaching on these texts as "sadistic humbug" (UR, 37).

that is, the earth itself. It does not point to the "lower parts" as a region belonging below the earth or some other such geographical place.[8]

The text of 1 Peter 3:18—4:6 better means that Christ went by the Spirit to those now in prison, in hell, in the days of Noah and preached to the wicked then in the preaching of Noah. There was not a subsequent preaching. Even if there were a preaching by Jesus between his death and resurrection, it is more likely that it was a proclamation of triumph, not an invitation to believe the gospel.

In addition, the Apostles' Creed was never used to teach a chance to repent after death but to proclaim Jesus' triumph over fallen demonic powers hostile to him. This same Creed and other early creeds clearly teach that Christ is coming again as judge. There is no further confession of universal deliverance from hell. I dealt in further detail with these creeds in chapter 8 above covering the early history of universalism.

A Fifth Major Claim of Universalism: No Final Judgment of Wrath

A fifth major claim of universal reconciliation is that there is no future, final judgment where the wrath of God is expressed. In his novel (*The Shack*, 120) Young has God assert: "I do not judge sin. Sin is its own punishment." In his other novel (*Eve*) Young devotes much of chapter 13 to this denial. In addition, Hosea Ballou in his *The Atonement*, argued that God is not angry toward sinners/sin.

Yet this assertion flies in the face of numerous statements about God's present and coming wrath. Wrath is God's predetermined response to a violation of his holiness. Paul warns of God's wrath as *already being experienced* by those who reject the revelation that God has given of himself in the creation (Rom 1:18). Paul warns of God's wrath coming on those who fail to live a life evidencing that they are saved (Rom 2:1–11, 16). Faith alone, not works, brings about justification, redemption, and atonement (3:24–31). At the cross God satisfied his "justice" by the death of Christ (3:25); it "satisfied" his anger toward sin. Christians have peace with God only by justification which is actualized by believing (5:1). Only then do they change from enemies to be reconciled to God (5:10–11). Paul says that all will stand before the judgment seat of Christ/God (Rom 14:10–12). Further discussion of passages from Romans are discussed in the pages below.

---

8. The Greek here is not a genitive of possession (the "lower parts" that belong to the earth) or a partitive genitive (the "lower parts" are part of the earth), but a genitive of apposition (the "lower parts" are the earth).

A Sixth Claim of Universalism: Love Triumphs over Justice

A sixth major claim of universal reconciliation is that God's love triumphs over his justice. This is a faulty translation/interpretation of James 2:13 (made also in *The Shack*, 164). In *Burning Down the Shack* I thoroughly show that this interpretation is faulty (116–8).

In 1878 the universalist ministers of Boston (see under the creeds of universalism in chap. 8) claimed that "divine justice" is "born of love and limited by love." This is the most fundamental claim of universalism. Yet it finds complete refutation in Paul's Second Epistle to the Thessalonians. This passage is so powerful and persuasive in its treatment of the justice of God that it alone is sufficient to refute the core doctrines of universalism. It is not surprising that it goes virtually unmentioned in universalist literature.

The weight, the significance, of 2 Thessalonians 1:5–12 is signaled by Paul himself when he says in a parenthetical remark (in v. 10): "and you in fact did believe our testimony." These words and its close parallel (1 Cor 1:6: "just as the testimony of Christ was established among you") intend to personalize the preceding statements regarding the justice and retribution of God to the situation of the readers. The remark covers the entire preaching and teaching ministry of Paul and his colleagues concerning Jesus Christ. That is, Paul is validating the content of the gospel that he preached and affirming that it was the basis of the believers' faith.[9] By these words Paul also connects the readers with the saints who have gone before and who with the Thessalonians will stand one day in the presence of Christ as their redeemer and vindicator. The emphasis in this passage on the justice of God is part and parcel of the gospel Paul preached and which led to the Thessalonians' faith. Universalism's claims redefining the relationship of justice and love crumble into dust in light of this text and its parenthetical remark.

An overview of this text includes recognition that there is a subtheme of reversal: while the Christians experience suffering now at the hands of their persecutors, their persecutors are doomed to experience suffering at the return of Christ. This reversal theme reminds us of the same theme found in the parable of the rich man and Lazarus (Luke 16) and to a lesser extent in the parable of the sheep and the goats (both discussed in chap. 12). This passage also gives support to the three elements of what hell is, as described in Christ's words (also in chap. 12). Hell is banishment or separation, destruction, and punishment.

---

9. See Wanamaker, *Thessalonians*, 232.

Another significant fact will become apparent as we address this text. It is heavily dependent on Isaiah 66, the last chapter of this great prophet. In the pages of the previous chapter I showed that Jesus often used the very last verses of Isaiah 66 to describe hell as the place where "the fire is not quenched" and "the worm does not die." Clearly, Jesus' understanding of future judgment influenced the early Christians in their understanding, and led them to reflect on the rest of Isaiah 66. Paul is part of that process of reflection. The Apostle is totally in line with Jesus' understanding.

All the above difficult texts dealing with supposed universal reconciliation find clarification in 2 Thessalonians 1. There cannot be universal reconciliation if some are permanently (v. 9: "eternal destruction") the objects of God's retributive justice. While universalists reject the terms, "retributive justice," they find clear expression in this passage.

The Severe Righteous Judgment from God in 2 Thessalonians

The first verses of this Epistle identify the issues at hand. The Thessalonians were flourishing in their faith and in their love toward one another. Their perseverance and faith in the midst of persecutions and afflictions were a cause of boasting on Paul's part (1:3–4). This situation leads Paul into the discussion about the nature of God who will take vengeance on their enemies.

Paul identifies the persecution and affliction of the Thessalonians as "evidence of God's righteous judgment, to make you worthy of the kingdom of God, for which in fact you are suffering" (v. 5). These words reflect a theology of suffering already in place prior to and during the first century AD.[10] This theology involved four elements and these are reflected in 2 Thessalonians 1.[11] (1) A strong sense of God's retributive justice (cf. vv. 6, 8–10); (2) present suffering by the saints was viewed as chastisement (or atonement) that would make them worthy of future glory (cf. v. 5); (3) the present "untroubled position of the godless and their future affliction by God" were viewed as the "reverse" of the experience of the saints (cf. vv. 6–7); and (4) the present "suffering of the elect was accepted as evidence of God's election and justice" (cf. vv. 3–4, 11–2). The Christians' suffering was making them worthy to share in the coming kingdom and those who were causing the suffering would undergo retributive justice and compensatory

---

10. Ibid., 222.
11. Ibid.

justice (vv. 6–7) at the time of Christ's coming again.[12] Paul seeks to assure the believers that their suffering was for the coming kingdom or reign of God about to break forth (v. 5 refers back to v. 4).

Verse 5 is a powerful reminder that God's judgment is "righteous." Contrary to universalism, there is no injustice in God's dealing with those who are unbelievers. There is no basis for a charge of distortion, unfairness, imbalance, and other attacks on God's character and actions. *God's love does not limit his justice; rather his righteousness limits his justice.*

In verse 6 Paul gives the negative dimensions of God's justice, while verse 7 gives the positive dimension. The conditional conjunction ("if," v. 6) introduces a first class conditional clause which means that the condition is not only assumed to be true for sake of argument but is true in fact: "if (= since) it is right for God to repay with affliction those who afflict you." What is said in verses 6–7 about the judgment of God is fair because it represents what is "right" or "just" with God. The word "right" is "righteous," the same word used in verse 5. The infinitive "to repay" expresses "God's decision" regarding both those who afflict the believers (they will be afflicted by God) and the believers themselves who are afflicted (they will be given rest, v. 7).

Verse 6 represents the OT law of retribution, the *lex talionis*. Here is the first contact with Isaiah 66, mentioned above. There it is said: "Hear the uproar from the city, hear that noise from the temple! It is the sound of the LORD repaying his enemies all they deserve." The enemies of the Thessalonians are the enemies of the Lord. Their just recompense is their being afflicted by God on the day of judgment (cf. v. 10). Verse 9 identifies their "just recompense" as "destruction and eternal exclusion" from the presence of God since they know not God and refuse to obey the gospel. The Christians may feel weak and impotent before their persecutors but the promise of retribution empowers them to persevere until the day when all will be reversed—they will find relief and their opponents will be afflicted by God himself. This is the first of several points of reversal.

On the day of judgment God will recompense the Christians who are in the process of being afflicted at the time of Paul's writing (note the present tense of v. 7). This is the positive aspect of the day of judgment. When Christ is revealed from heaven with his mighty angels he will bring to an end the time of "messianic woes" preceding his coming during which the faithful undergo severe distress.[13] In this judgment God will weigh the deeds of people to determine their retribution or recompense (cf. Rom 2:5–11; 1 Cor 3:12–15; 4:5; 2 Cor 5:10). The recompense for the afflicted Christians is to

---

12. Ibid., 223.
13. Ibid., 224–25.

receive "rest" from God. It is relief that parallels the great promises of peace and joy that characterize the kingdom (cf. Rom 14:17). By the words, "with us," Paul places himself as among those who will receive the same reward from God for suffering for Christ's sake (Col 1:24). By identifying with his readers Paul places their persecution in the larger context of a biblical, apocalyptic world view where the struggle for the truth of the gospel involves a struggle against the "forces of unbelief arrayed against it."[14]

Judgment on Universalists at the Second Advent of Christ

There is a clear implication here. *Believers who resist the heresy of universalism will be recompensed, rewarded, in the future day of Christ's return. The universalists themselves will receive deserved retribution for they know not God and do not obey the gospel (v. 8).*

The retribution and recompense occur when Jesus Christ is revealed at his second coming. Christ is currently hidden in heaven (cf. Col 3:1–4). Those who persecute believers are willfully ignorant of Christ's return and the impending judgment awaiting them (vv. 9–10); and the situations will be reversed. This promise of recompense is very similar to the promises made to the sheep in the parable of the sheep and the goats (see chap. 12 discussed above).

The participation of angels in the coming of Christ is a Jewish image intended to "heighten the drama and importance" of the event at the end of the age (cf. Mark 13:26–27; 1 Thess 3:13; Ps 68:18; Zech 14:5).[15] We saw angels identified in the parables of the rich man and Lazarus and of the sheep and the goats discussed in the pages above. They also appear in the parable of the tares as the harvesters at the end of the age (Matt 13:24–30, 36–43). The words at the end of the verse are best translated as the "angels of his power" rather than "his powerful angels" or "angels who exercise his power" to emphasize the character of the coming Christ rather than the nature of the angels.[16]

The next verse further describes Christ's coming. He will come "in flaming fire, meting out punishment on those who do not know God and do not obey the gospel of our Lord Jesus" (2 Thess 1:8; New English Translation). Clearly this verse paraphrases Isaiah 66:15–16: "See, the LORD is

---

14. Ibid., 225.

15. Ibid., 226.

16. Ibid. Thus it is a genitive of possession rather than a descriptive genitive, genitive of quality, or objective genitive.

coming with fire, and his chariots are like a whirlwind; he will bring down his anger with fury, and his rebuke with flames of fire. (16) For with fire and with his sword the LORD will execute judgment upon all men and many will be those slain by the LORD" (vv. 15–16). Indeed, in light of Psalm 104:4, the "flames of fire" may well be angels. It reads: "He makes winds his messengers, flames of fire his servants."

This reference to angels is supported by Hebrews 1:7 which follows the Greek Septuagint of Psalm 104:4. It renders this text: "He makes his angels winds, his servants flames of fire."

The word "punishment" is better rendered as "retributory punishment or vengeance," in light of the context. In Romans 12:19 Paul uses the same term twice with the sense of vengeance: "Do not take revenge, my friends, but leave room for God's wrath; for it is written: 'It is mine to avenge; I will repay,' says the Lord."

In addition to the immediate persecutors of the believers, others who do not know God nor obey the gospel will be subject to the same vengeance at the day of judgment. These words are probably not a reference to distinguish Gentiles from Jews but the clauses are synonymously parallel (which parallelism also occurs in v. 9). It is similar to hendiadys, where two words or clauses are meant to say the same thing (cf. 1 John 4:16: "know" and "believe" are one and the same thing). Those who do not know God are the same as those who do not obey the gospel.

There is a serious implication here for those who wish to redefine the gospel and yet maintain that they know God. Whether it be those in the emergent church or universalists, those who attempt such redefinition end up outside a genuine experience of God. While they seek to distance themselves from evangelicals (as the fiction writers McLaren and Young, who is also a nonfiction writer, seek to do), they find themselves excluded also from the presence of the Lord, as verse 9 makes clear.

I deal with further claims of universalism in the pages below where I discuss the special contributions of the Book of Hebrews and the Revelation.

A Survey of Convincing Texts from the Apostle Paul in Romans

In Paul's Epistle to the Romans, we have some of the strongest statements that seemingly support universalism, and some of the strongest statements against universalism. I will endeavor to address every one of them.

(a) Romans 2. The texts 2:1–16 and 3:19 teach that there is a final day of judgment coming which will settle the destinies of all people. It is a day of wrath and anger (vv. 5–6) for those who do not do the truth (vv. 8–9), who will perish (v. 12); but for the righteous, who persevere in good works, there is eternal life (v. 7).

(b) Roman 5. As shown above, universalists often cite verse 18 with its emphasis on "all." The Apostle contrasts how condemnation came to all by the trespass of one (Adam) with how justification to life came to all by the righteous act of one (Christ). Yet the surrounding verses more frequently state the comparison in the terminology of "many." In verse 17 Paul makes it clear that, as "death reigned by the one trespass of the one man," the contrast is with "those who *receive* the abundance of the grace and the gift of righteousness shall reign in life through the one, Jesus Christ." Here the "all" and the "many" in the context are defined as "those who receive." The contrasts of being in Adam and being in Christ are not equal: all humanity has corporate identity in Adam by choosing to sin in him and this is confirmed by committing daily sin in our experience. But all humanity is not corporately identified in Christ; only Christians are so identified. This is witnessed by the many exhortations to believe in order to be in Christ.

(c) Romans 8. The passage listing the five traits of believers in verses 28–30 all go together. God foreknew them (God enters into a loving relationship with them), predestined, called, justified, and glorified them. The chain is complete from beginning to end. There is no allowance for some falling out of the chain, or for some being later added. It is impossible that the text would allow all humanity to be included since Paul repeatedly makes a distinction between the elect and the non-elect (see texts below). This text teaches the sovereignty of God (cf. 9:1–29); the other side, human responsibility, is reflected in 8:4, 13; 9:30—10:21; 11:20–22.

(d) Romans 9. This passage which teaches so strongly the aspect of divine sovereignty implicitly argues against universalism. Verse 12 makes it clear that "the purpose of God according to election" or "by means of election" abides or remains, "not because of works but because of the one who calls."

This concept of election cannot be the basis for a charge that God is "unjust," Paul says (v. 14; cf. the charge of universalism), for God shows mercy and compassion to whom he wishes (v. 15). As God he is completely sovereign. So then "this compassion does not belong to the one who has an inner desire nor to the one who does outer works but to God who shows mercy" (v. 16). The example of Pharaoh shows, "therefore, that to whom God wishes to show mercy he shows mercy, and whom he wishes to harden, he hardens" (v. 18). *Thus universalism cannot affirm that the fires of hell will move people to repent and believe, for it is not within their power to do so since they are not part of his elect.* It is God who gives faith as a gift. It is God who circumcises hearts, in the circumcision of Christ, who buries believers, who raises them, who makes them alive with Christ (Col 2:11–13).

There is another point to make regarding Pharaoh. The greater affliction from God that he experienced, the more revelation he received regarding God's will, the more power from God that he experienced, the more hardened he became. He is a type of all the wicked who become even more wicked when confronted with the revelation of the truth, whether this side of hell or after. *Why and how are we to believe that entering hell will make the wicked respond differently?*

(e) Romans 10. This chapter strongly emphasizes human responsibility to believe the gospel and receive Christ (vv. 8–13). In verses 14–21 Paul sets forth four steps or conditions that must take place in the chain of faith: there must be one who sends the preacher; there must be the preacher who proclaims good news; there must be the hearing of the gospel; and there must be faith that results in calling upon God (vv. 14–15). These four steps are always operative for everyone who becomes a Christian. *If universalism teaches that those in hell will repent and believe the gospel, who will be there to preach it? For no believer will go to hell to begin the chain of steps that lead to faith. Also, since the Bible never says that God will send a preacher to hell who will send one?*

In Israel's case the Apostle says that the problem came with the fourth step: God sent the preacher of good news and Israel heard (completing three of the four steps). Yet she did not believe and call on the Lord. So God cannot be faulted. How did Israel hear? The gospel is similar to general revelation (v. 19; Paul cites Ps 19:4 where general revelation is the topic), for all to observe and respond to. All have heard in the sense that the mission to the Gentiles was designed to provoke the Jews to jealousy (v. 19; Paul cites Deut 32:21). Yet only the Gentiles, who really didn't seek God, responded to the proclaimed word in faith, along with a remnant of Jews (vv. 20–21).

The Challenge of Romans 10–11 for Universalism

What does all this have to do with universalism? There are several points. On the basis of the analogy with Israel, all humanity has heard the good news and is held responsible for believing (cf. Col 1:5–6). It cannot be said that some have never heard, and that in hell they will hear and respond. Universalism assumes, apparently, that the knowledge about the gospel will accompany or follow people to hell so that a preacher is not needed. But if this is so, this saving knowledge makes all those in hell culpable, as those who heard and did not believe. None can say that he/she did not have adequate knowledge to believe.

(f) In the powerful chapter of Romans 11, Paul explains the basis for the future restoration of Israel. Israel's present state is one of rejection: as natural branches she has been broken off from the cultivated olive tree. Yet this condition is only partial and temporary. Paul himself is an example and proof that there is a remnant that has believed. According to the special revelation given to Paul (the "mystery," v. 25), there is a time coming after the ingathering of the Gentiles, when Israel's "fullness" is realized, when "all Israel is to be saved" (v. 26). Applying this to universalism, (1) how can there be an additional ingathering of Gentiles out of hell, *when the earlier one is viewed as final and complete*? (2) How can there be additional Jews saved out of hell, when their "fullness" takes place at the end of this age? *How can a completeness be made more complete?*

Further, verse 29 powerfully affirms that the "gifts and calling of God are irrevocable." *If the elect are determined for this era, and this decision is irrevocable, how can this decision be later recanted, changed, or annulled, so as to include all?*

Yet Romans 11 contains one of the strongest texts attractive to universalism. It is the verse that Origen cited to justify universalism. "For God has consigned all to disobedience so that he may show mercy to all" (11:32). Yet in light of the context the second "all" cannot be everyone, including the wicked in hell, but must be interpreted to mean all who believe, whether Jews or Gentiles. To find universalism here contradicts the particularity that Paul has defended throughout much of Romans: it is only by faith that one is justified and discovered among the elect remnant (rather than the nonelect; see 9:20–29). In addition, Paul never hints anywhere that the mercy of God is experienced by any after death. The whole book deals with what people do with the knowledge of God before they die (cf. Rom.1:18–32). Another way to take the second part of the verse is to affirm that God's mercy has been shown to all in the sense of providing Christ as an atonement for all, offering salvation to all (note the context which refers to God's offer of salvation to the Gentiles), but only those who accept the offer of salvation will experience it (cf. vv. 7–10, 21–22).[17]

These texts are difficult to understand, for they ultimately concern divine sovereignty and human responsibility. These appear to be irreconcilable with our limited understanding of the ways of God. They are not reconciled in Scripture and we should not attempt to reconcile them, I believe. Instead, we bow, as Paul did, before the greatness of our God, whose judgments

---

17. See Erickson, *Theology*, 1032.

are unsearchable and whose ways are inscrutable. He is the source of all, the means of all, and the goal of all. To him alone is all glory forever due (11:33–36).

Other Pauline Texts

Colossians 1:19–23. This is one of the few passages that affirms that "all" in the universe have been "reconciled" to God. It is difficult for the traditional view and seems to support the "universalism view." In light of the fact that Paul uses "all" eight times in vv. 15–20, and that it consistently refers to the entire universe, "all" has to mean the entire universe throughout, including humanity, the inanimate creation, and Satan and fallen angels (note v. 16). So how can the traditional, evangelical view respond? From Romans 8 it is clear that only the inanimate creation is awaiting deliverance from its unwilling subjection to bondage (Satan and his angels are excluded, since they willingly revolted against God and did so prior to humanity's fall). Only this part of creation can be rescued by Christ's death for sin. It did not exercise a will to join in the rebellion of Adam and Eve, and it did not have the will to exercise in order to believe the gospel. Therefore, the promise that God was pleased through Christ "to reconcile all [things] to himself by making peace through the blood of his cross—whether things on the earth or things in heaven" (v. 20) cannot refer to the salvation of wicked angels (note my discussion above and below, from the Book of Hebrews regarding the impossibility of saving fallen angels on the basis of Christ's atoning death for human sin). "Reconciliation" has a saving connotation for fallen humanity and for fallen inanimate creation, but not for fallen angels and Satan. Furthermore, the text cannot be affirming that all of fallen humanity are reconciled to God. Otherwise, why would anyone have to go to hell first? Also, the very next verses affirm that the Colossians were once not reconciled, even though Christ had already died for them (hence the "reconciliation" of v. 20 did not include them). Yet now they are reconciled by Christ's death because they believe, and continue in faith (as vv. 21–23 affirm; see also vv. 4–5). Thus it seems that the "reconciliation" of verse 20 is not salvific, not saving, but refers to subjection and pacification brought about by a triumphant conquest. The apostle does not say that "all" have been forgiven and redeemed but only that the readers have been (cf. 2:11–14). The reconciliation of verse 20 is potentially salvific and redemptive, but such is only realized by those who willingly believe the gospel. God is not reconciled to anyone who has not believed.[18]

18. Contrary to the tenor of McLaren, and directly opposite to what Young has

Christ's triumph or conquest is what Colossians 2:15 affirms. The verse reinforces the kind of reconciliation intended in 1:19–20. Christ (or, God) has "disarmed the rulers and authorities and made a public disgrace of them, triumphing over them by the cross." This is not a salvific triumph, not one that is willingly embraced and that brings salvation and freedom from bondage, but like a military conquest it is one from which none ever escapes. This hardly pictures the freedom from the bondage of sin that accompanies the gospel when it is willingly believed and embraced.

The preceding is also the explanation for the somewhat parallel text in Philippians 2:9–11: "As a result God exalted him, and gave him the name that is above every name, so that at the name of Jesus every knee should bow—in heaven and on earth and under the earth, and every tongue confess to the glory of God the Father that Jesus Christ is Lord." In citing (or, alluding to) Isaiah 45:23, Paul is affirming that all the universe will come to acknowledge the supremacy, the triumph of Christ. Again this does not require a saving relationship. By his death Jesus consigns all to his wrathful day of judgment and vindicates his victory on the cross.

The context makes it clear that this victory had to be applied by the Philippians so as to save them. Christ's triumph did not make them Christians. They are to work out their salvation with fear and reverence (v. 12). They had to appropriate Christ personally by faith (1:29; cf. Rom 11:20–22) and contend for the faith (1:27).

In the related passage of 2 Corinthians 5:16–21 similar observations can be made. The text says: "All this is from God, who reconciled us to himself through Christ and gave us the ministry of reconciliation: that God was reconciling the world to himself in Christ, not counting men's sins against them. And he has committed to us the message of reconciliation" (vv. 18–19). The Corinthians were not reconciled until they heard the gospel and believed it. They were not earlier reconciled by the mere fact of Jesus' historical death about twenty-five years before. Hence Paul refers to his ministry as that of calling people "to be reconciled" to God (v. 20); his ministry is not to announce an accomplished reconciliation.[19] Several times in the context Paul acknowledges their coming to faith: (4:13–14: "It is written: 'I believed; therefore, I have spoken.' With that same spirit of faith we also believe and therefore speak"). Others are "unbelievers" whose "minds have been blinded" by Satan, the god of this world (v. 4).[20]

God say on p. 192 of *The Shack*.

19. Again, this is contrary to Young, *Lies*, 117–9, that the gospel, the "good news," is to announce to everyone that he/she is already saved, whether anyone believes this or not. Bell, *Love Wins*, 157, also asserts this.

20. Young rejects using the categories of "believer" and "unbeliever" (*Lies*, 57, 118).

The Book of Hebrews

The author of Hebrews gives a powerful witness to the eternal suffering of the lost. The author quotes or alludes to Psalm 110:1 five times (1:3, 13; 8:1; 10:12–13; 12:1–2). This OT text is the most frequently cited one in the NT. Psalm 110:1 is also cited in 1 Corinthians 15:27. The text clearly affirms that Christ's present position is on a throne at the right hand of God in heaven. He is waiting till the Psalm's promise is completed (note 10:13): "until his enemies be made the footstool of his feet." Thus the final picture of the triumphant Son is not that of the salvific, the saving reconciliation of all to him, so that there is only one group of saints or beings surrounding him in adoration and worship in heaven. Rather the final picture in these texts concerns that time, future to us, when all his "enemies" become totally subjected to him—they become a place for his feet to rest. The enemies are pacified by conquest. The contexts (esp. in 1 Cor 15) picture this as the final disposition of all things, so that when the Son yields all to the Father the subjected are still subjected or conquered—not saved (1 Cor 15:28). This hardly pictures adoration and salvation. *If universalism is correct, who will serve as the footstool of his throne?* While this is highly symbolic language, the meaning is clear. This interpretation agrees with that of other texts (Eph 4, Phil 2, and Col 1:19–20), as discussed above.

Israel's experience in the wilderness during the Exodus sets forth a pattern of God's dealing with people who disobey him. The event strongly argues against universalism. Israel's experience is set forth as a pattern that Christians should heed lest they fail to enter God's rest (Heb 3:14—4:13). According to Numbers 13 and 14 the Israelites refused to go into Canaan to possess the land promised to them because they disbelieved God. They heeded the majority "bad" report of the spies and rejected the minority "good" report from Caleb and Joshua. Consequently God doomed that generation to forty years of wandering till they all died in the wilderness. It is instructive to note the following. (a) Even after they repented and God forgave them (14:20–30), they could not alter their destiny. (b) One could claim that the judgment was disproportionate, for they spent one year in the desert for only a single day of testing God (14:34–35). (c) Even after they showed the sincerity of their repentance (they had confessed their sin, 14:40) by trying to go into Canaan (seemingly in obedience to God), the Lord was not with them and they were defeated (14:43–45). So they never entered rest (cf. Ps 95). The points against universalism are obvious. *Unbelief dooms one to a destiny, seemingly disproportionate (from our limited understanding) to the sin, which is unchangeable even with repentance and accompanying good efforts.* Apparently the repentance here is not genuine. This passage is similar to the parable of the ten virgins at the point where entrance to blessing is barred because of lack of proper preparation and obedience.

The Warning Passages in Hebrews

The warning passages of Hebrews are particularly pertinent to the question of the nature of God and the destiny of unbelievers (note 2:1–4; 3:7—4:13; 5:11—6:12; 10:26–39; and 12:25–29). Note in the third text that it is "impossible to renew to repentance those who fall away because they continually crucify the Son of God anew against themselves and make an open shame of him" (6:3, 6). The fourth passage warns that there remains no sacrifice for sin if people sin "willfully after receiving knowledge of the truth" (10:26); there is only a "fearful expectation of judgment and a fiery zeal that will consume those who oppose" (v. 27); they will be worthy of "more severe judgment" than those under the Mosaic covenant (v. 29). God is a God of vengeance who will repay (v. 30; cf. Deut 32:35–36). "It is a fearful thing to fall into the hands of the living God" (v. 31). The fifth passage warns that God is a "devouring fire" (12:29; cf. Deut 4:24; 9:3; Isa 33:14). All these passages have an air of finality and severe judgment.

The passage most in opposition to universal reconciliation is the third: "it is impossible to renew some to repentance" (6:3). *Apparently what is impossible for God to do, the proponents of universalism are able to do. This is an instance where the faulty logic of some leads them to assert that human beings are more compassionate than God!*

The Book of Revelation

The Book of Revelation also suggests a pattern for understanding how suffering and torment affect the wicked. Universalism asserts that the "fire of judgment" leads the wicked in hell (or the lake of fire) to repentance and faith, and hence acceptance into heaven. Yet the response of the wicked on this side of eternity, as a result of the series of the seal, trumpet, and vial judgments, does not lead to repentance. Instead, in response to the seal judgments, the wicked cry out for death to take them and they wish to hide from the wrath of God (6:16–17). After the trumpet judgments people "do not repent" of their evil deeds but persist in them—in idolatry, murders, magic, sexual immorality, and stealing (9:20–21). During the last, harsh, series of judgments, the bowl or vial judgments, the wicked "blaspheme God over these plagues and they would not repent and give him glory" (16:9; so also v. 11, and 21). The judgments are worse than any before, but the refusal to repent is even more entrenched and mentioned more frequently than ever.

Does this not suggest that the wicked are placed in a frame of thinking and doing which becomes more and more hardened age after age after age after age, etc.? Does this not support the principle: for those who begin to reject God while enduring suffering for their rejection only continue to reject God under additional suffering?

When the Scripture unfolds the final destiny of the bride as occupying the new Jerusalem and the new heavens and new earth (Rev 21:1—22:15), the final view that is given of the wicked is that they are "outside" the city into which the righteous "enter" (22:14-15). There seems to be no basis for a change in the position of either group.

Finally, the Book of Revelation gives us not only a glimpse of the final state of both the righteous and the wicked but perhaps indicates why the wicked are where they are. While the saints are in bliss enjoying the heavenly city (Rev 21:22—22:5) because they are cleansed (22:14), the wicked are outside the city still practicing their evil deeds (22:15; note that present tenses are used). *The text affirms that people continue to live, even after death, as they did before death.* Those who do wrong and are vile continue as such; those who do right and are holy continue on as such (22:11). This is the Bible's way of saying that all are confirmed in their choice! This context forbids the idea that some outside the city will be able to go into it through the open gates (21:25; 22:11, 14) as I noted in pages above.

Chapter 14

Sixteen Questions That Expose Universalism's False Beliefs about Hell

1. IF IN HELL Satan and his angels are "saved' or "reconciled" to God, as universalism asserts, what kind of reconciliation is this? People are reconciled on the basis of faith and trusting Christ for the forgiveness of sins, because he was made the "atoning sacrifice" ("propitiation") for sins, but never is this "atoning sacrifice" said to be for angels, nor is it offered to them. Jesus Christ became a human being, to atone for human sins; he did not take on the nature of angels to atone for their sins. How then could angels and Satan ever be reconciled to God? On what basis could they be? The Bible makes this very clear when it says that Jesus did not come "to help" (or, "show concern for") angels but came "to help" ("show concern for") the descendants of Abraham (so Heb 2:16 declares). The whole text of Hebrews 2:14–18 is worth considering as a rebuttal against universalism, emphasizing Jesus' incarnation and being tempted on behalf of human beings.

2. If Satan and fallen angels are to be reconciled to God, on what basis will this take place? What is the nature of their sin and how can it be removed? They are not of the present creation in bondage due to the fall of humanity in Adam (see Rom 8), since they fell before Adam's sin. Hence their restoration cannot be by the death of Jesus Christ, who came as God incarnate to die as a human being for the sin of Adam's race during the era of humanity.

3. If some other basis can be found for reconciling Satan and fallen angels, why cannot that basis work also for humans? This again suggests that within universalist teaching the coming and death of Jesus was not truly necessary after all. It becomes a divine feint.

4. How is it that people in hell will suddenly be able to "understand spiritual things" when natural people cannot understand them in this life (1 Cor 2:14)? How can they discern truth from falsehood when Satan the great deceiver will have a "free hand" in hell and be unrestrained by good, by the gospel, and by the Spirit (as 2 Thess 2 describes such constraint)? Sin is restrained now until the restrainer be removed, and then evil erupts on a greater scale than ever before. How can there be understanding in hell where there is no restraint to enable people to be able to resist the enormity of evil and repent?

5. Will not Satan, who blinds the minds of unbelievers now "so that they cannot see the light of the glorious gospel of Christ," so that "the gospel is veiled to those who are perishing" (2 Cor 4:4, 3), continue to do such blinding? What will hinder him from acting true to character in the lake of fire? Will those who are now "sons of Satan" (to use Jesus' words, John 8:44) suddenly change to become God's sons? Is it not necessary for Satan to be converted first for all of this to happen? Yet point 1. above places Satan outside the realm of the reconciled.

6. Is the faith of demons who "believe" now, yet "tremble" (Jam 2:19), saving faith? Obviously, it is not, for the Scripture neither says that the demons have saving faith, nor does it teach us anywhere to believe that they can be saved. If their kind of belief does not save now, how will it save in the future?

7. How can those in the lake of fire exercise faith when "faith is being sure of what we hope for, being convinced of what we do not see" (Heb 11:1)? That is, it seems that there is no longer the need for faith in the lake of fire, for hope has given place to reality (cf. Rom 8:24–25). Is this why universal reconciliation asserts that unbelievers in hell "will be saved by sight"?

8. When Paul speaks of the whole creation being reconciled does he not explicitly define this as all non-human creation, since it was subjected to frustration or bondage because of human sin (Rom 8:19–22)? He does not speak of the wicked or of angelic beings. At the return of Christ the creation is restored along with believing humans. There is no support for rational beings to be saved.

9. How can there be "restorative" or "remedial" punishment that leads to salvation? The purpose of pain or suffering seems to contradict universalism. Universalism argues that the torments of hell are meant to be "purifying" and "corrective," to cleanse people of their rebellion against God and to surrender to him to make them acceptable to heaven. The more the suffering the more certain is the repentance of even the most hardened sinners or fallen angels. Yet suffering in Scripture does not appear to have this purpose: to coerce people to put faith in God. Rather, suffering is intended to refine

believers, to act as discipline to cause them to live holy lives, not to enter into faith in the first place. Suffering is confirmation that we are already sons of God (cf. Heb 12:4–11).

Why should God have to coerce people into believing when faith is God's gift given to the elect (note the text below from Rom 10) and arises out of his love? Would not the unbelievers, when subjected to pain and suffering, simply blame God and rebel all the more, as they do now? The New Testament writers begin with faith, which when tested, leads to endurance and hope. They do not start with other things, such as trials or sufferings, that lead to faith (cf. James 1:2–4; 2 Pet 1:5–8; Rom 5:1–5; etc.). In Romans 10 the progression is not from suffering to faith but from God sending a preacher so that people can respond when they hear. This pattern cannot take place in hell. Universalism distorts the meaning of suffering and its relationship to saving faith.

10. If the suffering of pain and torment in hell becomes the catalyst for faith, isn't there the danger that suffering becomes the means of salvation, so that salvation comes about by works rather than by faith? This is theologically impossible and contradicts how people are saved before dying, that is, by faith (Eph 2:8–9). Does this process not result in there being two ways by which people are saved? Does this not mean that forgiveness and mercy and grace are all destroyed, since the sinner in hell suffers for himself and removes his own sins and their consequences by his own sorrows?[1]

11. If the suffering of pain and torment in hell constrains the wicked to repent and believe, does this not amount to divine coercion? Does not universalism become more constraining and determinative than the determination for which Calvinism is often faulted? Where in universalism is "free will to choose" or personal responsibility? The rejection of torture by universalism actually invents its own torture: suffering is used by God to bring repentance. Universalists are not ignorant of this significant distortion.[2]

12. It is claimed that it is unjust for God to leave the wicked in hell suffering punishment forever when they committed unbelief only during a human lifetime. Yet such punishment is not unjust if the unbelief and rejection continue for eternity. Indeed, with each passing moment, the judgment becomes more just because each passing moment is lived with the

---

1. This thought parallels that of Campbell and Skinner, *Discussions*, 429. See the rest of Campbell's helpful insights.

2. McLaren, *Last Word*, 187, cites Jonathan Kvanvig, *Hell*, as criticizing universalism for denying free will, for "all are forced into heaven." Kvanvig does not hold the conventional view.

consciousness of greater revelation regarding the wages or consequences of sin. The unrighteous are in a state of active rebellion.[3]

Similarly, from the opposite spectrum of eternity, it may well be asked if it is just for God to reward the faithful with an eternity of bliss for making a momentary decision to believe in Christ? The only reason that this is just, in both cases, is because of the saving work that God did in Christ. It cost God so much. He gave himself in Christ, his unique Son, to reconcile the world to himself; and this purpose is accomplished for the "world" that will believe and receive Christ. To reject the salvation offered in Christ is the crime beyond all crimes. The two thieves crucified with Christ represent the two responses to Christ and the consequences for the choices made. Jesus promised life in paradise only to the thief who acknowledged his sin.

One other thing should be said, as it has often been said before. Sinning against an infinite God has infinite consequences.[4]

13. Isn't the way that universalism deals with everlasting suffering—that the ungodly escape it—a poor alternative? Justice is not really served. There are other options besides universalism that meet the concerns about suffering everlasting torment. Another option is annihilationism or conditional annihilationism that asserts that the wicked are "consumed in the lake of fire." They cease to exist, either immediately upon death or after degrees of judgments appropriate to the works that all those outside of Christ have done (based in the just-ness of God: Gen 18:25; Rom 2).[5]

I suggest another option. Both annihilationism (in another form) and conscious existence are true. The wicked remain connected with the reality of this world and era alone; they do not enter the new reality of the world of bliss (the new heavens and new earth). From the standpoint of the former reality they continue to exist; but from the standpoint of the latter reality they "cease to exist"—they are forgotten. They are left behind in time, as it were, in a state of reality that cannot exist in the new reality. Time, if it exists at all, exists differently in the new era (see Rev 21:23; 22:5: God, not the sun,

---

3. Jewett, "Eschatology," 355. He adds that they in effect say, "Better to serve Satan than God, even if it be in hell," just as Satan has said, "Better to reign in hell than serve in heaven." The character that a person chooses in this life is "irrevocably confirmed in the life to come" (355).

Also, Powell, "Hell," 954, adds that the "punishment must continue as long as the sinful condition requiring it continues." It cannot come to an end until "guilt and sin come to an end." By rejecting Christ the person "has committed an eternal sin which deserves eternal punishment." It isn't the length of time that the sin consumes that matters but the kind, the severity of the sin.

4. Note the additional response to this issue that Shedd gives in the excursus after the Conclusion.

5. For a treatment of the four major views of hell, see Crockett, *Hell*.

is the light of the heavenly dwelling place). The present state of humanity is like being in the womb before birth. After birth this stage is virtually not remembered in light of the new reality of living. So it is with the future state of humanity. The new heavens and new earth will be so "real" that the present reality will seem unreal, and in a sense, is.

In this way those who reject God and his forgiveness do not hold God or the saints hostage to them in their suffering, as though the existence of evil is a constant reminder and remains unresolved. It is simply not part of a new, better reality.[6]

Another helpful (but not wholly satisfying) option is to affirm the possibility that in the end the number of those in paradise will be far greater than the number in hell. This is possible if those in paradise include all those children who die in the womb (perhaps as many as 40% of all conceptions become miscarriages), those who die before the age of accountability, all the infirm or mentally challenged, and those who respond by faith in the true God on the basis of general revelation.[7]

There is another phenomenon regarding statistics. It is said that today there are living on the earth a number (six billion plus) that is about the same number that have ever lived since the beginning of mankind until now. And statistics show that about 2.7 billion are Christians today. This means that about half of the world's people are Christians, and suggests that perhaps half of those living until now were Christians. If we couple this statistic with the observation just above, that all children who die in the womb or die before the age of accountability, and all mentally challenged or undeveloped adults also go to heaven, then probably well over 50% of the world's population, now and in the past, will or have gone to heaven. It may be well over 70%. While this means that there is still a large number who go to an eternity separated from God, it is not the proportion ("the vast majority") that universal reconciliation makes it to be.

14. Since Satan is the great deceiver, what will restrain him in hell from continuing his deceit? If even the faintest whisper of the gospel be heard, if even the smallest sliver of truth should break out, he will certainly block it, corrupt it, distort it, destroy it, so that no particle of truth will be tolerated

---

6. Wright, *Evil*, affirms the existence of people in hell, but they cannot exercise a veto over the enjoyment of heaven by the saints because Christ has triumphed over evil on the cross and God and his people have offered forgiveness to the rest, even though they reject it. By forgiveness, we are longer conditioned by the evil of others. Yet this approach cannot disallow the ultimate unity, either, by way of subjugation so that there is no longer any opposition to God's kingdom.

7. For further support for the greater number in heaven versus the number in hell see my paper: "The Sledgehammer of Universalism: Few will be in Heaven but Billions Will Be in Hell," at burningdowntheshackbook.com.

from which anyone could seize information regarding deliverance from sin and hell, and believe. How will his trait as the great deceiver be overcome? To suggest that perhaps he and his angels will be the first "to be reconciled" to God is an impossible idea. As the originator of sin in the universe, he has caused more havoc and evil than any human. Divine justice and his own extreme perversity by which he has deceived himself demand that he must suffer longer in hell and be the last to be reconciled. Is there anyone who would suggest that Satan should be reconciled before any human being? Yet if he is last then he is allowed to deceive all to prevent any from repenting. In this light it is impossible for any human to come to faith in hell.

15. If we should suppose that the devil (that is, Satan) does "repent" and has been received into heaven, what is to keep the devil from leading another rebellion against God and this time take a host of heaven's people and more angels with him? The universalist would say: "Well, the fallen angels once recovered will never fall again." But why should this be so? Evangelicals believe that the fallen angels cannot ever change their destiny of destruction, of hell. They made their choice, as did the "good angels," and this choice is irreversible. All humanity is relieved by this doctrine.

Universalism denies this doctrine. The fallen angels can (must) change and enter heaven. But this raises the horrible specter that, at some point in the future, they may rebel again. Universalism cannot deny this possibility by pleading some sort of doctrine that the fallen angels are confirmed in their choice (as evangelicals claim), because they deny this.

From the standpoint of universalism, the future for believers in heaven is scary and not at all safe and sure. What kind of heaven is this, when the potential of being with fallen-repentant angels who may rebel again is real? I dealt much further with this scenario in the excursus after chapter 5.

16. If universalism is true, why is there not a single, clear statement to the effect that all people in hell, after the judgment, will have the opportunity to put faith in Christ, be born again, and go to heaven?

The truth that does exist in universalism is that many people from every tribe and nation can and will be saved. But not all will be saved. It is not the case that the church does not wish to see that all are saved but that Scripture teaches that many will be lost.

In summary, the texts cited by universalists do not teach universal salvation but have other possible explanations.[8] They may refer to the following. (1) God's universal desire that none perish, not to a universal plan to save all. (2) God's universal purpose through the atonement to provide "the blessings of common grace to all." That is, all humanity without exception

---

8. Lewis and Demarest, "Spirit-Given Life," 489–90.

experience the providence of God, as the Bible teaches in many places (e.g., Matt 5:45; 6:25–33; Acts 17:24–28). (3) The universal sufficiency of Christ's atonement for all. (4) The universal pacification that disarms forces of evil but does not lead them to Christ (Col 2:15; Phil 2:9). (5) Christ's being the savior of the world, but this means only that Christ has provided sufficient salvation for the world. Its realization is limited to those who respond in repentance and faith.

Chapter 15

Eight Fatal Consequences Belonging to Universal Reconciliation and Summary of Nine Errors

THE FOLLOWING ARE THE fatal dangers that arise if one is going to embrace universalism. These consequences amount to a redefinition of the gospel taught by our Lord Jesus and his Apostles.

    1. In adopting universalism, one rejects the traditional view of the church through the ages, and embraces what the community of faith has identified as heresy (it is rejected by the Eastern, Roman, and Protestant churches).[1] Universalism has been close to Unitarianism in "sentiment and action." The Unitarians have become increasingly humanistic and reject the trinity and the deity of Christ. In 1825 they declared that they are not a part of the Christian church. In 1959 they voted to merge with the universalists.[2] The merger was accomplished in 1961. It is not surprising that Unitarians and universalists enjoy company, since they part company with the community of the faith over the destiny of the wicked. They end up disparaging the work of Christ. The more recent attempt to reform a Christian universalist denomination only reinforces the deliberate attempt to deceive the evangelical church.

    2. Universalism disparages the love of God by rejecting, in the end, the value of the greatest act of God's loving, namely the redemption secured by the sacrificial, substitutionary, atoning death of Jesus Christ. If in the end all people, and even Satan and his angels, are saved and enter heaven, what in the end is the value of Christ's death? His death cannot help fallen

---

1. Gerstner, "Universalism," 539.
2. Singer, "Unitarianism," 538.

angels and the devil. Upon serious reflection does it really matter that Jesus became incarnate and died if God is so loving that everyone without exception enters heaven? Does this view not subject God's justice and holiness to his love, as universalists claim, so that they are distorted? In neutralizing justice one also neutralizes, indeed extinguishes, grace.[3]

3. Ultimately the person of Jesus Christ is disparaged. His death and resurrection do not make a difference in the end. Yet he is worthy of all honor by all because of his death (Phil 2:11). The very text claimed as a basis for universalism, the reconciling of all to God, counts for nothing in the end, as far as exalting Jesus on a par with God the Father (giving him the name that is above every name—the name Yahweh). The history of universalism witnesses to this increasingly humanistic trend. Universalists tend to focus on God the Father to the blasphemous neglect of Jesus Christ—just as "Papa" (representing the Father), rather than Jesus, occupies center stage in Young's *The Shack*.

4. Evangelism is distorted. There is the real danger that the proclamation of the gospel will be considered less urgent because there is the ever-present option that people, all people, will ultimately be saved anyway. People are denied the knowledge that their rejection of Christ has everlasting consequences that cannot be altered after dying. The great commission is pointless; and the call to holiness is reduced in urgency as well.[4] The meaning of John 3:16 is abrogated. The promise that "whosoever believes in Christ might not *perish* but have everlasting life" is now understood in universalism to say that "perish" does not mean everlasting separation but that all will have a second chance after death and all will escape hell. *The verse now reads: "whosoever believes in Christ before or after death will not perish but have everlasting life."*

5. Universalism taints society's own sense of justice and retribution. Universalism teaches that even the most incorrigible of persons, the most leprous specimens of society (think here of Hitler, Pol Pot of Cambodia, Stalin, Mao Tse Tung, etc.), who have given themselves over to evil till the moment of death, still will be accepted one day into God's heaven. Does this not debase our human conception of fairness, of right and wrong—of justice?

6. If there is a legitimate place for the imprecatory Psalms of the OT, that implore God's judgment on his enemies, then it is possible to distinguish between the righteous and the wicked in this life and beyond. But

---

3. This idea is suggested by the evangelical Campbell in his dispute with Skinner, a leading universalist, in Campbell and Skinner, *Discussion*, 431.

4. See Keeley, *Christian Belief*.

universalism denies this. It maintains that all are God's people and he loves them equally. All are already reconciled to God.[5] Universalism extends this "equal love" to the devil and the fallen angels.

7. Promoters of universalism bear a special responsibility for promoting heresy. Writers of fiction (as McLaren and Young) are particularly clever to promote universalism to the unsuspecting who are caught up in the story. If tens of thousands, even millions, of people are reading their fiction books, and more recently the nonfiction of Bell and Young, should not the evangelical church warn the readers of the false doctrine that pervades them? Not since the time of the declaration of the universalist ministers of Boston in 1878, do these writers have the potential to do more to promote this heresy than any others in history.

8. Biblical interpretation, hermeneutics, is forever distorted if universalism is correct.[6] There is the repeated appeal to the argument of silence. There is a disavowal of half of the nature of God as wholly just so that the content of the Bible on this topic is ignored or deemed irrelevant. There is the "root fallacy" of insisting that a Greek word (*aiōn*) should have always and only the same interpretation in English. There is a rejection of the rule of interpreting by the wider context. There is rejection of interpreting according to the analogy of the faith—what the vast majority of Christians have always believed—what is in the Bible from cover to cover. There is the distortion of historical theology. There is failure to interact with strong proponents of contrary views. There is failure to consult the modern standard dictionaries and commentaries. There is rejection of the rule that one should generally go with the simplest interpretation. There is rejection of the principle that one should generally go with the interpretation on which there is general consensus.

If universalism is correct in its hermeneutics, the church will have to go back and argue over again all the decisions by the great councils of the church regarding the deity of Christ, his natures, and even the extent of the canon! Universalists, including Young and McLaren, are well informed advocates of universalism. Thereby they prove themselves unworthy interpreters of the Bible and teachers of falsehood and deceit. Their departure from the evangelical, apostolic faith proves that they are antichrists and deceivers (1 John 2:18–25; 4:1–6). *What they do is to rape biblical faith.*

---

5. See Young, *The Shack*, 155–64, 192; *Lies*, chapter 13.
6. See the hermeneutical principles that need to be observed, in Morey, *Faith*, 19-33.

SUMMARY OF THE NINE ERRORS OF UNIVERSAL RECONCILIATION

The claims of universalism rest on faulty bases. (1) There is no clear teaching in Scripture that affirms a "second chance" for people to alter their destinies after death, nor for the hearing of the gospel after death, nor for the exercise of faith in Christ after death, nor for repentance after death. Jesus himself is the strongest proponent (as in Luke 16; Matt 25) of eternal suffering in hell and thus the strongest opponent to universalism. The choice is to be either a disciple of Jesus Christ or of universalists. The choice is clear. (2) It is a falsehood that the church held universalism for the first five centuries. The earliest Apostolic Fathers do not support such a view. Instead, they affirm what the NT does: the wicked are lost in hell forever; they cannot change their destiny. (3) The only real basis of universalism is a distorted inference drawn from the love of God—distorted because, by its adherents' own assertion, God's justice must be subservient to God's love. The universalist ministers of Boston said that God's justice is "born of love and limited by love."[7] Yet the death of Christ was a satisfaction of both love and justice (Rom 5:6-11; 3:22-26), and neither can be limited by the other without losing its true value. Jesus Christ "loves righteousness" (Heb 1:9).

The summary of OT faith is found in Micah 6:8. God requires of his people that they "act justly, love mercy, and walk humbly with their God." It is not surprising that universalists never or rarely mention such verses!

Universalism asserts that the love of God could not allow people to go to everlasting judgment. But if this is so, why did not God's love constrain him at the beginning, to prevent the fall of humanity into sin and suffering and death and war and disease, etc., etc., over so many millennia? How could a loving God allow all of this?

(4) Universalism is the new face of the old opposition taken by the creature who defies the Creator, accusing him of injustice (Rom 9:14). *The devil is the mouthpiece of universalism.* When the latter asserts that there is not eternal death or judgment for the ungodly, they are saying as the serpent said to Eve: "You shall not surely die."

There are some things that God cannot do—to act contrary to his nature as God. If in the end even the devil and his angels are to be saved or reconciled into God's favor and heaven, what becomes of hell? Why did God

---

7. Note also the statements to the same effect, that God's justice is completely in service to his love, that the NT proclaims "nothing less than the total victory of his love," by Nels Ferre, *The Christian Understanding of God*, 228, 246-7, cited by Erickson, *Theology*, 1028-9. These statements bring the declaration of 1878 up to the current generation.

create Satan and allow him to fall, and bring such havoc into the world's history, if in the end even he is brought back? Why is there such an infinite cost requiring the death of the incarnate Son if in the end all reach heaven anyway?

(5) Universalism voids the accountability of every person to choose to accept forgiveness and reconciliation offered in Christ. *It withholds from multitudes the opportunity to be saved so that they perish in hell.*

(6) *Another thing that God cannot do is to void his will that people have a will to choose contrary to his will, to disbelieve.*

(7) Universalism minimizes the death of Christ. In the lengthy statement of the universalist ministers of Boston there is no mention of placing faith in Christ in order to be reconciled to God—not one word. Yet God has exalted Christ so as to make him worthy of the title of Yahweh (Phil 2:9). There is salvation in no other than in him alone (1 Tim 2:5; John 14:6). Even omnipotent love cannot transform the wicked into the righteous suitable for heaven, for the kind of righteousness required for heaven is only found by being justified by faith in Christ, a faith freely exercised without coercion or force by the fires of hell.

(7) Universalism is wrong in its doctrine about the fallen angels. They cannot ever be restored. The Bible offers no atonement, no forgiveness, no hope, no reconciliation for the fallen angels and for Satan. Jesus became human to save people; he did not become angelic to save angels (Heb 2:16). *He died to save people by becoming the God-man. He did not die to save angels by becoming the God-angel.* There is no Savior, no redeemer, no reconciler for them. They are lost forever.

And if the fallen angels are lost forever, then hell (or the lake of fire) is forever or everlasting. It is a place where lost humanity who join the devil's side will also go permanently. If hell is permanent for the devil and his angels (note that this is what Jesus asserted, Matt 25:41), it must be permanent for human beings who choose their side.

(8) Universalism fails to realize that "the fires of heaven . . . are hotter than the fires of hell" for those who have chosen to be God themselves.[8]

Universalism cannot draw back a step and say: "Let's make hell the permanent place only for the fallen angels, not for people." It cannot do this. For it argues that love limits God's justice, that love triumphs over justice. It argues that if there is permanency of separation for any creature then love has not won, then God has been defeated. According to universalism, it has to be the restoration of all creatures or it is the restoration of no creatures.

---

8. Willard, *Conspiracy*, 398.

Universalism is stuck in a position that ultimately drives its adherents into an impossible, because it is immoral and untruthful, position.

(9) Universalism's distortion of God's love bears its own demise. Such a concept holds God hostage to the enemies of Christ and the fallen angels and Satan. By this reckoning they win, not God.

Universalism Is Playing the Devil's Hand
De Young's Wager

The proponents of universalism are playing to the devil himself. Compare the differing consequences that attend the two options of evangelical faith or universalism. If evangelical faith is correct and preaches a place of everlasting separation from God, and many people respond and are saved, then they will go to heaven. The rest will go to hell and be lost everlastingly.

If evangelical faith is wrong and universalism is correct, and evangelical faith preaches the usual way, and people respond and are saved, then many will go to heaven. The rest will go to hell but later will repent and get to heaven anyway. No real harm is ultimately done.

If universalism is correct and preaches that there is a second chance after death, and many respond now, then many go to heaven, and others who go to hell now will later repent and get to heaven anyway.

But if universalism is wrong and preaches a second chance after death, and many respond now, then many go to heaven. But the rest will be given a false hope of a second chance and that false hope deceives them and leads them to neglect repentance now. This false hope dooms them forever. They will go to hell and never get to heaven. *Eternal harm is done.*

So which is the greater evil and which plays the devil's hand? Clearly, the greater consequence follows on the preaching of universalism if it is wrong in its doctrine than the consequence that follows on the preaching of evangelical faith if it is wrong in its doctrine. The devil would rather dupe people with the error of universalism (offering a false hope) than the error (so called by universalists) of evangelicalism.

The Greatest Sin

In his fiction, Young pervasively weaves his universalism into his story. He identifies independence from God as the evil of the Garden of Eden and the continuing greatest evil of fallen people. Yet by his and others' embracing universalism and rejecting the evangelical doctrines regarding the state of fallen man, by accepting the future reconciliation of the wicked in hell, by subverting justice to love, and by denigrating the institutional church they engage in their own independence from God. They embrace positions that find no clear support in Scripture and make them determinative for all that they think and do. They thereby subscribe to the very evil of independence they themselves condemn.

The Influence of Universalism

Both Young and McLaren have given personal testimony that universalism has made them more loving people and affects every area of their perspective, and much of their theology. From the foregoing it is clear that this impact on their theology is true. Not only are the cited doctrines affected—how people are saved, what the church is, how to preach and what the gospel to preach is, the meaning of the end times—but others are redefined. Universalism distorts who Christ is and what is the nature of his work (Christology), the nature of God (theology proper), the work of the Holy Spirit (pneumatology), the nature and destiny of angels (angelology), the nature of sin (hamartiology), the nature of Scripture (bibliology), and how Christians are to mature in their relationship with God (sanctification).

Virtually all of the areas of systematic theology and biblical theology are distorted by universalism. If one's view of God is distorted, then one's relationship with this God will be distorted.

Also the implications of the gospel are distorted by universalists. The latter, especially those converts from conventional evangelical proclamation, make much of the need to show greater social justice (note McLaren's remarks in the Introduction to this study). Yet true social concern proclaims the judgment of God. The words from Alexander Campbell are appropriate.[9]

> True benevolence . . . cries out, Danger! And would rather exaggerate than lessen its claims. There is not a spark of real philanthropy in the bosom of a thorough-going Universalist. Their philanthropy is spurious. Jesus the great philanthropist warned every sinner of "the worm that never dies," and of "the fire that shall never be quenched." His dogma was the *certainty* of future punishment: "*Unless you repent you shall all perish*" (italics his).

Some final quotes are pointedly pertinent, again (cited previously). C.S. Lewis remarked (in *The Great Divorce):* "There are only two kinds of

---

9. Campbell and Skinner, *Discussion*, 431.

people—those who say to God, 'Thy will be done,' and those to whom God says, in the end, 'thy will be done.' All that are in Hell choose it. Without that self-choice it wouldn't be Hell. No soul that seriously and constantly desires joy will ever miss it."[10]

Alister McGrath (*Justification by Faith*) has said: "Universalism perverts the love of God into an obscene scene of theological rape quite unworthy of the God whom we encounter in the face of Jesus Christ."[11] Indeed, the triune God has been violated.

---

10. From Keller, *Reason for God*, 79.
11. Ibid., 163.

Chapter 16

Universalism's Subversion of the Institutions of Society

IN ITS OPPOSITION TO the institutional church, and to institutions in general, universalism poses a grave threat to the future of society and civilization. Christian universalists have goals that parallel those of other forces seeking the destruction of culture, including terrorists and the LGBT forces. How can I say this? What's the connection? The whole connection goes to the very heart of what an institution is and why they are essential to the survival of a culture. In the next pages I wish to show why universalism is subversive to society's existence.

By its very definition, "universalism" reaches beyond any one way of salvation—the Bible's exclusive way. It wishes to include all in salvation, if not before death then also after death. Christian universalism simply argues that everyone everywhere must confess Christ in order to escape hell, sooner or later, in contrast to general universalism that teaches that there are many ways to God, to heaven, and Jesus is simply one of them.

What does this have to do with institutions? It is simply that separate individual churches that oppose universalism serve as an obstacle to the achievement of universalism. And the institution of the church in general is a similar obstacle to universalism. How is this?

We can learn how serious the challenge of universalism is to the church by considering the contemporary challenge to the institution of marriage. In a book about the institution of marriage, David Blankenhorn, along with others that he cites, gives a secular, yet compelling defense of marriage in opposition to those who would undermine marriage as an institution, namely the gay community and their forces seeking recognition of people of the same sex as having a marriage relationship. He points out that marriage is both a social institution and a personal choice. Why is this important?

What Blankenhorn says about marriage can also be said about government and the church, for they all are social institutions. What is a social institution? Blankenhorn defines it as a "relatively stable pattern of rules and structures intended to meet basic social needs."[1] He points out that an institution "is bigger than an organization or a process."[2] Thus social institutions create and maintain rules, including "rules for who is, and is not, a part of the institution."[3] In addition, social institutions create "authoritative public meaning." A "social institution builds and expresses shared agreements about what is important and what is to be valued."[4] Finally, and most importantly, "social institutions exist in order to solve basic problems and meet core needs."[5]

The parallels regarding universalism are several. It opposes the evangelical church, and all separate churches, because it wants to define itself so broadly that all could be attracted to it; and any who hold distinctive beliefs comprise an obstacle to the broad goal. Universalists, including Christian ones, don't submit to a creed. They don't want to be bound to a system of beliefs and practices—except the creed that that they don't have a creed! In *The Shack*, in *Lies We Believe about God*, and in *The Last Word and the Word After That*, the authors have a particular disdain for institutions—not only the church but also the government and, in Young's case, even the home and marriage.

What are the consequences? If universalism succeeds, there will be new rules, a new "authoritative public meaning," and new values. Basic problems and needs will go unresolved. In regard to marriage, the problem is to guide male and female behavior in sexual reproduction; and the need is for male and female to live together to successfully raise children. New values—actually a reversion to old ones—will be the consequences.

In a more particular case, Young in his novel opposes all institutions as power struggles for authority that destroy relationships. He prizes "pure relationships" with God and with people where there is no authority and no subordination. This description is parallel to the gay community's opposition to the institution of marriage—to make it a solely personal matter of relationships. Young unconsciously ends up arguing the same way that those

---

1. Blankenhorn, *Marriage*, 60.
2. Ibid.
3. Ibid., 61.
4. Ibid.
5. Ibid.

who practice a new kind of sexuality argue. In their aversion to institutions, universalists ally themselves with the most perverse opponents of marriage in the history of civilization.

Moreover, what will happen if Young's version of universalism is achieved? By opposing marriage and other institutions as institutions, he is changing the definition of them and they cease to exist. That's right. If marriage, government, and the church cease to be institutions, the result is that there is no marriage, no government, and no church. In their place come sexual promiscuity, anarchy, and irreligion and idolatry (theological promiscuity).

Instead of forecasting a brave new world of openness, freedom, and relationships centered around love, there will be enslavement, corruption, bondage, and the ensuing destruction of culture and civilization. It is not a better future; it is a reversion to what existed before 5000 years ago when people first began breaking from the mold of their long heritage to form social institutions.[6]

The biblical view is that God redefined the institutions of the cultures surrounding Israel, giving new rules and regulations for marriage, the state, and the church. With the coming of Jesus Christ these institutions received greater clarity and definition. Jesus spoke about each of these institutions in such a profound way that the church, his followers, has influenced marriage, the state, and the church around the world for two thousand years. In a sense it can be said that the Jews through Jesus bequeathed the heritage of its institutions to much of the rest of the world.

God has established or redefined all these institutions, and there is not a scintilla of evidence that the Jews or Christians sought to destroy any of these institutions. Indeed, all kinds of texts can be cited to show that Jesus and the Apostles call upon Christians to uphold these institutions, not oppose or destroy them. But universalists seek to destroy traditional institutions.

The Consequences of Destroying Institutions

The church, like government and marriage, involves both personal relationships and institutions.[7] To make any one of them a matter of personal defi-

---

6. Ibid., 57ff. Blankenhorn gives compelling evidence for the development of social institutions from the ancient Egyptians and Sumerians.

7. Blankenhorn, *Marriage*, 91, defines marriage thus: "marriage is socially approved sexual intercourse between a woman and a man, conceived both as a personal relationship and as an institution, primarily such that any children resulting from the

nition alone destroys the existence of marriage, government, and the church itself. It is not surprising that Young and other universalists oppose the rules and beliefs that churches embrace as detrimental to the achievement of their universal goals. Particular beliefs lead to particular creeds and churches, and to social ordering.

Blankenhorn cites others who give similar definitions that reinforce this understanding of institutions and their roles. North describes institutions as the humanly devised constraints that structure human interaction. They are made up of formal constraints (e.g., rules, laws, constitutions), informal constraints (e.g., norms of behavior, conventions, self-imposed codes of conduct), and their enforcement characteristics.[8]

For North institutions primarily concern what one *may not* do.

A.R. Radcliff-Brown defines social institutions as "the ordering by society of the interactions of persons in social relationships." The conduct of people is controlled by "norms, rules, or patterns." A person "knows that he is expected to behave according to these norms and that other persons should do the same."[9]

Social institutions carry public meaning. It is this that makes them objective and authoritative—and opposed by universalism. Without "specific rules and agreed-upon public purposes" the social institutions cease.[10]

Universalism becomes part of the general deinstitutionalization taking place in America today, including that of marriage. The three institutions go together, and all must change if universalism is to achieve its goal. For by denying a place to rules and beliefs in religion, the most important institution which defines all the others, I believe, there is no reason to hold on to rules and beliefs regarding marriage and government. It is religion or faith that provides the moral support to bring people into compliance with all the other institutions. It is not surprising that many universalists who argue for it as an option to believe and support also oppose nationalism and the institution of marriage. Young is quite explicit in his opposition to all institutions.

Yet, as with marriage, if these are only relationships to be defined privately, there is no need for these to exist. "The clear logic of deinstitutionalization is not transformation or even redefinition, but extinction."[11]

---

union are and understood by society to be—emotionally, morally, practically, and legally affiliated with both of the parents." He discusses at length each of the elements of this definition.

8. Ibid., 97.
9. Ibid.
10. Ibid., 98.
11. Ibid. While Blankenhorn uses these words to explain what happens when the

Thus in opposition to Young's and other universalists' assertions that rules and a creed of beliefs affirmed by institutions oppose freedom to be found in relationship are just the opposite of the truth. Ending rules and creeds will end the existence of the church, marriage, and government.

Young and other universalists oppose institutions, as though there are no benefits but only obstacles. But Blankenhorn describes the amazing benefits and pluses to institutions. He writes:

> A social institution is a pattern of rules and structures intended to meet basic social needs. Institutions are fundamental enablers of human sociality. They give humans the gift of knowing what to expect of others and what others expect of us. By reducing the burden of choice and permitting us to take some things for granted, institutions are essential pathways to higher and more complex forms of human creativity, deliberation, and cooperation. Finally, institutions guide behavior in specified pro-social directions. They wield authority in two ways. The first is when institutions provide meaning and aspiration that we experience as both natural and desirable. The second is when institutions pressure and coerce us.[12]

Institutions actually promote freedom for the common good, and hinder autocratic despotism within or without the church. Rules are beneficial, not harmful. Young and other universalists sound like spoiled children casting off the restraint that actually produces a greater good and freedom to do the good.

Young also describes what he calls a "circle of relationship" in which there is mutual parity among humans and the Trinity. There is no subordination of anyone to anyone else; otherwise relationship would cease, he maintains (in *The Shack*, 122–4; *Lies*, chaps. 4, 7, 9).

But is this the case? Interestingly, Blankenhorn takes up the issue of a "pure relationship." He finds fault with the idea that a "pure relationship" without the institution is to be preferred. He writes, in part quoting Anthony Giddens, as follows:

> A pure relationship is just us, for us, made by us, and without the encumbrances of socially defined meanings, forms, and purposes. A pure relationship, says Giddens, "is one in which external criteria have become dissolved." It is "entered into for its own sake, for what can be derived by each person from a sustained association with the other." Its central motif is the search

---

institution of marriage is opposed, they are appropriate to all social institutions.

12. Ibid., 168.

for emotional intimacy." Two of its primary traits are instability and impermanence: "It is a feature of the pure relationship that it can be terminated, more or less at will, by either party at any particular point." Giddens reports, not surprisingly, that enshrining the pure relationship as our primary model of intimacy not only seriously undermines marriage as an institution, but also is likely to prove "a subversive influence on modern institutions as a whole."[13]

Giddens foresees the far reaching effects of opposing the institution of marriage on other institutions. But I think the priority lies with the church. Universalists, in refusing to be bound by rules, creeds, and institutions, embrace a similar scenario for their relationship with God as Giddens has traced it for marriage. I maintain that undermining the institution of the church, which sanctions government and marriage, will have even more severe consequences for society. I would argue that the very undermining of the institution of marriage presently going on by the gay community and the government is a result of the undermining and compromise of the church that preceded it. After all, it is the church that defines what is moral and sin, and homosexual behavior is condemned in Scripture. Yet many churches are embracing certain forms of same-sex behavior. It is these churches that are to blame for the erosion of the institution of marriage.

Young and other universalists have a faulty view not only of relationships but of the role of social institutions in society. To make a mutual relationship with God in a "circle of relationships" the supreme value and goal is a distortion of truth and violates the Scripture with its recognition of the role of laws, rules, and regulations for the common good. *Universalists are the anarchists of our day in league with others including modern terrorists and LGBT forces.*[14] Universalists could learn much from social scientists. But then again universalists oppose institutions—including schools of higher learning—and the wisdom they could impart, and so they languish in self-deluded understanding of their own making! The Apostle Paul condemned such arrogance of human wisdom (see 1 Cor 1–2; Col 2:16–23).

By way of significance for contemporary America, the foregoing discussion allows this observation. In its attitude toward the three primary

---

13. Ibid., 168–9.

14. Young exhibits anarchist tendencies when he asserts that today evangelical "structures" (note the word in light of the above discussion) are crumbling and that he stands on the cusp of a "new reformation" (see Miller, "Controversial Book," last four sentences/paras).

institutions, universalism is anti-church, anti-marriage, and anti-American. In the euphoria often attending the emergent church and the novels and film of Paul Young, the celebrants are unwittingly contributing to the destruction of their culture and thus to the anarchy and bondage that most certainly will follow.

Biblical Warnings

The following texts from Proverbs are appropriate for the end of this Section. They deserve sober attention.

> "The path of the righteous is like the first gleam of dawn, shining ever brighter till the full light of day. But the way of the wicked is like deep darkness; they do not know what makes them stumble" (4:18-19).

> "The way of the LORD is a refuge for the righteous, but it is the ruin of those who do evil" (10:29).

> "Be sure of this: The wicked will not go unpunished, but those who are righteous will go free" (11:21).

> "In the way of righteousness there is life; along that path there is immortality" (12:28).

> "There is a way that seems right to a man, but in the end it leads to death" (14:12).

> "The LORD detests all the proud of heart. Be sure of this: They will not go unpunished" (16:5).

> "The Righteous One takes note of the house of the wicked and brings the wicked to ruin" (21:12).

> "He who pursues righteousness and love finds life, prosperity (or, righteousness) and honor" (21:21).

Conclusion

Responding to Universalism in Fiction, Nonfiction, and Film

UNIVERSALISM IN ALL ITS forms poses a serious challenge for the evangelical church today as it always has. Yet the current resurgence of universalism is probably the greatest in the history of the America church. What are the implications of the foregoing study?

There are several. First, we evangelicals need to resuscitate the preaching and teaching of hell and eternal punishment. Second, we need to warn about the pernicious evil of universalism in all its forms, including Christian universalism (so-called) or universal reconciliation. When such is incorporated in popular fiction and film or popular church movements, it is especially seductive and captivating.

We can gain insight from the past. In an old book, Matthew Smith writes some helpful instructions regarding universalism. He himself became a convert to evangelical faith after preaching universalism for a dozen years. He came to experience deliverance from the conviction of his sin and placed his faith in Jesus Christ. At the end of his lengthy autobiography, he gives weighty advice to evangelicals, to the orthodox.

But first he gives these powerful reasons why there must be a "future state of rewards and punishments." [1] Each one is expanded by the author. (1) It alone can answer the universal faith placed by God in the heart of every person. (2) Our own sense of justice demands it. (3) Perfect justice cannot be attained in this life, neither by law nor by Divine arrangement. (4) Men cannot be known in this life. (5) Actions of men live after the actor is dead.

---

1. Smith, *Universalism*, 219ff.

Since universalism is in our midst and is seductive, there are some compelling guidelines that Smith suggests that evangelicals should observe.[2] These incorporate some very sober warnings. (1) "It is impossible to write the history of universalism without saying much that seems to be severe or unkind." He calls universalism "this ministry of death" and notes that "Much domestic, social and national evil, has already sprung from universalism."[3] He adds: "No policy is more fatal than that which allows this error to settle in a community, and send out its deadly leaven, undisturbed."[4] (2) "Equally unwise, I believe, save in very extraordinary circumstances, is the custom of open debate with the preachers of universalism."[5] (3) "Have nothing to do with the system by way of countenance. Call it by its right name."[6] (4) "Know what universalism is."[7] (5) "Recognize the ministry of universalism only as the ministry of Satan" (cf. 2 Cor 11:15).[8] (6) "Beware of universalist books in disguise," including story-books and books of *poetry and fiction*" (italics mine).[9] (7) "From Romanism this country has much to fear; but as much, I believe, from universalism."[10]

Some Final Evaluations of Universalist Fiction

The writers of fiction and nonfiction and the makers of film seductively seek to promote universalism. Yet the fiction of universalism is the more dangerous, and it is just that: *it* is a fiction.

By its nature, fiction tends to capture the reader in its plot, its creative story, its graphic pictures, and its easy flow that appeal more to the emotions than critical thinking. When adapted to the screen the message is even more powerful. And therein lies its seduction. This is certainly so with the speeches of the characters that Young uses to portray the Trinity; and the characters McLaren creates to aid his much-maligned, "too good to be true" pastor: a black man, an "intersexual" person, a black woman. Their many characters are caricatures of conventional Christians.

2. Ibid., 247–55.
3. Ibid., 248.
4. Ibid., 249.
5. Ibid.
6. Ibid., 251.
7. Ibid., 252.
8. Ibid., 253.
9. Ibid., 254–5.
10. Ibid., 255.

Universal reconciliation is the current equivalent of the devil's old lie, "You shall not surely die." It is as horribly evil now as it was then.

The fiction of universalism almost never engages contemporary evangelical scholarship. Is it because evangelicals have responded to all of this before and their response is powerfully persuasive?

There is a certain comfortable luxury that accompanies the advocating of universalism. That is, it is easy to advocate this teaching from the wealth and luxury of America and the West in general, but in China, Nepal, Afghanistan, and other parts of the Muslim world Christians are being persecuted and dying for their faith. I suspect that heaven and hell mean much more to them than they do to us here. The enormity of evil is more a reality there than here. But it is no less real here.

Fiction allows its authors to get away with all sorts of things, including outrageous statements. Consider McLaren: "whether your words were right, your heart was right, and I think that's what matters most" (32). Here is Young "quoting" Jesus: "*My* life was not meant to be an example to copy. Being my follower is not trying to 'be like Jesus'" (149). They use profanity (McLaren has many instances of this, but Young has it too). Universalism also ignores significant counter teachings to their views; it misrepresents history, modernism and postmodernism; it has a distaste for taking ownership of any particular view on the future of unbelievers; and there are all kinds of caricaturizing and stereotyping.

Examples of caricatures abound. These usually mock examples of evangelical faith, including the "Four Spiritual Laws"; the "Left Behind" series; Christian radio broadcasting; appreciating John Phillip Sousa and jazz music; election; evangelical's interpreting Scripture apart from context and literary genre; God as Judge represented as being bound by some mechanism; God's judging more cruel than any human's; the "Bible Evangelical Fellowship"; preaching fire and brimstone; God's judging presented as an exam to see if we believe the "right notion of salvation"; failure of seminaries; evangelicals as believing in the end of the world and not believing in the salvation of the world, as atheists do; Christians being more culpable than atheists; Catholics, Episcopalians, post-Protestants, and inner city churches presented as looking better than conservatives, evangelicals, and suburban churches; recovering fundamentalists questioning the reality of hell; doctrine counting not nearly as much as love and relationships; interpreting literally the book of Revelation; and many more.

Common points among universalist authors such as Young, McLaren, and Bell and their stereotypes involve many things. They all redefine the gospel and evangelical and are rethinking doctrines; they rewrite the Christian's view of history as escaping from this world; they redefine the kingdom of God; they have been personally transformed by universalism; they are anti-government and anti-American; they blame evangelicals for the ills and tortures of society including Hitler; they believe that being relational and spiritual will change the doctrine of hell and the concept of God; they deny hell as eternal suffering; the evangelical view of hell means that humans treat their children better than God does his; they present no urgent need to believe the gospel; they make reconciliation unconditioned by believing; they redefine "Christian"; they oppose the church as an evil system; and others.

Stereotypes of the characters include a black person as the most authoritative teacher in both fictions from McLaren and Young. Both feature Asians in significant roles. McLaren's Dan (the pastor) is being contested by a rightwing person. Dan is repeatedly praised for his honest search for truth and other things. It is all so very predictable!

Oswald Chambers Warns Us about Misunderstanding the Love of God

It is fitting that I bring this conclusion to a close by citing again the thoughts of Oswald Chambers whom I briefly cited in the Preface. Chambers and his wife bequeathed to the Christian world the most widely read devotional today. Chambers died in Egypt in 1914. Completed by his wife prior to 1935, *My Utmost for His Highest* continues to lead people back to the Lord Jesus and back to the cross. Chambers had wrestled with those in his day who tried to diminish the justice of God and subject it to the love of God. His words at several places still go to the heart of the matter today—how to understand biblically the meaning of the love of God. They form a fitting reminder of what is at stake should universalism overwhelm Christian belief. So many of the issues with which I deal in this book are answered by Chambers.

For November 19 the reading is titled, "When He Is Come." Note how forgiveness is related to the cross and to relationship with God. Chambers writes: [11]

> The great miracle of the grace of God is that He forgives sin, and it is the death of Jesus Christ alone that enables the Divine nature to forgive and to remain true to itself in doing so. It is shallow nonsense to say that God forgives us because He is love. When we have been convicted of sin we will never say this again. The love of God means Calvary, and nothing less. The only ground

---

11. Chambers, *My Utmost*, 324.

> on which God can forgive me is through the Cross of my Lord. There, His conscience is satisfied.
>
> Forgiveness means not merely that I am saved from hell and made right for heaven (no man would accept forgiveness on such a level); forgiveness means that I am forgiven into a recreated relationship, into identification with God in Christ. The miracle of Redemption is that God turns me, the unholy one, into the standard of Himself, the Holy One, by putting into me a new disposition, the disposition of Jesus Christ.

Young and other universalists do not own the corner on relationship with God. Chambers correctly relates it to our forgiveness—a term rarely found in universalist literature—because of the cross. Without it there can be no relationship with God. Recall that universalists consider that the cross is man's idea, not God's (so Young, *Lies*, chap. 17).

Chambers expands on this idea of forgiveness and its relationship to universalist thinking about the love of God. For November 20, under "The Forgiveness of God," he writes:[12]

> Beware of the pleasant view of the Fatherhood of God—God is so kind and loving that of course He will forgive us. That sentiment has no place whatever in the New Testament. The only ground on which God can forgive us is the tremendous tragedy of the Cross of Christ; to put forgiveness on any other ground is *unconscious blasphemy* (italics mine). The only ground on which God can forgive sin and reinstate us in His favour is through the Cross of Christ, and in no other way. Forgiveness, which is so easy for us to accept, cost the agony of Calvary. It is possible to take the forgiveness of sin, the gift of the Holy Ghost, and our sanctification with the simplicity of faith, and to forget at what enormous cost to God it was all made ours.
>
> Forgiveness is the divine miracle of grace; it cost God the Cross of Jesus Christ before He could forgive sin and remain a holy God. Never accept a view of the Fatherhood of God if it blots out the Atonement. The revelation of God is that He cannot forgive; He would contradict His nature if He did. The only way we can be forgiven is by being brought back to God by the Atonement. God's forgiveness is only natural in the supernatural domain . . . When once you realize all that it cost God to forgive you, you will be held as in a vice, constrained by the love of God.

---

12. Ibid., 325.

In several ways universalists mock such words. They deny the need to be forgiven since there is no original sin; there is no judgment for sin at the cross. By making the love of God the supreme attribute of God's nature, and by redefining God's holiness they deny that Jesus suffered the judgment of God by paying the price for our sins. They deny penal substitution, calling it "one of the most diabolical doctrines ever" (so Young). The only advance that modern universalists have made over those of Chambers' day is that now the views of universalists have become "conscious blasphemy" (rather than "unconscious blasphemy")!

One more time it is helpful to cite Chambers in light of how universalists treat the holiness of God and pit the love of Jesus against the judgment of God. Under "It Is Finished," he writes:[13]

> The Death of Jesus Christ is the performance in history of the very Mind of God. There is no room for looking on Jesus Christ as a martyr; His death was not something that happened to Him which might have been prevented: His death was the very reason why He came.
>
> Never build your preaching of forgiveness on the fact that God is our Father and He will forgive us because He loves us. It is untrue to Jesus Christ's revelation of God; it makes the Cross unnecessary, and the Redemption "much ado about nothing." If God does forgive sin, it is because of the Death of Christ. God could forgive men in no other way than by the death of His Son, and Jesus is exalted to be Saviour because of His death. "We see Jesus . . . because of the suffering of death, crowned with glory and honor." The greatest note of triumph that ever sounded in the ears of a startled universe was that sounded on the Cross of Christ—"*It is finished.*" This is the last word in the redemption of man.
>
> Anything that belittles or obliterates the holiness of God by a false view of the love of God, is untrue to the revelation of God given by Jesus Christ. Never allow the thought that Jesus Christ stands with us against God out of pity and compassion; that He became a curse for us out of sympathy with us. Jesus Christ became a curse for us by the Divine decree. Our portion of realizing the terrific meaning of the curse is conviction of sin, the gift of shame and penitence is given us—this is the great mercy of God. Jesus Christ hates the wrong in man, and Calvary is the estimate of His hatred.

---

13. Ibid., 326.

Chambers' words deeply stir me. His thoughts are right on target regarding universalists. When the latter would even have us think of God as a "cosmic abuser" because of the cross of Christ (so Young and Bell), Chambers is correct when he writes: "All the pleading which deliberately refuses to recognize the Cross is of no avail; it is battering at another door than the one which Jesus Christ has opened . . . The apparent heartlessness of God is the expression of His real heart, there is boundless entrance in His way."[14]

A Short Lesson on Greek Prepositions

At the heart of understanding how faith, love, grace, and the event of the cross all relate is the meaning of prepositions and case functions in biblical Greek. While these may be quite varied they are also quite informative. The NT teaches that the cause, the basis, the ground of salvation is the death of Christ on the cross. Faith is the means of appropriating the salvation—often expressed by a dative/instrumental of means case or by the preposition *dia* with the genitive case. Thus in Ephesians 2:8–9 Paul writes: "For by grace are you saved through (or by) faith." Thus faith is the means of appropriating salvation; it is never the basis or cause of our salvation. Rather the sacrifice of Christ on the cross is—Jesus paid the price to redeem us (Col 1:13: "in whom we have redemption, the forgiveness of sins"). The basis or cause of our salvation is expressed by the accusative case, sometimes with or without a preposition. Nor is love the basis or cause of our salvation. Love is the motivation that compelled God, who is love in his nature and does loving acts, to provide a way whereby to save us, but love is not the cause or basis. Thus we can say that we are saved, we are justified ["declared righteous"], not because of faith but through faith because of the cross. These ideas are never confused in the NT.

Note how frequently the Apostle Paul reiterates this distinction for faith in one verse. Galatians 2:16 says: "Know that a person is not justified by [or, through] the works of the law, but by faith in Jesus Christ. So we, too, have put our faith in Christ Jesus that we may be justified by faith in Christ and not by works of the law, because by the works of the law no one will be justified."

---

14. Ibid., 343.

A Personal Word

A final personal word is appropriate. I owe final allegiance to Jesus Christ, and to him alone. What I have written is for his glory. I seek to follow his ways and his teachings. From all that I can interpret from the NT, I believe in the reality of hell because Christ did. If he counts for anything, he counts for everything. If any part of his teaching counts, all of it does. Nothing else matters except that "he is all things and in all things" (Col 3:11).

Excursus

An Older, Persuasive Voice Defending Everlasting Punishment

WILLIAM G. T. SHEDD was born to New England Puritan parents in 1820 and devoted his life to the teaching of theology. Among many works his *The Doctrine of Endless Punishment* was published in 1886, eight years before his death. He wrote this book because already universalism was being introduced into the Presbyterian church in Scotland and being accepted in America.

Shedd's work is a brilliant, persuasive defense of the doctrine of everlasting punishment. He is well acquainted with the history and influence of universalism and gives an able defense of the biblical truth from the standpoint of the Bible, reason, and history—the same three appeals that universalists use.

Shedd's Introduction

In his introduction Shedd reflects on how significant the issue of the hereafter is. He writes: "The fall and eternal ruin of an immortal spirit is the most dreadful event conceivable." That some of God's "rational creatures" will forever be at enmity with God "cannot be thought of without sorrow and awe" (v). He points out that this doctrine of endless punishment did not come from the ministry nor from the church but from the Lord Christ himself. And he adds that this One who has suffered for man's sin more than any man has or ever will "surely has the right to determine the method and extent of his own self-immolating compassion" (v). Jesus Christ has the right to determine the method and extent of his love. For support, Shedd here cites the words of Jesus from Mark 1:40 and Matthew 20:15.

Dealing with the issues of belief, Shedd observes that "in order to escape danger, one must believe in it. Disbelief of it is sure destruction" (vi). He applies this principle to eternal punishment. Those who believe that there is a hell, following Christ's words, will escape it; those who deny hell's existence and ridicule it, will fall into it (vi). The reader can here recall the denial of hell by McLaren, Young, and Bell.

Shedd asserts that there is no doctrine more serious. The rejection of the doctrine of endless punishment "cuts the ground from under the gospel" (vi). If the denial of the doctrine is the truth, one needs no salvation. But if the denial is an error, the "error prevents penitence for sin, and this prevents pardon" (vi). "No error, consequently, is more fatal than that of Universalism" (vi). He continues (vi):

> It blots out the attribute of retributive justice; transmutes sin into misfortune, instead of guilt; turns all suffering into chastisement; converts the piacular work of Christ into moral influence; and makes it a debt due to man, instead of an unmerited boon from God. No tenet is more radical and revolutionizing, in its influence upon the Christian system. The attempt to retain the evangelical theology in connection with it is futile.

Universalism's Practical Effects

Shedd turns next to show the destructive impact that universalism has on practical theology (vii). He points out that if this doctrine is correct then havoc would come to all the liturgies and literature of the church. As examples, he cites how this would deny the contents of the "Morning Prayer for Families" in the book of Common Prayer used in the Episcopal church, the Litany, and devotional literature. He asks: If endless punishment is removed from Augustine, Chrysostom, Thomas a` Kempis, Bunyan's *Pilgrim Progress*, Taylor's *Holy Living and Dying*, and Baxter's *Saints' Everlasting Rest* "what is left?" (vii).

Shedd carries out the content of *The Doctrine of Endless Punishment* in three parts: the history of the doctrine, the biblical argument, and the rational argument. Since I have already deal with much of this I will cite only those special arguments that Shedd brings forward.

Overall, as I concluded above with the work of Isaac Backus (the excursus after chap. 8), contemporary or modern universalists do not offer up any new supports for their error that have not already been refuted in the past—as early as the early church and the Apostolic Fathers.

Shedd's Chapter I: History of the Doctrine of Endless Punishment

In his first part, Shedd offers some new evidence for the historical reach of universalism (UR). As I tried to prove above, contrary to what UR asserts, the "common opinion in the Ancient church was that the future punishment of the impenitent was endless" (p. 1). Thus the claim of UR to the contrary is patently false. Shedd backs up his claim by noting that comparing this doctrine with that of the Trinity, there was far more dispute over the latter than over the former. Shedd notes that UR, having so little support in Scripture and reason, "gradually died out of the Ancient church by its own intrinsic mortality" (2). Neander in his history acknowledges that there was more "restorationism" in the period of 312-590, mainly due to the influence of the Alexandrian school under the influence of Clement and Origen, than earlier. Yet eternal punishment was the dominant view (2). Hagenbach agrees that during the period up to 250 most of the fathers held to eternal punishment.

The Basis of Origen's Views

Shedd notes that Origen's views grew out of his view of human liberty: "free will may fall into sin at any time; and free will may turn to God at any time" (3). This led Origen to his theory of "the endless alternation of falls and recoveries, of hells and heavens; so that practically he taught nothing but a hell" (3). The latter remark comes about, as Augustine argues, because heaven becomes misery if it can be lost repeatedly.[1] Traces of Origen's influence in restorationism can also be found in Didymus of Alexandria, the two Gregories, and also in Diodore of Tarsus and Theodore of Mopsuestia—both leaders of the Antiochian school. Shedd asserts that the views of Origen were strongly combatted by contemporary church leaders and subsequently by church leaders such as Epiphanius, Jerome, and Augustine (4).

As far as the medieval church is concerned, it was virtually united in support of endless punishment. The Reformation churches, both Calvinistic and Lutheran, held the same position (4).

---

1. Interestingly this is the same argument I discovered and write about in the excursus after chapter 5.

Universalism Since the Reformation

Since the Reformation many individuals and some sects have embraced various views of the afterlife: universalism, restorationism, and annihilation. Church denominations have never embraced these views, but some within them have done so. Evangelical churches have not embraced them [even into the 21st century, I would add]. Shedd notes that denial of endless punishment usually accompanies denial of original sin, vicarious atonement, and regeneration (5). [In the chapters above I've noted this same phenomena, which isn't surprising]. Shedd notes that one who denies the personal penalty for sin must logically deny also vicarious penalty (5). Suffering that is only educational—remedial, corrective—does not require "a vicarious atonement in order to be released from it" (5). [Again the universalists McLaren and Young make this quite explicit. In interviews Young denies penal substitution, and such substitution is inconsistent with his claim that the cross was man's idea, not God's (*Lies*, chap. 17). He redefines sin and asserts that it does not separate from God (*Lies*, chap. 27).]

Shedd continues his overview of the history of UR by noting that in his time (the 19th century) it had grown stronger in Germany as it connected with rationalism and pantheism. He notes how the former is strongly anti-evangelical and asserts the recovery of all from sin. He points to the influence of Schleiermacher who blended the gospel with pantheism in his support of universalism. He interpreted Jesus' words (as in Matt 25:46) as figurative, defended other texts (such as 1 Cor 15:25, 26) as universalist, and argued that people in hell experience less and less suffering by their endurance and suffer more remorse over time so that people in hell are better people in hell than upon the earth. He also argued that the sympathy that people in heaven will have with their former friends in hell will prevent their happiness. Shedd dismisses such logic as flowing from questionable reasoning and contrary to Scripture (7).

Shedd concludes his history by citing some Trinitarian theologians (such as Nitzsch) and others who accept some form of UR, but he notes that their universalism has "a slender exegetical basis" (9). Instead, such writers appeal to human feeling and sympathy. They especially fail to explain the meaning of Christ's words pertaining to future destinies. Either these words are taken figuratively or they are severed far from the context. Ingenuity unfavorable to sound exegesis, and even caprice in interpretation, occur. An example is how Romans 6:23, the "wages of sin is death," comes to mean that sin abolishes itself (10–1). Shedd would not be surprised that modern UR interpreters, as I've shown in these chapters, would continue to promote such hermeneutics.

Shedd's Chapter II: The Biblical Argument

In this chapter, Shedd addresses virtually all of the arguments that UR raises as based in Scripture. These are the same that I've discussed in the chapters above, so it is not necessary to linger here in this review of Shedd's work. But Shedd's newer evidence deserves mentioning.

He begins by noting that the strongest support for the doctrine of endless punishment comes from Jesus Christ himself, the Redeemer of men. Though the Apostles clearly teach the doctrine, they give far less detail about it in comparison to Jesus. This is appropriate, Shedd observes, because none but God has the right to sentence a soul to hell, to execute the sentence, to delineate the nature of the suffering, and more. And Jesus took it upon himself to sound the warning. "He, the Judge of the quick and the dead, assumed the responsibility of teaching the doctrine of Endless Retribution" (13). It is inconceivable (my interpretation of Shedd's words) that Jesus would warn of such a destiny or exaggerate the suffering if hell wasn't real (14). The Jews would believe his words to be true when he knew them to be false (by the view of universalism)!

The Jews' Belief

At this point Shedd documents in a footnote (14) what the Jews believed at this time. He cites Edersheim (*Life of Jesus*, 2:789) as affirming that the schools of Shammai and Hillel, along with the synagogue, all taught eternal punishment during the first century. In the second century Rabbinic opinion relaxes on this doctrine. But in the third century there is a return to the former view. This information contrasts especially what McLaren says about Jewish understanding during this period.

The Biblical Witness

Shedd cites the texts that include Jesus' words about endless punishment: at least twenty-two texts (15–9). He then turns to the terms employed that deal with the abode of the lost and the nature of the punishment. First, he gives a very thorough explanation of *sheōl* in the OT, translated by *hades* in the Greek translation (the Septuagint). Similarly, he discusses the NT use of *hades*. He points out that these words mean either (1) the place of future retribution or (2) the grave, as the context makes clear. Shedd points out that the Early Patristic and Reformation churches held to these two states and places, and spurned that a third idea could be found, a middle state of purgatory. Shedd takes exception to those modern translations that remove definition (1) and simply find only the (2) meaning, thus obliterating the place of torment for the wicked.

Sheôl As the Place of Judgment

In contrast, Shedd proceeds to give very detailed explanation for the term *sheôl* (22–8) and insists that the term often signifies the place of future retribution. Three texts in the OT (Job 26:6; Prov 15:11; 27:20) and one in the NT (Rev 9:11) link *sheôl* to *abaddon* (destruction), and the last reference is to "the angel and king of the bottomless pit" (23). Thus *sheôl* must refer to the place of judgment and not simply the grave. Also, Shedd observes, it is improper to divide *sheôl* into two parts—*hades* and paradise. Such an idea is unbiblical and imported from the Greek and Roman classics (24). Both senses of *sheôl* are threatened to "the wicked but never to the righteous" (24). If one reads simply that the "wicked go down to the grave," a common death, how does this constitute a judgment or destiny differing from the righteous? Shedd cites Calvin on Psalm 9:17 as making a similar argument (25, note 1: Calvin did not hesitate to translate the word as "hell" instead of "grave"). Interestingly, the NIV usually renders the term "the grave" while the ESV renders it *sheôl*. A clinching text seems to be Revelation 21:8 which rehearses that the wicked are assigned to their part in the Lake of Fire (28).

What Shedd seems to be saying is this. The earlier text (20:13-14) refers to "death and *hades*" as being cast into this Lake; and this wording can only refer to the wicked—only the wicked, not righteous dead, are in the context of the Great White Throne judgment in chapter 20. Here *hades*, mentioned twice, must be the abode of the wicked only. It's inconceivable that the text could mean that only part of *hades* gives up its dead and only part is cast into the Lake of Fire.

As his second proof that *sheôl* is the proper name for hell Shedd notes the following (28–9). If *sheôl* is not the place of the wicked then there is no place name given for their destiny in the entire OT. A third proof is that the OT speaks of the contrary abode of the righteous, namely heaven, an abode of blessedness (30–1). A fourth proof is the inseparable connection of *sheôl* "with spiritual and eternal death" in many texts (32–4).

Sheôl As the Grave

Shedd proceeds with his second major point: *sheôl* signifies the grave to which both the good and evil go. But only the body goes there (34–42). The bodies of the righteous are resurrected out of *sheôl* in a glorified form, which takes place prior to the wicked's judgment at the Great Judgment mentioned above.

Shedd notes that the NT terms for future punishment are *hades, gehenna,* and *tartarus*. Interestingly, Plato affirmed everlasting (*ton aei chronon,* literally "the time always") suffering for transgressors; and he and Homer both cite the term *hades* as the place of suffering. For them *tartarus* was one part of hades (42).

The NT Hades

Shedd next provides the support needed to show that the NT term *hades* means the same that the Hebrew *sheôl* meant in the OT: it is both the place of retribution and the grave. The meaning of it as a place of retribution is more frequent than its meaning as the grave, contrary to the ideas of *sheôl* in the OT. As he did for the OT word *sheôl*, Shedd cites several supports for *hades* being a place of torment (43–6): the rich man in the parable is in torment there (Luke 16:22–4); it is the opposite of heaven (Matt 11:23); it is Satan's kingdom (Matt 16:18); it is the prison of Satan and the wicked (Rev 20:1–3, 12–4); it is connected with spiritual death (many references including Rev 1:18; 6:8; 20:13). Only three times is it the grave (Acts 2:27, 31; 1 Cor 15:55). Shedd explains that the larger number of uses for the place of punishment is due to the fuller revelation given by Christ in the NT (47).

Shedd insists that *hades* "is the *disembodied* (italics his) state for the souls of the wicked between death and the resurrection," as Paradise (a part of heaven) is for the souls of the righteous (48). Both await a resurrection. But this state is not incomplete for either. The wicked experience full misery and the righteous full happiness (56). When the church treated this disembodied state as more and more incomplete then an intermediate state was propounded and the doctrine of purgatory arose to cleanse believers from any remaining corruption (58). The Catholic Church grasped this idea and found support seemingly in 2 Maccabees 12:45 (61). The Reformed churches corrected this error and affirmed that the souls of believers at death are made perfect in holiness and immediately pass into glory (59). Both the Larger and Shorter Catechisms read this way (59). The souls of the wicked are at death cast into hell and their bodies kept in their graves till the resurrection at the final judgment (Rev 20).

In all of his careful discussion, Shedd's point is to reject the pagan Greek and Roman view of a "nether world" in which all departed souls reside. There was one *hades* for all (61). Shedd argues that this is unbiblical.

A Descent of Christ to Hell?

Shedd takes several pages (69–74) to show that there was no descent of Christ to hell, as universalists assert. Such a descent was not part of the original Apostles' Creed. [I've already dealt with this matter in preceding chapters]. In a footnote over several pages (74–7), Shedd lists major theologians who throughout the history of the church have explained how the Biblical texts do not support this event.

What Is Hell Like and How Long Is It?

Here Shedd moves to another significant point (75). He takes up the nature and duration of the suffering of hell. He points out that the various metaphors that describe the suffering are all toward one direction—it is suffering and punishment. Metaphors to represent hell as remedial and temporary are totally lacking.

Shedd moves to a discussion of the duration of hell. Young and other universalists make much of the argument that the Greek words behind "age" and "eternal" mean only a limited time, an age, and do not mean "eternal." Shedd points out that the Bible speaks about only two ages, one limited and finite, the other unlimited and infinite or endless and future. There are many texts that teach both. For example, the twofold mention of "age" (Matt 12:32) first refers to the present, limited age and the second to the "age to come." Plurals are sometimes used for both concepts for rhetorical effect; they are not arithmetical but rhetorical in their use (86). Similarly we use the English "forever" in both a limited and an unlimited sense.

Shedd takes several pages (89–94) to give eight reasons to show that suffering for the lost continues indefinitely after death; the theory of annihilation is false.

The False Claim of Universalism about an Intermediate State

What makes universalism especially evil and unbiblical is its claim that there is another, a third aeon or age between the present and the future, final one. In this intermediate state, between time and eternity, the vicarious atonement is applied to dead but repentant people. Shedd gives several reasons to show that death is the marker between the Bible's two aeons or periods (95–100). Death is part of the final, endless state of the soul. Significantly, in the parable of the rich man and Lazarus the rich man asks that his brothers be warned *before* they die and enter *hades*. Shedd also points out that the mediatorial work of Christ as redeemer is limited to this age and ceases at the end of this age when the Trinity becomes supreme: "that God may be all in all" (1 Cor 15:28) (100). Shedd cites many texts that speak of redemption belonging to this age alone, and the total absence of texts speaking of redemption after the grave (102–4).

Even prior to Jesus' first advent into the world people "are condemned already" (John 3:16). Thus people have no claim on God; forgiveness is undeserved. God's exercise of mercy is optional (105). For UR to claim that God's love compels him to save those after the grave is baseless.

What about the Heathen and Infants? Are They Lost?

The extension of redemption into the future world rests much on the cases of the heathen and infants. Somewhat surprisingly, Shedd (109) argues on the basis of several texts that God has elected to salvation some unevangelized heathen even though they have not heard the Word. The inward disposition involves penitence for sin and the longing for its forgiveness and removal. He cites several texts (John 9:36–8; Gal 3:7; Matt 8:11). It is not because such people are virtuous, which arises from egotism and self-righteousness, Shedd observes, but that they are repentant, penitent, and of a contrite spirit (note Matt 5:3; Acts 10:35). The former condition is one of works, which can never save (110–4).

Shedd points out two errors regarding the salvation of the heathen: first, that all people are saved; and second, that only a few are saved (114–5). In his last chapter, Shedd will show that there are many more who will be in heaven than those who are in hell—perhaps 1000's of times more! The opposite view rests on such texts as "Many are called, but few are chosen" and that there are many on the broad way to destruction (Matt 7:13–5). The Bible often speaks of the great numbers in heaven (Rev 5:11–3; 7:9; 19:6) but never uses such terminology for those in hell.[2]

Regarding the salvation of infants, Shedd makes it clear that all such are lost because of original sin. All have a will inclined toward sin. The fact that all evangelicals believe that infants are elect rests on the unmerited and

---

2. I suggest that this view is correct in light of the fact that "every creature in all creation" is found in heaven joining in the praise of Rev 5:11–3.

optional grace of God. God does as he pleases and in accord with his nature (116–7).

Shedd's Chapter III: The Rational Argument

Shedd's final chapter is one of the strongest ever written to employ reason to show that hell must be real and forever. His arguments are sober and weighty. One comes away from reading this section with a deepened sense of how desperate is the state of the lost and why a sin by a mortal can have everlasting consequences. In vain universalism struggles to answer his arguments. I dealt with many of these arguments in the excursus after chapter 5 but Shedd goes much further.

For the most part the following outline of Shedd's material is that of my own creation. Shedd argues that everlasting punishment is certain, not only from the Biblical evidence, but also from a rational standpoint. He says that punishment rests on three truths of theism: there is a just God; man has a free will; and sin is voluntary action—unforced human agency (whether inward inclination or act) (119). All three points are necessary to support everlasting punishment. And in the end all three are denied by universalists.

Endless Punishment Is Retribution and Just

Shedd's first major point concerns the nature of punishment. Endless punishment is retribution (120–3). It is not undeserved calamity which is not due to particular sinning, and it is not correction which has as its goal to cause one to change his ways (Heb 12:3–7).

Rather everlasting punishment is retribution intending to vindicate law, to satisfy justice (121). It is wholly retrospective; it is not prospective concerned with improving moral behavior, to deter, to improve society and the public good. These are utilitarian purposes, not moral ones (123–4). This idea of punishment finds precedence in the Bible and in history (so Plato, Cicero, Grotius, Bacon, Blackstone, Herbart, Woolsey and others; see footnote 1, 123). But modern jurisprudence has largely abandoned this view.

Everlasting punishment prevents the two extremes of indulgence and of cruelty (124–6). It honors human nature. Seeking justice treats people as people, with free will and as responsible. Seeking the public good treats people as chattel, as things, as brute beasts.

Punishment is Endless from the Nature of the Case:

Sin Incurs Everlasting Guilt

Shedd lays much stress on guilt, the result of sin (127–9). Suffering must continue as long as the reason for it, guilt, remains. Transgression against God brings guilt, and guilt never ceases to exist unless one receives Christ as the one who made penal substitution for sins (Rom 6:23). Further, punishment is everlasting because guilt is indivisible or everlasting. One is infinitely guilty and too long a punishment of sin is impossible (131). In dealing with a so-called "finite sin" bringing infinite guilt, Shedd points out that the "infinite incarnate God suffered more agony in Gethsemane, than the whole finite human race could suffer in endless duration" (131, note 1). Suffering is everlasting to correspond with everlasting guilt because God takes into consideration (which humans cannot do) the inward motives (government can only deal with outward crimes, not inward sins), the outward rebellion, and the "infinite perfections and adorable majesty of God" (133). Thus hell is not a penitentiary but righteous retribution. "In the justice of God there is a gradation of punishment exactly proportioned to the guilt of the offender" (138).

Endless Punishment Is Rational Because Conscience Supports It

Retribution, Shedd remarks, is endless because the human conscience considers it reasonable and right to be such (140). Human conscience approves God's judgment (the parable of Luke 16:19–31; Rom 2:16; 13:3, 4). A guilty conscience expects endless punishment, has no hope of release, and is filled with despair. Dante wrote over the portal of hell: "All hope abandon, ye who enter here" (143). In the Bible there is no such thing as "eternal hope."

This dread of conscience is universal and never ceases. If hell were not real, is only a chimera (impossible fancy) or a figment of the imagination, it would've vanished long ago. The ongoing denial of hell shows how entrenched it is in man's moral constitution. People don't keep on trying to denounce belief in centaurs! The ongoing demand for justice on earth proves that retribution is grounded in the human conscience. I observe that even liberals denounce a Hitler!

Endless punishment Is Rational Because of the Endlessness of Sin

Second, Shedd argues that punishment is rational because of the endlessness of sin (145). Sin is infinite in duration but not in intensity. James (2:5) says that one sin makes one guilty of all the law. Yet there are degrees of suffering due to the degree of light one receives on earth.

Also, sin is endless because of the nature and power of self-determination (147). Stubborn willfulness to sin intensifies itself perpetually. Left to itself, pride increases and never diminishes (so Pharaoh). It is impossible for the one who wills to sin to find repentance and reformation.

Also, sin is endless because the sinful will is in bondage to sin (148). One is not forced to sin but if one sins he cannot by himself get back to where he was. The effect of a vicious habit is to diminish one's ability to resist temptation. He cannot reverse himself and conquer his self-determination. Sin is the "most spontaneous of self-motion"; and moral bondage is one of the consequences (150). [I think that Shedd's observations are especially pertinent to various sexual sins]. In hell, the sinful propensity, unresisted, slowly but surely eats out all virtue until the will becomes "all habit, all lust, and all sin" (150). In hell, resistance to evil ceases and surrender to evil becomes demoniacal (Prov 7:22–3) (150).

Finally, sin is endless because rebellious enmity toward the law and its Source is not diminished but increased by the righteous punishment experienced by the impenitent (151). Note how the rich man never did repent in hell (Luke 16:19–31).

Endless Punishment Is Rational Because Sin Is an Infinite Evil Against an Infinite Being

Shedd goes on to identify another reason why sin is so deserving of everlasting judgment (152). It is because sin is an infinite evil, done against an infinite being. Shedd makes the comparison: the greater worth and dignity of the being the greater is the gravity of sin committed against him (compared to acts committed against humans or animals).

This argument goes to the heart of the gospel. The incarnation of Almighty God and his vicarious satisfaction for sin demonstrates the infinity of the evil (153). Thus it is correct to conclude that the doctrine of Christ's vicarious atonement logically stands or falls with that of endless punishment. If punishment is not endless, then Christ's substitutionary atonement is unnecessary.

The objection is often made: It is unfair to suffer infinitely for an offense committed in a finite time. Shedd (153) observes that such an idea implies that crime is measured by the time occupied in its commission. But government makes no reference to the length of time taken to commit a crime. A murder may take but a few seconds while a theft may take minutes if not hours.

Endless Punishment Is Reasonable Because the Wicked Themselves Prefer It

Shedd brings forward a somewhat surprising argument to support endless punishment (153). The "unsubmissive, rebellious, defiant, and impenitent spirit prefers hell to heaven" (154). As Milton's Satan said: "It is better to reign in hell than to serve in heaven" (154). Indeed, the submission to God and love of him that characterize heaven are more hateful to Lucifer and his angels than even the sufferings of hell. Shedd writes: There is not a "single throb of godly sorrow, or a single pulsation of holy desire, in the lost spirit." Rather the temper "toward God in the lost is angry and defiant" (as it was while Jesus was on earth: John 15:24, 25; 3:19) (155).

Endless Punishment Is Rational As Proven By the History of Morals

Shedd notes that the history of civilization shows that the nations opposed to penalty and endless retribution are the most lawless and vicious (157). On the other hand, a virtuous and religious nation fears "God the Judge of all the earth who will do right" (Gen 18:25; Isa 5:20). It was evangelical faith that gave the American Revolution, Shedd observes, its moral force. In contrast, the French Revolution lacked this force because evangelical faith was lacking (158). Shedd concludes with an observation about the culture of the 19th century which is even more true today. There is "no more important theological tenet than eternal retribution to those modern nations" that indulge in riches, luxury, earthly power, and "in bestial and shameless vice" (158). Shedd could hardly have spoken more strongly about the need for belief in endless punishment. Our day has exploded with "shameless vice."

Shedd's Conclusion: In the End How Many Will Be Saved?

Shedd concludes with some final, somewhat surprising observations that are as needful now as when he wrote. First, people need to consider the limited extent and scope of hell. It is only a spot in the universe. In the immense "range of God's dominion, good is the rule, and evil is the exception" (159). Hell is a "pit," a "lake," not an ocean. It is bottomless but not boundless.

In addition, the number of unfallen angels and the redeemed greatly exceeds the enemies of God (Ps 68:17; 103:21; Deut 22:2; Matt 6:13; 1 Cor 15:25; Rev 4–5; 14:1; 21:16, 24–5). More of mankind will be saved than lost. This was the belief of Calvin, Zwingli (many die in childhood), Edwards, Hopkins (by a ratio of 1000 to 1), Hodge, and others.

Second, it is important to remember that the mercy of God and his desire to save is infinite. This point is proven by three great truths (162–3). (1) The eternal Judge took the place of the human criminal. (2) God substituted his own satisfaction for that due from man, without relinquishing any claims of law and justice and did it by drinking the cup of "punitive and inexorable justice to the dregs." (3) God has made deliverance from endless punishment available to anyone who simply avails himself of the gospel by means of penitent faith.

In their discussion of endless punishment Christians should never forget these lasting truths that Shedd has well written. They are as pertinent today as before, if not more so! It is a fitting way to bring this book to a close.

Epilogue

THIS IS NOW MY third book written to expose the false claims of universal reconciliation (UR) as found in various writers of fiction and nonfiction, past and present. It is not something I set out to do in a vacuum, but I was prompted by a friend's rejection (so Wm. Paul Young) of evangelical faith and truth and his embrace of UR. His novel (*The Shack*) also became a movie. During the last decades other writers advocating UR have appeared, including Brian McLaren, Rob Bell, and Thomas Talbot. They made their case for a "new form of Christianity" by citing the Bible, by appealing to emotion and reason, and by appealing to church history. I found these appeals to be both troubling and unsupportable: troubling because they captured immature Christians unawares and deceived them; and unsupportable as demonstrated by a serious, deliberate research of every one of their appeals.

What comes next? I fear that in America and in the West there will be significant impairment of the evangelical church to dislodge all UR thinking as it should be. There is too much in UR that appeals to the basic, fallen nature which for many is too attractive to abandon. More and more writing will appear embracing this approach and finding fault with evangelical faith.

The phrase, "the deception of universal reconciliation," has a double meaning. UR both deceives others and is itself deceived. It deceives Christians yet is itself deceived by the great deceiver, the "father of lies" (John 8:44).

The Challenge of Writing This Book

It is difficult from a human, natural standpoint to write content that emphasizes the judgment and wrath of God rather than the love and mercy of God. But it is not difficult from a biblical standpoint. As an evangelical Christian, I am compelled to be faithful to the total self-disclosure of God as revealed in Scripture. I am compelled by the love that God has shown me by bringing me into a saving and growing relationship with him on the basis of the death of Jesus Christ. He has chosen me. I serve him as my Savior and Lord. Therefore, I feel compelled to end this book with two appeals to those who are not yet persuaded that universalism is a false hope and is heretical, and are not yet Christians, or are wavering Christians. The first appeal is based in the Bible, the other based in logic and reason.

The Seriousness of Denying the Reality of Sin Against God

The first concerns what the Apostle John wrote in his First Epistle—a text I have not cited in full in the book before but I believe it is extremely important. It deals with the nature of sin, its reality, false claims about it, and its remedy. The Apostle John had to deal with false teachers in his day who denied the true meaning of sin and its consequences. Today all universalists underplay or redefine sin; and Young in particular devotes a whole chapter (*Lies*, chap. 27) to redefining sin and denying that sin separates anyone from God. His major idea in all his writings is that all people are in relationship with God—and other universalists make this a supreme value. Yet without a true and full knowledge of what the sin nature is, what acts of sin are, and the acknowledgement of sin/sins, *there can be no fellowship with God*. Note these verses (1 John 1:5–2:2):

> This is the message we have heard from him and proclaim to you, that God is light and in him is no darkness at all. (6) If we say we have fellowship with him while we walk in darkness, we lie and do not practice the truth. (7) But if we walk in the light, as he is in the light, we have fellowship with one another, and the blood of Jesus his son cleanses us from all sin. (8) If we say we have no sin, we deceive ourselves, and the truth is not in us. (9) If we confess our sins, he is faithful and just to forgive us our sins and to cleanse us from all unrighteousness. (10) If we say we have not sinned, we make him a liar, and his word is not in us. (1) My little children, I am writing these things to you so that you may not sin. (2) But if anyone does sin, we have an advocate with the Father, Jesus Christ the righteous. He is the propitiation for our sins, and not for ours only but also for the sins of the whole world.

This is a carefully constructed text. The three false claims ("if we say") are what universalists are saying. They make false claims to have fellowship with God (v. 6), to be without a sin nature (v. 8), and not to commit acts of sin (v. 10). Thus the consequences given in each of these verses follow: they lie and don't practice truth; they deceive themselves and the truth is absent from them; they make God a liar and his word is not in them. The alternating verses give the remedy, the correction for such doctrinal errors.

There is no clearer text in the Bible, I think, that shows the seriousness of what it means to deny the full reality of sin. Such denial of sin has several consequences: it makes any claim to have fellowship with God a lie; living in darkness prevails; deception is involved; truth is abandoned; God is slandered; there is no forgiveness; there is no propitiation or sacrifice for sin available.

This is what UR is and does.

A Reasoned Appeal to Believe in Jesus Christ:

Consider This Logic If You Are in Process of Rejecting the Christian Understanding of the Bible in Its Witness to the Truth about God

Second, I extend the following line of reasoning, apart from citing the Bible, to those who yet are not Christians or perhaps are wavering Christians. I do this because the most important matter in the whole world, and at the heart of the whole discussion of UR, is whether a person truly knows God, has been forgiven, and is ready to meet him.

1. Christians, at least evangelical Christians, interpret the Bible literally—that is, taking the words of Scripture in their normal, grammatical-historical-contextual meaning without imposing some outside meaning on the text. We let the Bible speak for itself. From the entire context of the Bible we find the love and the holiness of God clearly taught.

2. Where else will you go? To some sect or religion that interprets the Bible on some other basis? But then which of the contending interpretations will you follow, and what provides the standard for setting one interpretation over another?

3. What other religion will you turn to? There are many: Islam, Hinduism, Buddhism, Janism, spiritism, animism, agnosticism, atheism, etc.

   a. Do these have a satisfactory world view covering what is truth, what is moral, what is reality? Where does truth, the good, the real come from?

   b. Do these have a sufficient appreciation of history—able to find a narrative that makes sense throughout the course of time?

How do they understand the beginning? Where do they think history is going?

c. Do these have a sufficient understanding of what a human being is? What is the nature of people that distinguishes them from animals?

4. Finally, the most important question of all is: What will you do with Jesus Christ?

a. There is sufficient evidence outside the Bible that he actually existed.
b. Both the Old and New Testaments affirm him to be the unique Son of God who came to earth by a physical birth to redeem humanity by his death on the cross which took the form of a sacrifice for sin. After three days, he came alive and lives for evermore.
c. No other religion or sect has a leader who went through death and lives in a resurrected body.
d. All of Christianity hangs on the reality, the truth of Jesus Christ's resurrection. The Apostles invite all humanity to examine this issue. For example, Paul the Apostle wrote a whole chapter (1 Corinthians 15) that has as its basic thesis: if it is not true that Jesus Christ came to life again then Christianity is false and the Apostles are false witnesses.
e. If Christianity embraces a resurrected Christ, then what are you going to do with the claims and truth he communicated as recorded in the Four Gospels—claims about who he is, what the cross (his death) is all about, the reality of sin and forgiveness, the reality of heaven and hell, and he as the only way to God his Father in heaven? And what are you going to do with his command: "Believe in me"? (John 14:1). He also claimed that he is coming again to right all the wrongs of earth and bring in everlasting peace (John 14:3ff.).

5. The answer is on your, the reader's, shoulders. What will you decide about Jesus Christ?

An Appropriate Prayer Regarding the Ultimate Issues Involved in This Book

There is perhaps a no more appropriate prayer by which to close this book than that which the Apostle Paul made on behalf of the Ephesian believers. It expresses his deep concern that early Christians experience the fullness of God. He brings together faith, love, knowledge, discernment, and the power of the Triune God. He wrote (Eph 3:14-19):

> For this reason I bow my knees before the Father, (15) from whom every family in heaven and on earth is named, (16) that according to the riches of his glory he may grant you to be strengthened with power through his Spirit in your inner being, (17) so that Christ may dwell in your hearts through faith—that you, being rooted and grounded in love, (18) may have strength to comprehend with all the saints what is the breadth and length and height and depth, (19) and to know the love of Christ that surpasses knowledge, that you may be filled with all the fullness of God.

Bibliography

Ahlstrom, Sydney E. *Theology in America*. Indianapolis, IN: Bobbs-Merrill, 1967.
"*aiōn*." In *A Greek-English Lexicon of the New Testament and Other Early Christian Literature (BDAG)*. Translation and revision of Walter Bauer's 5th ed. by Frederick Danker, et al, 27-28. Chicago: University Press, 1979.
"*aiōn*," "*aiōnios*." *The Greek New Testament*. Edited by Barbara Aland, et al. 5th Revised Edition. Stuttgart: Deutsche Bibelgesellschaft, 2014.
Armstrong, Chris R., ed. "The History of Hell: A Brief Survey and Resource Guide." In *Christian History Magazine*. Worchester, PA: Christian History Institute, 2011.
Backus, Isaac. *The Doctrine of Universal Salvation Examined and Refuted, containing A concise and distinct Answer to the Writings of Mr. Relly, and Mr. Winchester, upon the Subject*. Providence: n. p., 1782.
Ballou, Hosea. *Ancient History of Universalism*. Boston, MA: n. p., 1872.
Balz, Horst. "*aiōnios*." In *Exegetical Dictionary of the New Testament (EDNT)*. Edited by Horst Balz and Gerhard Schneider. Grand Rapids: Eerdmans, 1990. 1:46-48.
Barclay, William. *A Spiritual Autobiography*. Grand Rapids: Eerdmans, 1977.
Beal, Timothy. "Theology for Everyone." *The Chronicle Review* (Jan. 15, 2010) B16-17.
Bell, Rob. *Love Wins: A Book About Heaven, Hell, and the Fate of Every Person*. New York: HarperCollins, 2011.
Blankenhorn, David. *The Future of Marriage*. New York: Encounter, 2007.
Bock, Darrell. *Luke Volume 2: 9:51-24:53*. Baker Exegetical Commentary on the New Testament. Edited by Moises Silva. Grand Rapids: Baker, 1996.
Brown, Francis, S. R. Driver, Charles A. Briggs. "*sheôl*," In *A Hebrew and English Lexicon of the Old Testament (BDB)*. Oxford: Clarendon Press, 1907, rep. 1972. 982-83.
Buis, H. "Punishment, Everlasting." In *The Zondervan Pictorial Encyclopedia of the Bible*. Edited by Merrill C. Tenney. Grand Rapids: Zondervan, 1975. 4:955.
———. "Hell." In *The Zondervan Pictorial Encyclopedia of the Bible*. Edited by Merrill C. Tenney. Grand Rapids: Zondervan, 1975. 3:116.
Cairns, Earle E. *Christianity Through the Centuries*. Grand Rapids: Zondervan, 1954.
Campbell, Alexander, and Dolphus Skinner. *A Discussion of the Doctrines of Endless Salvation in an Epistolary Correspondence*. Utica: C.C.P. Grosh, 1840.
Carson, D.A. *Matthew*. The Expositor's Bible Commentary. Edited by Frank E. Gaebelein. Grand Rapids: Zondervan, 1984.
Cassara, Ernest. *Universalism in America: A Documentary History*. Boston: Beacon, 1971.

Challies, Tim. www.challies.com/book–reviews/what-does-the-shack-really-teach-read-lies-we-believe-about-god/ (March 9, 2017).

Chambers, Oswald. *My Utmost for His Highest*. Grand Rapids: Discovery House, 1935.

Charles, J.D. "Pagan Sources in the New Testament." In *Dictionary of New Testament Background*. Edited by C. Evans and S. Porter. Downers Grove: InterVarsity, 2000. 756–63.

Chrysostom, John. "Homily IV: Romans 1:26, 27." *Epistle to the Romans*. Cited in James B. De Young. *Homosexuality: Contemporary Claims Examined in Light of the Bible and Other Ancient Literature and Law*. Grand Rapids: Kregel, 2000.

Clark, G.H. "Eternity." In *The Zondervan Pictorial Encyclopedia of the Bible*. Edited by Merrill C. Tenney. Grand Rapids: Zondervan, 1975. 2:384.

Collins, J.J. "Eschatologies of Late Antiquity." In *Dictionary of New Testament Background*. Edited by C. Evans and S. Porter. Downers Grove: InterVarsity, 2000. 330–37.

Cooper, John W. "The Bible and Dualism Once Again: A Reply to Joel B. Green and Nancey Murphy." *Philosophia Christi* 9/2 (2007) 459–69.

Crockett, William, ed. *Four Views on Hell*. Grand Rapids: Zondervan, 1966.

Crockett, William V., and James G. Sigountos, eds. *Through No Fault of Their Own? The Fate of Those Who Have Never Heard*. Grand Rapids: Baker, 1991.

Crouzel, Henri. *Origen*. Translated by A.S. Worrall. San Francisco: Harper & Row, 1817.

De Lubac, Henri. *Origen on First Principles*. New York: Harper & Row, n.d.

De Young, James B. *Burning Down the Shack: How the "Christian" Bestseller Is Deceiving Millions*. Washington, DC: WND Books, 2010.

———. *Homosexuality: Contemporary Claims Examined in Light of the Bible and Other Ancient Literature and Law*. Grand Rapids: Kregel, 2000.

———. *Lies Paul Young Believes about God*. Abbotsford, WI: Aneko, 2017.

———. "The Meaning of 'the Law' in 1 Corinthians 14:34: With Implications for General and Special Revelation." Paper presented to the Evangelical Theological Society, San Diego, CA, November, 2007.

———. "The Number in Heaven vs. the Number in Hell; The Sledgehammer of Universalism." Paper on the web site of James De Young, burningdowntheshackbook.com. (March 28, 2017).

Ellicott, Charles J. *A Critical and Grammatical Commentary on the Pastoral Epistles*. Boston: Draper and Halliday, 1861; rep. Minneapolis: James Family, 1978.

Elwell, Walter A., ed. *Evangelical Dictionary of Theology*. Grand Rapids: Baker, 1984, 2001.

E., R. "Universalism," and "Universalists." In *Cyclopaedia of Biblical, Theological, and Ecclesiastical Literature*. Edited by John M'Clintock and James Strong. Grand Rapids: Baker, 1881, rep. 1970. 10:657–63.

Erickson, M. *Christian Theology*, 2nd ed. Grand Rapids: Baker, 1998.

———. "Is There Opportunity for Salvation after Death?" *BSac* 152:606 (Apr 1995) 131-44.

Ferre, Nels. *The Christian Understanding of God*. New York: Harper & Brothers, 1951.

Gaustad, Edwin S., ed. *A Documentary History of Religion in America*. Grand Rapids: Eerdmans, 1982.

Gerstner, John H. "Heaven and Hell." In *Baker's Dictionary of Theology*. Edited by E. F. Harrison. Grand Rapids: Baker, 1966. 38.

———. *Heaven and Hell: Jonathan Edwards on the Afterlife*. Grand Rapids: Baker, 1980.

———. "Universalism." In *Baker's Dictionary of Theology*. Edited by E. F. Harrison. Grand Rapids: Baker, 1966. 539-40.

Hanson, John Wesley. *Aiōn—Aiōnios*. Chicago: Jansen, McClurg, 1880.

———. *Universalism: The Prevailing Doctrine of the Christian Church During Its First Five Hundred Years*. Boston: Universalist, 1899.

Holmes, Michael W., ed. and rev. "The Didache." *The Apostolic Fathers*. Grand Rapids: Baker , 2002.

Holtz, Traugott. "*aiōn*." In *Exegetical Dictionary of the New Testament* (*EDNT*). Edited by Horst Balz and Gerhard Schneider. Grand Rapids: Eerdmans, 1990. 1:44–46.

Jacobsen, Wayne. "Is *The Shack* Heresy?" www.windblownmedia.com/shackresponse. html (10/21/2008).

Jeffrey, Katherine. "I Am Not Who You Think I Am." *Books & Culture* (Jan/Feb 2010) 33–34.

Jewett, P. "Eschatology." In *The Zondervan Pictorial Encyclopedia of the Bible*. Edited by Merrill C. Tenney. Grand Rapids: Zondervan, 1975. 2:342–58.

Jobes, Karen H. *1 Peter*. Baker Exegetical Commentary on the New Testament. Grand Rapids: Baker, 2005.

Josephus, Flavius. *Antiquities*, 18.1.4 In *Josephus Complete Works*. Translated by William Whiston. Grand Rapids: Kregel, 1960.

Josephus, Flavius. *Against Apion*, 2.32. In *Josephus Complete Works*. Translated by William Whiston. Grand Rapids: Kregel, 1960.

Keeley, Robin, ed. *Eerdmans Handbook to Christian Belief*. Grand Rapids: Eerdmans, 1982.

Keller, Timothy. *The Reason for God: Belief in an Age of Skepticism*. New York: Dutton, 2008.

Kelly, J.N.D. *Early Christian Doctrines*. New York: Harper & Row, 1960.

Knight, George T. "Universalists." In *The New Schaff-Herzog Encyclopedia of Religious Knowledge*, 1908. 12:95–96.

Kruger, C. Baxter. "The Genius of The Shack." Perichoresis: https://www.perichoresis. org/the-genius-of-the-shack/ (February 28, 2017; accessed May 31, 2017).

———. "William Paul Young Orthodox Novelist." Perichoresis: https://www. perichoresis.org/william-paul-young-orthodox-novelist/ (Feb. 28, 2017).

Kvanvig, Jonathan. *The Problem of Hell*. Oxford: University Press, 1993.

Lewis, Gordon R., and Bruce A. Demarest. "Spirit-Given Life: God's People Present and Future." Vol. 3. in *Integrative Theology*. Grand Rapids: Zondervan, 1994.

Louw, Johannes P., and Eugene A. Nida, eds. *Greek-Lexicon of the New Testament Based on Semantic Domains*. 2nd ed. New York: United Bible Societies, 1989. 1:489-91.

Ludlow, Morwenna. "Universalism in the History of Christianity." Chapter 10 in *Universal Salvation?* Edited by Robin Parry and Christopher Partridge. Grand Rapids: Eerdmans, 2003.

Marshall, I. Howard. *The Gospel of Luke: A Commentary on the Greek Text*. Grand Rapids: Eerdmans, 1978.

McLaren, Brian D. *The Last Word and the Word After That: A Tale of Faith, Doubt, and a New Kind of Christianity*. San Francisco: Jossey-Bass, 2005.

Mead, Frank S. *Handbook of Denominations in the United States*. 2nd revised edition. New York: Abingdon, 1961.

Merrill, Eugene H. "*sheôl.*" In *New International Dictionary of OT Theology & Exegesis (NIDOTTE).* Edited by Willem A. VanGemeren. Grand Rapids: Zondervan, 1997. 4:6.

Miller, Emily McFarlan. "Controversial Book *The Shack* Makes the Leap from Page to Screen." Religious News Service: https://religionnews.com/2017/03/03/controversial-book-the-shack-makes-the-leap-from-page-to-screen/ (March 3, 2017; accessed May 31, 2017).

Morey, Robert A. *Death and the Afterlife.* Minneapolis: Bethany, 1984.

Morgan, Christopher W., and Robert A. Peterson, eds. *Hell Under Fire: Modern Scholarship Reinvents Eternal Punishment.* Grand Rapids: Zondervan, 2004.

Neufeldt, V., and D. B. Guralnik, eds. "eternity." In *Webster's New World Dictionary.* New York: Simon & Schuster, 3rd ed., 1988. 466.

Orr, James. "Punishment, Everlasting." In *The International Standard Bible Encyclopedia*, 4:2503. Edited by James Orr. Chicago: Howard-Severance, 1937.

Osborne, G.R. "Resurrection." In *Dictionary of New Testament Background.* Edited by C. Evans and S. Porter. Downers Grove: InterVarsity, 2000. 931–36.

Plato. *The Laws.* Translated by R. G. Bury. The Loeb Classical Library. Cambridge: Harvard University Press, 1967.

Powell, Ralph E. "Hell." *Baker Encyclopedia of the Bible.* Edited by Walter A. Elwell. Grand Rapids: Baker, 1988. 2:953–54.

Reitan, Eric. "Human Freedom and the Impossibility of Eternal Damnation." In *Universal Salvation? The Current Debate.* Edited by Robin A. Parry and Christopher H. Partridge. Grand Rapids: Eerdmans, 2003.

Roberts, Alexander, and James Donaldson, eds. *The Ante-Nicene Fathers.* Grand Rapids: Eerdmans, rep. 1967. 1:188, 190, 191.

Robinson, David. *The Unitarians and the Universalists.* Westport, Conn: Greenwood, 1985.

Sasse, Hermann. "*aiōn,*" "*aiōnios.*" *Theological Dictionary of the New Testament (TDNT).* Edited by Gerhard Kittel. Grand Rapids: Eerdmans, 1968. 1:197–209.

Shedd, William G. T. *The Doctrine of Endless Punishment.* New York: Charles Scribner's Sons, 1886; rep. Klock & Klock, 1980.

Singer, C.G. "Unitarianism." *Baker's Dictionary of Theology.* Edited by E.F. Harrison. Grand Rapids: Baker, 1966. 538.

Smith, Matthew Hale. *Universalism Not of God: An Examination of the System of Universalism; Its Doctrine, Arguments, and Fruits with the Experience of the Author, During a Ministry of Twelve Years.* New York: American Tract Society, 1847.

Talbert, Charles H. *Reading the Sermon on the Mount.* Grand Rapids: Baker, 2004.

Talbott, Thomas. *The Inescapable Love of God.* n.p.: Universal, 2002.

Towner, Philip H. *The Letters to Timothy and Titus.* Grand Rapids: Eerdmans, 2006.

Turner, David L. *Matthew.* Grand Rapids: Baker, 2008.

Walker, Williston. *A History of the Christian Church.* New York: Scribner's, 1959.

Wanamaker, Charles A. *The Epistles to the Thessalonians: A Commentary on the Greek Text.* Grand Rapids: Eerdmans, 1990.

Willard, Dallas. *The Divine Conspiracy.* San Francisco: Harper, 1998.

Wilson, Andrew. "The Strongest Argument for Universalism in 1 Corinthians 15:20-28." *JETS* 59/4 (2016) 805–12.

Wright, N.T. *Evil and the Justice of God.* Downers Grove: InterVarsity, 2006.

Young, Wm. Paul. *Crossroads: A Novel.* New York: Faith Words, 2012.

———. *Eve: A Novel.* New York: Howard Books, 2015.
———. *Lies We Believe about God.* New York: Atria Books, 2017.
———. *The Shack: Where Tragedy Confronts Eternity.* Newbury Park: Windblown media, 2007.
———. "Universal Reconciliation." Paper delivered to an open forum, Portland, Or., Spring, 2004.

www.ingramcontent.com/pod-product-compliance
Lightning Source LLC
Chambersburg PA
CBHW071236230426
43668CB00011B/1465